MW01157060

The Catholic Experience in America

Recent Titles in
The American Religious Experience
Philip Goff, Series Editor

The Buddhist Experience in America
Diane Morgan

The New Religious Movements Experience in America
Eugene V. Gallagher

The Latter-day Saint Experience in America
Terryl L. Givens

The African American Religious Experience in America
Anthony B. Pinn

The Catholic Experience in America

Joseph A. Varacalli

The American Religious Experience
Philip Goff, Series Editor

Greenwood Press
Westport, Connecticut • London

Library of Congress Cataloging-in-Publication Data

Varacalli, Jospeh A.
  The Catholic experience in America / Joseph A. Varacalli.
    p. cm.—(The American religious experience)
  Includes bibliographical references and index.
    ISBN 0–313–32583–9 (alk. paper)
    1. Catholic Church—United States—History. 2. Catholic Church—United
States. I. Title. II. Series: American religious experience (Greenwood Press
(Westport, Conn.))
BX1406.3.V38 2006
282'.73—dc22   2005019206

British Library Cataloguing in Publication Data is available.

Library of Congress Catalog Card Number: 2005019206
ISBN 0–313–32583–9

First published in 2006

Greenwood Press, 88 Post Road West, Westport, CT 06881
An imprint of Greenwood Publishing Group, Inc.
www.greenwood.com

Printed in the United States of America

The paper used in this book complies with the
Permanent Paper Standard issued by the National
Information Standards Organization (Z39.48–1984).

10 9 8 7 6 5 4 3 2 1

To the men of my life: my deceased father, Joseph; my deceased intellectual mentor, Monsignor George A. Kelly; my brother, Nicholas John; my father-in-law, Douglas J. Worthington; and to my two sons, Thomas F. X. and John Paul

Contents

Series Foreword

Philip Goff

Some years ago, Winthrop Hudson, a leading religious historian, began his survey book on religion in America with a description of a London street. "When Americans walk down the street of an English city," he wrote "they will be reminded of home . . ."[1]

Few would dispute that for many years this was the case. Multiple faith traditions in today's United States trace their roots to English lineage, most notably the Episcopal, Methodist, and Baptist Churches. But that sort of literary device would not hold up under the pressure of today's diversity. Lutherans, Presbyterians, and Dutch Reformed adherents would balk at such oversimplification—and those are just a few among only the Protestant Christians. Add the voices of Jews, Eastern Orthodox, Muslims, Buddhists, and Irish, Italian, and Polish Catholics, and we would have a powerful chorus demanding their stories be told. And their stories do not begin on the streets of London.

Of course, Hudson knew that was the case. His point was not that all significant American religions began in England, but that, "with only a few exceptions, the varied religious groups of America have their roots abroad."[2] But clearly the "abroad" Hudson worked with was predominantly European, even if not entirely English. Today's scholarship has broadened that focus to include African, Asian, Central and South American, as well as Canadian and some "home grown" traditions that are on their way to becoming worldwide faiths. If ever scholarship in American religion has reflected the lineage of its people, it is in the recent writings that have moved beyond conventional ideas of faith traditions to include non-Anglo peoples who, while often existing off the radar screen of the establishment, have nonetheless formed much of the marrow of American religious life.

Although our studies of American religion have expanded to include more migrating faith groups from more areas of the world, the basic question that divided historians early in the twentieth century remained: namely, are traditions of American life (religion, politics, economics, etc.) transplants from the Old World, or did something entirely new and unique form in the New World? That is, should we seek to comprehend America's present religious scene by understanding its roots? Or should we try to understand it by looking at its transformations?

Of course, the truth lies somewhere in between. One cannot understand present-day Methodists or Buddhists by knowing their Old World beginnings in England and China or Japan. Nor can one determine the transformations those faith traditions underwent in America without knowing a good deal about their Old World forms. The American experience, then, is one of constancy of tradition from one angle and continual revision from another. The fact that they may look, think, and sound different than their Old World forms does not negate the fact that they are still recognizably Methodist and Buddhist in their new contexts.

This book series is meant to introduce readers to the basic faith traditions that characterize religious life today by employing that continuum of constancy and change. Each volume traces its topic from its Old World beginnings (when it applies) to its present realities. In doing so, readers will see how many of the original beliefs and practices came to be, as well as how they transformed, remained nearly the same, or were complemented by new ones in the American environment. In some cases—African Americans and Mormons most clearly—the Old World proved important either implicitly or imaginatively rather than explicitly and literally. But even in these cases, development within the context of American culture is still central to the story.

To be sure, each author in this series employed various approaches in writing these books. History, sociology, even anthropology, all play their parts. Each volume, then, may have its idiosyncrasies, as the authors chose which approaches worked best at which moments for their respective topics. These variations of approach resemble the diversity of the groups themselves, as each interacted in various ways at different stages with American society.

Not only do these volumes introduce us to the roots and development of each faith group, they also provide helpful guides to readers who wish to know more about them. By supplying glossaries and time-lines, the books give a deeper sense of beliefs, behaviors, and significant figures and moments in those religions. By offering resources for research—including published primary and secondary sources as well as helpful websites—the series presents a wealth of helpful information for formal and informal students of religion in America.

Clearly, this is a series conceived and published with the curious reader in mind. It is our hope that it will spur both a deeper understanding of the varieties of religious experience in the United States and better research in the country's many and always changing traditions.

Notes

1. Winthrop Hudson, *Religion in America*, 4th ed. (New York: Macmillan Publishing Company, 1987), 11.

2. Ibid., 11–12.

Preface

The purpose of *The Catholic Experience in America* is to provide the reader with an introduction to and overview of the history and contemporary situation of what is now America's largest religious group. It is written with an eye to multiple audiences. It is primarily geared to the advanced high school and beginning college and seminary student, although hopefully it can also serve as a valuable reference tool for the scholar and educated lay person. The first nineteen chapters plus the conclusion and postscript, written in a very straightforward fashion, provide the basic material for the introductory student. Chapters 20 and 21 provide more detailed information and analysis that might be of special interest to the those already familiar with the basic history and divergent interpretations of the American Catholic experience. The volume also includes a series of appendices that provide useful background information as well as tools that can assist the reader in comprehending the line of argumentation in the text (e.g., listings of key Church documents; definitions of terms and phrases; basic information on Church organizations; demographic and statistical information about the Church community; a listing of some key locations and centers of religious, cultural, and intellectual life; a notation of some key archival depositories; a resource guide pointing out some key resources on the Internet, and an historical time line).

Like any written work of analysis, this volume has a definite orientation with its corresponding strengths and weaknesses. It has four intended strengths.

First, the approach is *thematic*. Betraying the sociological training of its author, the attempt is made to identify trends and generalizations objectively discernible at a particular juncture in American time and place produced by specific and constantly changing sets of social and historical factors. The emphasis, then, is not on "naming names" and discussing the particularities of individual actors but on identifying events, issues, and philosophical positions that measure up to the standard of perennial relevance for the experience of being Catholic in America. Historical "players" come and go, but what sociologists term the "unit ideas" of social analysis remain the same. Four themes are highlighted throughout the text.

One crucial theme is taken from the important work of Michael Zoller who points out in his book, *Washington and Rome: Catholicism in American Culture* (1999) that Catholicism in this country tried to tread a balance between loyalty to the nation and the imperatives of the religion as set down by papal authority. Sometimes this balance tilted toward assimilation to Protestant norms and at other times to secular norms. Yet, at other times assimilation was consciously tied to creating an authentic multicultural variation, that of simultaneously being *both* American and Catholic and in yet others, to mirroring Roman understandings of the faith. There are good historical reasons, for instance, why the stance of most early Maryland Catholics was cautious, accommodationist, and Anglicized in an overwhelmingly Protestant country during the colonial and early Republican eras of the American nation. Likewise, it is not too hard to explain the sense of confidence and, at times, militancy held by many Catholics raised in an internally cohesive and expanding subculture gaining in political and cultural strength in the 1940s and 1950s, in which Catholics were intent to be American, but in "the Catholic way." Neither should it be hard to understand both the significant ignorance of and rejection of the basic essentials of the Catholic faith by the present generation of young and quite secularized Catholics given the decomposition of that very same Catholic subculture—or "ghetto" as its detractors like to characterize it. As David R. Carlin has persuasively noted in his *The Decline and Fall of the Catholic Church in America* (2003), three key factors were involved in this decomposition: (1) the prevailing progressive interpretation of the Second Vatican Council (1962–65), (2) the secularizing and antiauthority social protest movements of the contemporary era starting in the mid-1960s and (3) the post–World War II move of Catholics from the inner city to the suburbs of America. The decomposition of the self-contained Catholic social universe of the 1940s and 1950s brought modern American culture into the internals of the Catholic Church and into the psyches of millions of Catholic Americans. This explains *both* the greater receptivity of many Catholics to the ideas of an unfettered individualism and freedom as well as the sexual permissiveness that is at least one cause of the recent priests' scandals of the turn into the twenty-first century.

Another and related theme, discussed in the recent work of John T. McGreevy (*Catholicism and American Freedom* 2003), is the constant debates in American history between Protestant and secular scholars, on the one hand, and Catholic thinkers, on the other, over the meaning of the concept of "freedom" (or as this author prefers, over "individualism"). The former group sees an authentic exercise of freedom/individualism in terms of "autonomy" while the latter views freedom/individualism linked inextricably to truth and objective morality. As Lord Acton, the Catholic liberal of the nineteenth century, argued in making the Catholic case, freedom is not the freedom to do what we want but to do as we ought. This is an idea most recently reinforced by John Paul II in one of his recent encyclicals, *Veritatis Splendor* (1993). As John T. McGreevy makes clear in his impressive work, a Catholic understanding of the human being with its emphasis on the "common good," social dependency and connectedness with social institutions clashed, and has continued to clash, in the American context with either the religious individualism of the "Protestant principle" or the secular liberal emphasis of a radical individualism. In the pages that follow, you will see this debate unfold subtly and otherwise in the controversies between Protestant/secular and Catholic thinkers over issues involving democracy and the separation of Church and State, formal education and religious dissent, birth control and abortion, and homosexuality and the sexual abuse scandals, among many others.

Yet another related and major theme that runs through the volume comes from my own work, *Bright Promise, Failed Community: Catholics and the American Public Order* (2001), which, in turn, applies and adapts the sociology of knowledge concept of a "plausibility structure"—first developed by my former mentor, Peter L. Berger—to the case of the Catholic community in American society. In brief, a "Catholic plausibility structure" refers to a subcultural set of social institutions (e.g., parishes, schools, seminaries, mass media outlets, health care facilities, professional and academic associations, etc.) capable of socializing individuals into a willing acceptance of the basic tenets of the Catholic faith and worldview.

The existence and state of the Catholic plausibility structure is a crucial consideration precisely because the dominant or mainstream culture of the United States has never been Catholic, influenced variously by versions of capitalism and soft socialism and by Protestantism and liberal secularism. In the early part of American history, Catholics lacked a sufficiently integrated and comprehensive plausibility structure to allow the Catholic religion to compete successfully in an overwhelmingly Protestant America. Conversely, the contemporary Catholic plausibility structure has been severely weakened in the present post–Vatican II period, the result of a widespread institutionalized dissent existing within a significant number of Catholic institutions. It was only during the middle period of American Catholic history—the fruits of the organizational blueprint laid down by the bishops through the provincial and plenary councils of Baltimore that spanned the years 1829 to 1884—did the Church possess a comprehensive set of social institutions that effectively transmitted the Catholic faith to a majority of the Catholic populace. Sociological and historical research does, indeed, clearly document the severe decline in, first, knowledge of the Catholic faith and, second, assent to Catholic teaching that has occurred between the generations of Catholics socialized during the immediate pre–Vatican II, Vatican II, and post–Vatican II eras.

Finally, a fourth and, again, related theme is that, despite the unprecedented accomplishments made during his reign (1978–2005), John Paul II was no disciplinarian. He failed, for the most part, at what sociologists would term "social control," as dissent within the Church continued in an institutionalized state during his pontificate. While continuing overall the policies of John Paul II, his successor, Pope Benedict XVI (the ex-Cardinal Joseph Ratzinger of the Congregation for the Propagation of the Faith) is expected to address the issue of dissent head on. The resulting reduction in the quality and degree of institutionalized dissent is expected to strengthen, to some degree, the "plausibility structure" of the Catholic Church in the United States and throughout the global Catholic community. The election of Pope Benedict XVI is clearly seen as a victory for the "restorationist" camp of the Catholic Church.

All thematic generalizations, however defensible and useful, admit of exception—hence the corresponding weakness of the thematic approach. Missing from this volume, for the most part at least, is any significant discussion of the seemingly innumerable, controversial, colorful, idiosyncratic, and singular individuals who are such an essential part of American Catholic history and who, undeniably, made a significant impact, for better or worse, on the Church's history in this country. There are many other excellent introductions to the Catholic experience in the United States that do include substantial discussion of such personalities. One can point to, for instance, the relatively recent and imposing publication of Charles R. Morris, *American Catholics: The Saints and Sinners Who Built America's Most Powerful Church* (1997) and the older and shorter but still useful work by Father Andrew M. Greeley, *The Catholic Experience: An Interpretation of the History of American Catholicism* (1967). What this volume provides—and I contend is more appropriate for an initial introduction—is the broader framework (primarily sociologically informed but interdisciplinary in nature) from within which these startling personalities can be "plugged in," depending on the later need and interest of the reader in question.

The second and third intended strengths of the volume are, respectively, its *historical openness* and its attempt at *objectivity* and even-handedness. Regarding the second, the volume doesn't pretend to be able to predict the future course of events for the Catholic Church or for its millions of individual Catholics. Rejected is any a priori assumption, many times held by "progressive" Catholics, that there is some natural, inevitable, and permanent evolution for the Catholic Church to a religious version either of socialism or of individualism. The question here is whether the period of American history from the 1960s to the present has set the historical mold or, as testified by the contemporary growth of Catholicism and the religious resurgence around the non-Western, so-called "Third World" (as discussed, for instance, by Philip Jenkins in his treatise, *The New Christendom* [2002]), is an abnormal, temporary historical blip on the radar screen. I make no pretense to knowing the answer to this question; time and future events will tell the story. For that matter, conversely, neither is it assumed, the recent election of Pope Benedict XVI notwithstanding, that there must be some traditional restoration for the American branch of the Church Universal as is predicted by some of the more optimistic followers of Pope John Paul II and Pope Benedict XVI and their common agenda. Rather, the position taken in this volume is that the future—especially as one moves further from the present situation—is inherently open, subject to a variety of forces, individual, social, and religious, some of which are unpredictable and seemingly, at least to the secular eye, mysterious in nature.

Third, every attempt will be made to portray objectively and accurately the likely short-term outcomes of the controversies discussed and the prospects of the various groups analyzed (thus granting these groups what Peter L. Berger has referred to as "cognitive respect") that are part and parcel of the Catholic experience in the United States. Readers, if they so desire, can judge for themselves where they might stand on any of the myriad number of religious and cultural issues discussed in this volume.

It is important to point out that my reliance on standard and respected scholarly sources and my conscious attempt at even-handedness notwithstanding, this work is nonetheless an *interpretation* that bears, at least subtly, the mark of its author. This is especially the case for the material presented in chapters 20 and 21, which is more advanced and is, relatively speaking, geared to those more familiar with the issues involved in American Catholic history. Therefore what the scholar Chester Gillis says about his own work, *Roman Catholicism in America*, is directly applicable to my own attempt: "Thus I have made choices concerning inclusion and exclusion, description and analysis, highlights and background" (1999, 6). It is fair to point out to the reader that this author has assumed that the normative standard of the Catholic religion is defined by the Church's magisterium or official teaching authority. It is, of course, the case that millions of Catholics in the United States have been either supremely indifferent, hostile, or selectively accepting of that authority; these realities necessarily constitute a major part of the analysis contained within *The Catholic Experience in America*. All in all, this work moves away from those typically so one-sided in a progressivist direction and that characterized scholarship in the immediate post–Vatican II period. This volume can be viewed as one of many more balanced and orthodox pieces of scholarship that can be expected to gain ascendancy during the pontificate of Pope Benedict XVI and should be viewed, partly at least, as a result of the intellectual legacy of Pope John Paul II.

Fourth and finally, this reference work is, relative to much other published work in the specialized world of the academy, *interdisciplinary*. While the basic stamp of the sociologist is evident, I have ventured into the terrains, among others, of the theologian, philosopher, historian, and social-psychologist. This attempt, of course, runs the risk of exposing the author's ignorance in fields outside of his own training. However, I remained convinced that no one disciplinary perspective can encompass successfully the complex reality of the Catholic Church in American civilization and the American psyche. I believe (and hope) the reader considers the risks of such an ecumenical academic exercise to be justified intellectually.

I would like to thank the following professional colleagues and friends for their useful critiques of earlier and partial drafts: Dr. Jack Schrems (Political Science, Villanova University), Dr. John Quinn (History, Salve Regina University), Dr. Donald J. D'Elia (History, SUNY–New Paltz), Dr. Brian Simboli (Library, Lehigh University), Father Edward Krause (Theology, Gannon University), James Likoudis (former president of Catholics United for the Faith), and Monsignor Robert A. Batule (Diocese of Rockville Centre). The Reverend Deacon Nicholas Daddona (of St. Andrew the Apostle Church, Westbury, New York), Dr. Maureen Daddona (Biology Department of Nassau Community College) and Dr. Richard Renoff (Sociology Department of Nassau Community College–SUNY) offered critical comments on Chapter 17, "Eastern Catholicism." I accepted some but not all of their various suggestions for revision. This reference work is clearly better for their various critiques. Of course, I remain solely responsible for the line of argumentation put forth in the following pages.

Some parts of the material in the text were previously published in different versions in the journals the *Catholic Social Science Review* (CSSR), the *Homiletic and Pastoral Review* (HPR), and *Faith and Reason* (F&R). I have made liberal use of my previously published articles "Gibson's *Passion* and the American Culture War" (CSSR 2005, vol. 10); "The Cultural and Political Impotence of Catholics in Contemporary American Life" (CSSR 2004, vol. 9); "Dissecting the Anatomy of the Sexual Scandal" (HPR January 2004); "Neo-Orthodoxy, the Crisis of Authority, and the Future of the Catholic Church in the United States" (F&R summer/fall 1989); and "Obstructing *Ex corde Ecclesiae*" (F&R fall/winter 1997–98). They appear here with the permission, respectively, of Stephen M. Krason (publisher of the *Catholic Social Science Review*), Father Kenneth Baker, S.J. (editor of the *Homiletic and Pastoral Review*), and Dr. Timothy O'Donnell (president of Christendom College and former editor of its journal, *Faith and Reason*). Readers will also see evidence of basic continuity and subtle changes in my thinking that spans over two decades of scholarship in the area of American Catholic studies and includes hundreds of published articles, commentaries, book reviews, and well as to the volumes, *Toward the Establishment of Liberal Catholicism in America* (1983), *The Catholic and Politics in Post–World War II America* (1995), and *Bright Promise, Failed Community: Catholics and the American Public Order* (2001). Finally, I express the hope that this reference work will make some small, but real, contribution to the vast and impressive corpus of scholarship in the area of the relationship of the Catholic Church and American civilization.

TWO THOUSAND YEARS AND COUNTING: THE CATHOLIC EXPERIENCE

Part I will provide a very general and brief introduction to three central issues concerning the Catholic religion on a worldwide, universal basis. The first is to provide a general sense of the overall theological and philosophical vision of the Catholic faith as articulated officially by what is called the Magisterium, or teaching authority, of the Catholic Church. It should be immediately stated that these views have been "unofficially" modified, either consciously or unselfconsciously, by individuals and groups in light of their acceptance of various ideologies, cultural worldviews, and individual psychological requirements. In some cases, these ideologies, worldviews, and requirements are objectively consistent with the Catholic faith; in other cases, there is the attempt to superimpose ideas that are intrinsically at odds with the essence of the religion. In the former case, one can argue that certain individuals and movements have attempted what Catholic thinkers refer to as an "organic" development of Catholic doctrine; in the latter, their attempts are truly revolutionary vis-à-vis the faith.

The second issue is to briefly describe the organization of the Catholic Church headed by the pope and bishops, each bishop spiritually and legally leading a certain local jurisdiction called a diocese or archdiocese or some other religious entity. Included also will be a discussion of various other components of the religious organization such as religious orders and other groups with specialized tasks called ministries and apostolates.

Third, there will be a necessarily short introduction to the implication of the fact that the Catholic Church has "spanned the ages" in many various geographical areas of the world. The purpose of this brief historical analysis is simply to make the points that different historical

eras and different cultures have produced significantly different interpretations of the Catholic faith and that, therefore, the Catholic experience in the United States, as internally complex as it is, represents only
a small patch of the overall mosaic of the Catholic Church viewed historically. Indeed, if the thesis of Philip Jenkins, is correct, it may very
well be that the American and Western versions of the Catholic faith
will fast shrink in numbers and importance in comparison to the newly
emerging manifestations of the faith quickly spreading in the Third
World and southern hemisphere.

Chapter 1

The Catholic Theological and Philosophical Worldview

For the believing Catholic, the "Catholic vision" is a wondrous thing to contemplate in its complexity and majesty. Given its complexity and the less than perfect nature of human beings, it is a worldview even harder to realize in society, in social relationships, and within the individual.

Theology

Theologically, Catholic doctrine centers around the claim that things in the natural, social, and cosmic universe center around the reality of a Triune God, the Second Person of Whom, Jesus Christ, Divine Son of the Father, died on the cross to save humankind from original sin. Catholics believe that Jesus Christ founded the Catholic Church as *the* Church of Christ, headed by a pope, who as the "Vicar of Christ," is guided and protected by the Holy Spirit through the exercise of "magisterial authority," or, the decision-making authority of the pope and those bishops in loyal communion with him. In the Catholic tradition, while popes are viewed as spiritual descendants of Peter, the "rock" upon which Jesus Christ promised that He would build His Church, bishops are seen as successors to the other original apostles of Jesus and whose authority, as such, is based on the idea of "apostolic succession." In what is considered perhaps the key document of the Second Vatican Council (1962–65), *Lumen Gentium* ("Dogmatic Constitution on the Church," #25, in Abbott, 1966), magisterial authority is explained as follows:

> Bishops, teaching in communion with the Roman Pontiff, are to be respected by all as witnesses of divine and Catholic truth. In matters of

faith and morals the Bishops speak in the name of Christ and the faithful are to accept their teaching and adhere to it with a religious assent of soul. This religious submission of will and mind must be shown in a special way to the authentic teaching authority of the Roman Pontiff, even when he is not speaking *ex cathedra*. That is, it must be shown in such a way that his supreme magisterium is acknowledged with reverence, the judgments made by him are sincerely adhered to, according to his manifest mind and will. His mind and will in the matter may be known chiefly from the character of the documents, from his frequent repetition of the same doctrine, or from his manner of speaking. (Abbott 1966, 48)

The Catholic position on religious authority can be compared to the quintessential Protestant perspective in which the Holy Spirit is viewed as being in a direct and unmediated relationship with the individual believer. From the Protestant perspective, Catholicism is characterized by what Peter L. Berger (1969) has referred to as a "cosmological baggage" that hinders the relationship between God and the individual believer by constructing an allegedly unnecessary and man-made cultural (or "pagan") lense that diverts the individual away from God. In contrast, the Catholic worldview, while acknowledging a real and legitimate relationship between the Holy Spirit and the individual, nonetheless posits a special and definitive relationship for the Catholic religion between, on the one hand, the Holy Spirit and, on the other, the pope and the Church's magisterium, teaching in Christ's name and with His authority. Put another way, Catholicism is a religion that is not only inherently communal and social but also is one that argues that the official institutional Church is a nonnegotiable and indispensable mediator between God and the individual believer.

Catholic theological doctrine concerns itself with issues of *faith* (or belief), *liturgy* (or rituals), and *morals* (how to live a proper life in society). The theological task takes into account the essentials of the faith as propounded, for instance, in first, the Apostles Creed (c. 200 A.D.) and, then later, the Nicene-Constantinopolitan Creed (381 A.D.). It also involves an understanding both of how God channels grace (special supernatural gifts) to His Church and to His followers through, especially, what Catholics and some other Christians refer to as the seven sacraments (i.e., Baptism, Confirmation, Eucharist, Penance/Reconciliation, Anointing of the Sick, Holy Orders, and Matrimony). Sacraments are viewed, in the

Catholic worldview, as life-enhancing spiritual powers given by God to support individuals through their earthly existence. And theological activity also involves the manner in which individuals petition the Lord through prayers, such as the *Our Father*. Starting with the Ten Commandments given by God to Moses, Catholic theological doctrine provides a blueprint for living a correct Christian life in this world leading to eternal happiness in the next. Regarding this latter point, as the *Catechism of the Catholic Church* points out, "if faith is not expressed in works, it is dead and cannot bear fruit unto eternal life" (1994, 5).

Under the interpretation of the Church's magisterium (teaching authority), the source of Catholic theological doctrine is to be found in God's revelation to man—completed with the coming of the Messiah, Jesus Christ—and encoded in the teaching of *Sacred Scripture* (the Holy Bible), and the *Apostolic Tradition of the Church* (explored in the deliberations of ecumenical councils and meetings of various synod of bishops and national episcopal conferences). This lived apostolic tradition is also seen in the spiritual heritage of the early Church fathers, doctors of the Church, and a long litany of those who, in crucial respects, imitate Christ, that is, the saints. Although the divine deposit of revelation was fully completed by the end of the apostolic age and can never be contradicted, there is nonetheless, a continual *development of doctrine*, as enunciated most famously by John Henry Cardinal Newman in his *An Essay on the Development of Christian Doctrine*, which noted that the absolute truth handed down by God through this Church is itself mediated in different sociohistoric contexts. With appropriate qualifications, one can speak, then, of the Catholic Church's self-understanding of an evolutionary movement within her tradition over time in the direction of the perfection of an objectively valid religious truth that is both cumulative and irreversible. Guided by the ability of the Catholic magisterium to sift the chaff from the grain, Catholic theological doctrine constantly accrues and adds what it considers historically valid historical interpretations of the faith to its evolving tradition, thus continually expanding the ability of the Catholic Church to better understand the will and design of God.

Philosophy

Philosophically, Catholicism starts with a realistic anthropology, one that avoids defining human beings as completely "spiritual" or "mate-

Pope John Paul II offering communion during World Youth Day, Denver, Colorado, 1993.

rial," "good" or "bad," "reasonable" or "irrational," and "free" or "determined" (Varacalli 2001). Human beings are viewed, in a significant sense, as spiritual beings whose destiny as beings, ideally and following St. Augustine in his famous *Confessions* (1998), is to have one's soul rest with the Lord in Heaven. However, Catholicism by no means deprecates the material, the physical, the bodily. From the Catholic worldview, our souls animate physical bodies that themselves are divine creations, reflections of a supernatural design that commands respect and inspires awe. Key here is the Catholic importance placed on a holistic understanding of man's reasoning potential which, in principle, is capable of both acknowledging but subordinating the nonrational (e.g., emotional, erotic, intuitive) faculties.

Somewhat paradoxically, the nature of the individual is portrayed as basically one oriented to do good but, as a result of original sin, always capable, at a moment's notice, to descend into sin. Man is capable of exercising reason in the attempt to discover God, truth, and the good life. Faith and reason are complementary and never contradictory. While shaped by both supernatural and social influences, the human being is depicted as having free will, which allows him to choose his own course either to follow or reject the will of God. In the Catholic worldview, individual conscience is properly formed by an authentic Catholic theological doctrinal sensibility that is philosophically consistent with the natural law.

Natural law—that is, the idea that there is imposed into human organization a certain moral logic and structure—exists and has perennially existed. This philosophical anthropological position finds biblical and literary expression in St. Paul's assertion that morality "is written into the heart." Both individual and societal survival requires a minimal conformity to this moral logic and structure while spiritually healthy and flourishing individuals and societies require an even fuller conformity. The natural law asserts that the human mind can grasp, at least roughly, through reason and its associated and subordinate faculties, the very nature of this logic and structure. The idea of natural law historically had been accepted by most thinkers, atheist and non-Christian included, until the end of the eighteenth century. As Rev. John Courtney Murray, S.J., so lucidly put it in his *We Hold These Truths*, "the life of man in society . . . is founded on truths, on a certain body of objective truth, universal in its import, accessible to the reason of man, definable, defensible" (1964, 8). The natural law, for Father Murray, makes the case "that man is intelligent; that reality is intelligible; and that reality, as grasped by intelligence, imposes on the will the obligation that it be obeyed in its demands for action or abstention" (1964, 113). Similarly, Paul E. Sigmund speaks of "a central assertion expressed or implied in most themes of natural law. This is the belief that there exists in nature and/or human nature a rational order which can provide intelligible value-statements independently of human will, that are universal in application, unchangeable in content, and morally obligatory on mankind. These statements are expressed as laws or as moral imperatives which provide a basis for the evaluation of legal and political structures" (1971, viii).

However, as the Catholic logic unfolds, given that the human being's reasoning ability is mitigated by his sinfulness and by the surrounding culture that may, in varying degrees, be inconsistent with Catholic theological doctrine and the natural law, the grace of God and an active participation in the sacramental life that God has bestowed upon his Church are additionally necessary to keep human beings more fully on course with their intended supernatural destiny.

The created order, likewise, has a logical and structured purpose and inherent beauty and is, at base, good. Ideally, individuals, who are naturally social beings or who are made to be in a fundamental solidarity with other individuals, relate to each other in an interdependent or "organic" fashion. Put another way, the ordering principle of the Church—the "Mystical Body of Christ" or the idea that all Christians should work cooperatively in solidarity under the leadership of Christ— finds its contemporary social analogue, albeit a pale reflection, in a healthy, functioning organic civilization that is based both on natural law thinking and the social doctrine of the Church.

Suggested Readings

Abbott, Walter, ed. *The Documents of Vatican II*. Washington, DC: America Press, 1966.

Augustine, Saint. *Confessions*. Reprint ed. Translated by Henry Chadwick. Oxford: Oxford University Press, 1998.

Catechism of the Catholic Church. New York: Catholic Book Publishing, 1994.

Murray, Rev. John Courtney. *We Hold These Truths: Catholic Reflections on the American Proposition*. New York: Image Books, 1964.

Newman, John Henry Cardinal. *An Essay on the Development of Christian Doctrine*. Reissue Edition. Notre Dame, IN: University of Notre Dame Press, 1989.

Sigmund, Paul E. *Natural Law in Political Thought*. Lanham, MD: University Press of America, 1971.

Varacalli, Joseph A. *Bright Promise, Failed Community: Catholics and the American Public Order*. Lanham, MD: Lexington Books, 2001.

Chapter 2

The Formal Organization of the Catholic Church

The Catholic Church, at base, is a hierarchical institution led by the pope and by those bishops in loyal communion with the pope. The Catholic Church's authority structure is referred to as the Church's magisterium. This theological concept is legitimated by the claim of "apostolic succession," that is, that the popes throughout history succeed the first pope, Peter, and the bishops stand in line of succession from the other original apostles. The authority of the pope as the vicar (or prime representative) of Christ implies a special and unique position among the other bishops, that is, as possessing a universal authority and jurisdiction over all bishops, priests, and the ordinary faithful. His unique authority is based upon the instruction of Jesus Christ to his chief apostle, Peter: "Thou art Peter, and upon this Rock I will build my church; and the gates of hell shall not prevail against it. And I will give unto thee the keys of the Kingdom of heaven; and whatsoever thou shalt bind on earth shall be bound in heaven; and whatsoever thou shalt loose on earth shall be loosed in heaven" (Matthew 16:18–19). However, given the Catholic understanding that the Holy Spirit does not have an exclusive relationship with the pope, but can enlighten bishops, priests, other religious, laypersons, and even nonbelievers, both pope and bishops as rulers of the Church are expected to listen attentively to the theological reflections of all. Put into the language of modern cybernetics theory, the magisterium as the Church's "command post" is expected to receive openly "input" and even be energized from nonmagisterial sources but, in the final analysis, is to decide what constitutes or does not constitute ideas and practices that belong within the parameters of Catholic orthodoxy.

The pope primarily relies on the theological assistance of his fellow bishops who occasionally meet together in Ecumenical Councils. Cardinals are usually bishops who have distinguished themselves in some positive way in service to the Church and are appointed by the pope to assist him through the worldwide College of Cardinals in his responsibilities as bishop of Rome. The College of Cardinals also has a specific duty: to choose, through the inspiration of the Holy Spirit, the next pope when the present occupant passes on to the next life. Synods of bishops are gatherings of bishops who are convened to help the pope deal with some practical issue that the Church must address. Throughout the history of the Church, popes have convened major worldwide meetings called Ecumenical Councils that include all the bishops of the world, important theologians, and also sometimes leading religious, intellectual, and cultural figures. Councils historically have been called to settle some crucial issue dealing with the dogma and doctrine of the Church as with, for instance, the condemnation of the Arian heresy (which proclaimed that Jesus was merely a man and not God). The most recent council, Vatican II, convened in Rome for three months each year from 1962 through 1965 and was viewed as a "pastoral council," concerned with the key issue of the how the Church should relate to the historically unique condition called "modernity." Administratively, the pope and the bishops are assisted by the Church's central bureaucracy located in the Vatican, called the Roman Curia.

In addition to his universal jurisdiction over all the faithful, the pope also serves as the local bishop of Rome. Indeed, it is the diocese—a geographical and juridical domain consisting of many parishes, religious orders, and Church organizations—that is the central organizational unit of the Church. Each diocese is headed by a bishop, with especially large dioceses or, more accurately, archdioceses led by archbishops. According to the *Catholic Information Project* (United States Conference of Catholic Bishops, December 2003, www.usccb.org/comm/cips.html), within the Catholic Church of the United States there are presently 195 dioceses/archdioceses, 19,081 parishes, 43,634 priests, 5,499 religious brothers, 73,316 religious sisters, 585 hospitals, 7,142 elementary schools, 1,374 high schools, and 230 colleges and universities, as well as hundreds of religious orders of men and women, and other entities too numerous to mention attempting to fulfill the various religious and social mandates of the Catholic religion in America.

As of January 1, 2003, and within the diocese of Rockville Centre, for instance—which was founded in 1957 and encompasses the two

Avery Cardinal Dulles, S.J. is a member of the
College of Cardinals, which has the task of ap-
pointing the next Pope upon the death or res-
ignation of the present occupant. He was part
of the conclave of Cardinals that elected Pope
Benedict XVI on April 19, 2005 after the
death of Pope John Paul II on April 2, 2005.
Copyright Peter Freed.

large counties of Nassau and Suffolk on Long Island, New York—there
are 134 parishes in a total of 119 towns. Headed by Bishop William F.
Murphy and serving a Catholic population of 1.5 million Catholics (out
of a total population of approximately 3 million citizens), the diocese
presently has 408 priests, 63 priests from other countries, 240 permanent deacons, 89 religious brothers, 1,333 religious sisters, and 19 seminarians. There are 75 Catholic elementary schools and high schools
(2,622 students in kindergarten, 26,738 in elementary schools, and
11,979 in high school). The two Catholic colleges within the diocese
are administered by religious orders (St. Joseph's College, run by the
Sisters of Saint Joseph and Molloy College, run by the Dominican Sis-

ters) and educate a total of 9,310 students. In addition to numerous other diocesan organizations, Catholic Health Services of Long Island consists of 5 hospitals, 3 nursing homes, 2 home care agencies, 2 senior housing complexes, a community-based home for those with special needs and a hospice that served a total of 743,000 people in the year 2002 ("About the Diocese of Rockville Centre," January 1, 2003, www.drvc.org/stats.html). Most of the other dioceses in the country are smaller than that of Rockville Centre with about a half dozen representing larger religious jurisdictions.

The Second Vatican Council (1962–65) served, with significant qualifications, as a democratizing agent within the Church's formal organization in that it called for the creation of advisory structures. In one of the council's key documents, *Christus Dominus* ("On the Pastoral Office of Bishops in the Church [1965],") there was the call, for instance, for the creation of regional (e.g., Latin America) and national (e.g., Ireland) episcopal conferences in which individual bishops who lead dioceses are expected to consult other Bishops of the same geographical or political area (Abbott 1966). The major advisory structure in the Catholic Church in the United States, initiated almost immediately in the wake of Vatican II, is now the United States Conference of Catholic Bishops (USCCB). The conference has been extraordinarily active promoting important activities. Some have been quite controversial, and, some would say, divisive, such as the Bishops' Bicentennial Celebration with its focal point event, the 1976 Detroit "Call to Action" Conference (Varacalli 1983; Zoller 1999). The national conference published, during the 1970s and 1980s, a host of statements dealing with the American economy, nuclear weapons, the Church's response to AIDS, and other social justice issues that were not only very progressive in orientation but also, perhaps, as some conservatives argued (Kelly 1990; Hitchcock 1984) secularized the Catholic message contained within the social doctrine of the Church.

Implemented in the name of the Second Vatican Council have been other consultative structures such as priests' senates, to represent the needs of priests to their bishops; sisters councils, to represent the voice of religious sisters and nuns; and parish pastoral councils, to communicate the desires and advice of parishioners to the local pastor, among other more ad hoc and informal groupings.

A key issue here is whether or not these advisory structures will be content merely to offer their perspectives to appropriate religious authority but rather see fit to challenge it. Will these new structures attempt to reverse the basically "top-down" authority structure of the Church, pushing for what scholars of religion such as Julia Mitchell Corbett (2000) call a more "congregational" style of authority, in which the local parish makes all key decisions or, slightly less revolutionary given the hierarchical authority structure of Catholicism, a "connectional" style of authority, in which the pope and the bishops essentially share authority with lower echelon clergy and religious laity? Indeed, the progressive Catholic theologian Monica Hellwig, noting that the Catholic Church in the United States is embedded in a culture emphasizing such values as democracy and individualism, states that:

> It is not surprising, therefore, that American Catholics . . . have begun to wonder why we do not see more local initiative in church policies and actions, why the faithful have no voice in choosing their pastors at the parish and diocesan level, and why questions of the orthodoxy of theologians are not referred to consultation with their peers. Such attitudes and questions can, of course, be seen as acts of insubordination to church authority in its present patterns, but it may be wiser to consider whether they might be a prophetic challenge concerning the nature of the church. (1990, 74)

As we shall see in subsequent chapters, the "Call to Action" Conference and the recent Voice of the Faithful (VOTF) movement energized by the recent sexual scandals in the Church, call for a type and nature of democratization of Church structure that would require a revision in the basic doctrine and understanding that the Catholic Church has held.

Suggested Readings

Abbott, Walter, ed. *The Documents of Vatican II*. Washington, DC: America Press, 1966.

Corbett, Julia Mitchell. *Religion in America*. 4th ed. Englewood Cliffs, NJ: Prentice Hall, 2001.

Hellwig, Monica. "American Culture: Reciprocity with Catholic Vision, Values, and Community." In *The Catholic Church and American Culture: Reciprocity and Challenge*, edited by Cassian Yuhaus. Mahwah, NJ: Paulist Press, 1990.

Hitchcock, James. *The Pope and the Jesuits: John Paul II and the New Order in the Society of Jesus*. New York: The National Committee of Catholic Laymen, Inc., 1984.

Kelly, Monsignor George A. *Keeping the Church Catholic with John Paul II*. Garden City, NY: Doubleday, 1990.

Varacalli, Joseph A. *Toward the Establishment of Liberal Catholicism in America*. Lanham, MD: University Press of America, 1983.

Zoller, Michael. *Washington and Rome: Catholicism and American Culture*. Notre Dame, IN: University of Notre Dame Press, 1999.

Chapter 3

The Universal in the Particular: The Universal Catholic Church in Time and Space

There is a great deal of pluralism and diversity within the Catholic Church of the United States. The purpose of this necessarily short chapter, however, is to suggest that the range of pluralism and diversity internal to the Catholic experience in America is far less than that of Catholicism throughout global and historical experience. There are two immediate points to be made here, points in tension but not in contradiction with each other. The first, and less important, is that the American Catholic experience, in part, is as broad as it is, because America, as a "nation of immigrants," has brought to its shores many of the various global and historical versions of Catholicism available. These various Catholic traditions brought over may, in some cases, have been muted, "low culture," premodern "peasant," versions of the Catholic faith and may have, in some cases, succumbed quickly to the assimilation processes of America but they still brought some real diversity to the Catholic Church in America. The second, and larger point, is that the American Catholic experience—as interesting and complex an expression of the Catholic faith as it is—falls far short of representing the total Catholic experience. As a matter of fact, because of their claims of a contemporary pervasive secularization in the United States (and of modern Europe, also) and in spite of the Church's wealth and massive physical plant in this country, some scholars believe that the future of Catholicism belongs to other sectors of the global community. Regarding the position downplaying the future importance of a European/American Catholicism at the expense of developments in Africa, Asia, and Latin America, one can refer to the thesis put forth by Philip Jenkins in his volume *The Next Christendom* (2002). Speaking of the historical ability of the Catholic religion not to depend on its survival by concentrating in any one general geographical area, David R. Carlin notes that:

> Catholicism has collapsed in this place or that place in the past without collapsing altogether. . . . In the centuries following the Arab conquests, it gradually collapsed in Western Asia and North Africa, while at the same time surviving in Europe. In the sixteenth century, it collapsed very suddenly in much of Northen Europe, but it survived in Southern Europe, in Poland, in Ireland, and in Latin America; it even showed some promise (a promise that eventually fizzled out) of expanding into East Asia. Today it shows great promise in Africa. Catholics are aware of this. They know that their Church can afford to lose a province here and there—even so magnificent a province as the United States, and nonetheless go on living and eventually thriving. (2003, 309)

Another important foundational issue that should be brought up at the beginning of both this volume and this chapter is the intimate relationship between religion and culture. Whatever else it means from the perspective of the religious believer, sociologically *religion constitutes some part of culture.* In some societies, such as contemporary Saudi Arabia or, to a lesser degree, in contemporary Ireland, religion (Islam and Catholicism, respectively) and culture are closely intertwined. In such a situation, religion is obviously the key central force in shaping the thought and behavior of individuals. In other societies, such as contemporary England or Sweden, the culture is pervasively nonreligious with the result that relatively few individuals are affected seriously by, variously, the Anglican, Lutheran, other Protestant, or Catholic heritages. Indeed, it is probably fair to state that one of the few cases in which one can detect a sense of serious religious commitment on English shores has been that of the Muslim faith, recently brought into the country through immigration. *The relevance for this volume is that, both globally and historically, the Catholic Church simultaneously has both shaped and been shaped by the culture and civilization in which it is embedded.* In some cases, Catholicism has been more producer than produced, in other cases, the reverse relationship has been characteristic. Another related observation is that, in some cases, one can say that Catholicism has been central and defining to the dominant civilization as it was in the high Middle Ages in Europe. In other cases, it has been viewed and treated as a despised counterculture as it was in Elizabethan England or in America during the colonial era. In yet other instances, like that of the United States during the post–World War I era, it has served as an effective subculture, encouraging the Catholic individual simultaneously to maintain a vital sense of being Catholic while still actively encouraging participation and advancement in the life of the larger civilization. Some Catholic commentators of that era argued that the Church was successful in its attempt to produce individuals who were very "American," but "American in a decidedly Catholic way."

Indeed, some Catholic observers have made the case that the Catholic religion is at its best and its most effective when it masters the ability, in a particular sociohistorical situation, to "evangelize through inculturation," that is, to spread the faith by building on and converting whatever is true, holy, beautiful, and functional in cultures, subcultures, and countercultures. This was certainly part of the vision of the Church's recently deceased pontiff, John Paul II (d. April 2, 2005). During his reign, Pope John Paul II attempted to apply this philosophical and methodological approach to Catholic efforts at evangelization on the African continent.

Empirically, however, the Catholic Church has not always mastered this specific and positive relationship between faith and culture as envisioned by John Paul II and many others in the Catholic tradition. In many historical instances, the faith has been allowed to have been reduced to the surrounding culture and in others, it has taken on a radically inward, "world-rejecting" posture. Regarding the first possibility, for instance, Harry Crocker (2001) argues that the Catholicism of the Greek-speaking eastern half of the Roman Empire during the first thousand years of Christianity had a tendency to lose its integrity in various mystery cults, syncretic belief systems, elaborate and ornate forms of materialism, and to *caesaropapism* and emperor worship. (It was the Roman Emperor Diocletian [emperor from 284 to 305 A.D.] who had split administratively the Roman Empire into eastern and western halves, thus increasing the degree to which respective local cultures could shape the empire.) For Crocker, the western or Latin or Roman part of the Empire, with its belief in natural law and reason, proved to be a more natural carrier of the truth claims of the religion. Somewhat similarly, in the contemporary United States, traditional defenders of the Catholic faith argue that Catholicism has been cut down to the contours of an American culture emphasizing individualism, utilitarianism, relativity, and materialism.

Regarding the possibility of world rejection as a conscious option, the famous query of the early Christian theologian, Tertullian, "What hath Athens to do with Jerusalem?" reflected the sentiments of many in the early Christian community. Many early Christians basically posited a fundamental disjunction between Christianity and the world, rejecting anything of a this-worldly nature. In the famous classificatory scheme of the liberal Protestant theologian H. R. Niebuhr (1951), such a position represented the "Christ against culture" option, an option still accepted today by certain Protestant groups, like the Amish, who are within the Anabaptist tradition (Zellner 2001). The Catholic Church, at least since the third century A.D., has rejected the "Christ against culture" option, accepting officially as an ideal, at least, the idea that the Catholic faith should enrich whatever civilization it is embedded within. Certainly, in a Protestant and, later, secular America, the Catholic Church has never manifested any serious movement to anything remotely approaching a "world-rejecting" stance; indeed, if anything, the reverse tendency is the case. As a matter of fact, in 1899, Pope Leo XIII issued his famous statement *Testem benevolentiae* ("On the Heresy of Americanism") in which, among other things, the pope warned against the tendency in civilizations like the United States to emphasize the "active" and ignore the "passive" virtues. The Catholic Church *did* adopt, however, during the nineteenth century, *as a tactical strategy*, a policy of rejecting the pervasive movements of the modern world at the time and did, at least for a period, withdraw upon itself. Such outside movements, whether in the form of the rise of such ideational currents as scientism, liberalism, Marxism, Progress, or Social Darwinism or such social structural developments as the rise of autonomous nation-states and a statism as fostered by an extremely progressive understanding of Church-State separation were clearly seen by Church officials as intrinsically hostile to the faith. As such, the Church of the time tended to reject such developments. For instance, in the 1864 publication of the *Syllabus of Errors*, Pope Pius IX listed the "eighty principal errors of the age." To bring home the point to readers, error number eighty read: "The Roman Pontiff can, and ought to, reconcile himself and come to terms with, Progress, liberalism, and modern civilization as recently introduced."

In fairness to a liberal or progressive Catholicism, it is important to point out that it would say that the official Church's position wasn't merely a "tactical" move in response to a hostile situation, but it represented a prototypical expression of an essentially narrow and needlessly triumphalist institution. In the progressivist Catholic worldview, this intrinsically inward posture would require the impact of the Second Vatican Council (1962–65) to turn Catholicism toward what it views as a more open and wholesome attitude and relationship with the outside non-Catholic worldview. Vatican II, progressives claimed, opened up the Catholic Church to such cultural/religious realities as democracy, individualism, freedom, the sciences and the social sciences, and other world religions and secular philosophies.

The traditional Catholic response to this is that the developments in the eighteenth and nineteenth centuries that the Church rejected *were* inherently irreconcilable with the faith. According to such a logic, it would be impossible to be both a sincere Catholic and, for instance, a sincere Marxist, Socialist, liberal, feminist, or Freudian psychologist. The position here was that the underlying assumptions of the Catholic and secular worldview were, in the phrase of the University of Notre Dame philosopher, Alasidar MacIntyre, "morally incommensurate."

Some, but not all, Catholic traditionalists leave open the possibility that the Church can work with some contemporary attenuated and modified forms of these modern secular ideational (e.g., feminist) and social-structural (globalization) developments. Despite disagreeing with much that is advocated by the contemporary United Nations, for instance, in its abortion and population control policies, the present day Catholic Church actively participates in this world body through its papal representative and Vatican delegation and selectively and judiciously supports some of its activities, that is, those that are viewed as compatible with the natural law. The Catholic Church today is very actively providing a critique for what today passes for as "globalization," supporting those developments that promote the spiritual and material needs of all, but especially the poor, throughout the globe but critical of those developments and ideologies that perpetuate the maintenance or increased dominance of any socioeconomic elite (whether communistic/socialistic, capitalistic, aristocratic, etc.). Mention here should be made of an important Catholic research and policy organization, located at the United Nations, the Catholic Family and Human Rights Institute. While formally independent of the Vatican, it has been an effective proponent of Catholic public policy on the world scene and, conversely, a general thorn in the side of very secular and progressive organizations that promote legal and policy recommendations that are contrary to what the Church sees as a universal morality and the natural law.

There are many other ways in which the Catholic experience in America is not representative of a global Catholicism. Sticking to the theme of the relationship of religion and culture, the cultural mediator for the Catholic faith in America has been either Protestantism or secularism. This will obviously differ in implication from, respectively, those situations in which the Catholic faith is mediated in a Latin-based European culture, or a Greek-based culture in the eastern half of what once was the Roman Empire, or the tribal-based traditional orientations of the sub-Saharan African continent, or the pragamatic this-worldliness of the Chinese civilization, or the syncreticism characteristic of the Spanish and native Indian cultures of the Latin American experience. An important question, raised by the "pro-Roman" or "pro-Latin" perspective of Harry Crocker Jr. (2001), is whether or not some cultural mediators (e.g., a classical "Greco-Roman"one) represents a more natural carrier of the Catholic worldview than do others).

The American Catholic experience differs from others in that the Catholic community has existed politically under a (continually changing) democratic form of government. This differs in implication from those situations in which the faith exists within authoritarian (e.g., monarchial) and totalitarian (Nazism or socialist) frameworks. The Catholic Church teaches that it can exist in any sociopolitical system that respects the "fundamental dignity of the human person." This would exclude any active, positive participation with the totalitarian regimes of Nazism and communism. And as John Paul II, among other Catholic leaders, had constantly reminded the world, the Catholic Church admits that its historical record has not been one innocent of perpetuating injustice, violence, and involvement with authoritarian forms of government that have not manifested any concerted effort on behalf of the common good. Historically, the Church has suffered under monopolistic forms of government and has benefitted—at least superficially—in other cases. Harry Crocker Jr. notes the fundamental watershed importance of the Edict of Milan that first gave Christians in the Roman Empire religious freedom and tolerance and eventually led to the establishment of "Catholic Christianity as the religion of empire" (2001, 5).

Another key issue that differentiates the Catholic experience in America from selected sociohistorical periods in global history is that of an anti-Catholicism that, empirically speaking, has overlapped into a simple genocide. As readers of this volume will learn, there is much utility in Michael Schwartz's (1984) claim that "the persistent prejudice" in American history is anti-Catholicism. That said, Protestant/secular antipathy and discrimination toward Catholics pale in comparison with the persecution of the Christian martyrs under such Roman Emperors as Nero (reign 54 to 68 A.D.), Domitian (81 to 96 A.D.), Decius (249 to 251 A.D.), and Diocletian (284 to 305 A.D.). Neither has American Catholicism witnessed the hatred and destruction against the Church and the Catholic faithful ushered in during modern times by right-wing secular nationalists such as Adolf Hitler in Nazi Europe in the years during World War II or left-wing secular socialists like Joseph Stalin or Mao Tse-tung in the post–World War II era. And while American Catholics have certainly and occasionally experienced violent relationships with their conationals, the United States has thus far dodged the bullet—for a variety of reasons that include philosophy, government, and economic prosperity—of unrelenting conflict and mutual atrocity committed by Catholic and Protestant alike during, for instance, the Protestant Reformation and its aftermath and, more recently, in Northern Ireland. Neither has the American Catholic population experienced or participated in the mutual evils committed between Muslims and Catholics during the Crusades or in contemporary Africa.

The Catholic, or more accurately, the human response, to being at the receiving end of violence and discrimination ranges the whole gamut. Some *convert* (or "go to the winning side"); others are *intimidated* (and "go into hiding into the catacombs in order to survive and keep the faith alive"); yet others *privatize* their faith ("downplaying their identity to improve their chances of societal survival or success"— as some scholars have characterized the modal response of many Catholics during the early colonial period of a Protestant-dominated America); yet others *organize* in reaction ("fighting back" in the sense of creating antidefamation leagues like the Catholic League for Religious and Civil Rights and fraternal organizations like the Knights of Columbus) to, finally, an openness to *martyrdom* (e.g., manifesting a steadfast loyalty to one's faith in the face of likely death and/or torture). Those Catholics in America who love their faith have been able to avoid, at least thus far in their history, the necessity of serving as martyrs for the faith.

Suggested Readings

Carlin, David R. *The Decline and Fall of the Catholic Church in America*. Manchester, NH: Sophia Institute Press, 2003.

Crocker, Harry, Jr. *Triumph: The Power and the Glory of the Catholic Church—A 2000-Year History*. Roseville, CA: Forum, 2001.

Jenkins, Philip. *The Next Christendom: The Coming of Global Christianity*. Oxford: Oxford University Press, 2002.

PART II

CATHOLICISM AND CIVILIZATION IN THE UNITED STATES: A CHRONOLOGICAL OVERVIEW

Part II (Chapters 4–7) provides a chronological overview of the history of Catholicism in the United States. There are four basic identifiable stages to this history. Chapter 4 details the "less than auspicious beginnings" of a minority Catholic Church—basically immigrant with little wealth, power, and prestige—trying to establish itself in a society where a generic and hegemonic Protestantism reigned. It was a Protestantism with a vivid memory of Protestant-Catholic clashes and hostility in Europe, which were carried over to the New World.

Buttressed by the mass migration of the Irish in the early to mid–nineteenth century and by the organizational blueprint of the Baltimore provincial and plenary sessions that started in 1829 and ended in 1884, Chapter 5 focuses on the slow and tortuous process—"brick by brick and by the grace of God"—by which American Catholicism built up its organizational infrastructure. Parishes, schools, seminaries, colleges, hospitals, mass media outlets, and professional associations of all sorts were created to set up a supportive subcultural environment in which the Catholic faith could be successfully propagated to its own members. The organizational response of the Catholic bishops to the sociological reality that the Catholic faith was embedded in a then Protestant and a mostly unsympathetic civilization reached its historical maximum effectiveness during the immediate post–World War II period of American history. In the words of Bishop Gerald Shaughnessy, Catholics had, indeed, "built better than they knew."

Chapter 6 suggests that a combination of internal and external forces (Carlin 2003) led to a severe weakening of the Catholic subcul-

ture from the mid-1960s through to the turn of the twenty-first century
(Varacalli 2001). Internally, the desire for "success" on the part of a
significant percentage of the upwardly socially mobile American Catholic population (as determined by the secular cultural gatekeepers of
the outer, non-Catholic society) was combined with a progressive reading of the message of the Second Vatican Council (1962–65) that downplayed the importance of a distinctively Catholic identity and presence
in the society-at-large. Externally, there was a post–World War II move
to the suburbs and exodus out of the more cloistered inner-city Catholic neighborhoods that was combined with an increasingly powerful
secular, that is, nonreligious culture (again, at least as defined by the
cultural elites at the time) with a great ability to shape the worldview
of individuals who participate in it. This increasingly secular American
culture was itself shaped by the elective affinity between the social
change and protest movements of the era with its burgeoning youth
subculture, itself an inevitable demographic consequence of the post–
World War II "baby boom" generation. The effects of these internal
and external considerations was to produce a Catholic population not
only highly educated, affluent, and influential but also increasingly assimilated into philosophies and perspectives that were neither Catholic
nor fundamentally religious.

Chapter 7 discusses the efforts of the pontificate of Pope John Paul
II (1978–2005), and the "restorationist" movement he has inspired, to
reverse in the United States the movement toward what was perceived
by traditional Catholics as religious indifference and secularism. Such
efforts have, for better or worse, been at best mixed. The prognosis of
many of the participants in this restorationist movement range from the
guardedly optimistic to those who see a long winter in the foreseeable
future for a traditional understanding of the Catholic faith in American society. The more guardedly optimistic have recently been buoyed
by the election to the thrown of Peter of Pope Benedict XVI, an even
more staunch restorationist than was Pope John Paul II.

Chapter 4

Less Than Auspicious Beginnings: A Minority Church in a Protestant Culture

The following ten themes or propositions are important in order to understand the general situation of the Catholic Church and Catholics in both colonial America and the early American Republic up to the mid–nineteenth century. All in all, they point to the tremendous obstacles and challenges the early Catholic Church had to face in order to survive in its new home.

The first theme is that American civilization was generically Protestant at the outset and hostile to the Catholic faith. Approximately 99 percent of the original colonists were Protestants of one sort or another with only a tiny fraction of Catholics and a smattering or Sephardic Orthodox Jews to be found in what would later become the United States of America. Speaking of the early American nation, David R. Carlin notes that while it had no established church, it *did* have an informal, unofficial one which he calls "generic Protestantism" (2003, 118). As Carlin quickly adds, however:

> But there was at least one great negative article . . . [in the generic creed]: that the Church of Rome was a false church, that the Pope was a fraud, that the religion taught by Rome and its pope was a terrible distortion of true Christianity. Protestants could not agree among themselves as to what "true Christianity" was, but they could all agree on one thing: whatever it was, it was not Roman Catholicism. (2003, 119)

The second theme is that the earliest Catholics came to America, Protestant hegemony notwithstanding, first, to escape Protestant persecution in England and later, secular persecution in the France of the

Revolution (Hennesey 1981). (The smattering of Jews came to America, ironically, to escape Spanish Catholic authorities in Europe.)

The third fact of importance was that English Protestant America was surrounded by Catholic influence in the North (i.e., by French Canadians) and South and Southwest (i.e., by the Spanish in Florida and the southwestern rim of Texas, Arizona, New Mexico, and California). As a matter of fact, the first Catholic parish in the New World was established in the year 1565 in Saint Augustine, Florida. James T. Fisher notes an important distinction among the Spanish colonizers, that "tensions unavoidably erupted among the Spaniards in North America . . . pitting those who viewed their mission as primarily religious against the many *conquistadores* [conquerors] whose motives were more personal, political, and economic in nature" (2000, 13–14). He also notes a similar dichotomy between the French missionaries and fur traders up North:

> While the Spanish focused their colonizing efforts on the "borderlands" of Mexico, the 17th century saw the French concentrate on Canada. From that base, adventurers and missionaries explored parts of the future states of Maine, New York, and Michigan, as well as the Mississippi Valley. . . . French Canada became dominated by Catholics, many of whom hoped to build a Christian society in the wilderness, while others—notably the fur traders—came seeking riches. (2000, 20)

This potentially threatening geographical reality, whether based on religious or economic interests or both, did nothing to lessen anti-Catholic feelings in the American colonies. Threatening or not, Catholic religious, cultural, and political forces would not win the day on the American landscape in the seventeenth and eighteenth centuries. "The rising British Empire," James T. Fisher observed, "had designs on North America that not only changed the political and diplomatic landscape of the New World but introduced a dramatic new religious component as well. Long before the advent of American independence, English Protestants become the dominant power in the new civilization" (2000, 23).

A fourth theme to note is that European events exacerbated even further the tenuous situation of Catholics in America. In England, for instance, the Anglican persecution of the more radical Protestant ele-

Oldest church in America, St. Augustine, Florida in a Civil War era photograph. *Courtesy of the Library of Congress.*

ments of the Reformation encouraged the migration of the more anti-Catholic Protestants to the New World. As Carlin notes:

> This profound English anti-Catholicism came to America with the English settlers of the seventeenth and eighteenth centuries. This was particularly true in the northern colonies, above all in New England, where Puritans dominated. All English Protestants, regardless of specific denomination, were, of course, anti-Catholic; but the more thoroughgoing their Protestantism, the more anti-Catholic they were likely to be. . . . By the time of the American Revolution, more radical forms of Protestantism had spread even to the southern states—not Congregationalism, which never flourished outside New England, but Baptist and Methodist churches. On average, then, the Protestant "temperature" of the New Republic was much higher than it was in England. For in England, the great majority of people still belonged to the established church, which was far less intensely Protestant than were the dissenting churches—Congregationalists, Presbyterians, Baptists, Quakers, and Methodists—while in the United States, almost everybody belonged to a dissenting church. So as anti-Catholicism was a strong prejudice in England, it was even a stronger prejudice in America. (2003, 128)

The fifth key point is that the early American Catholic Church was small in numbers, with tiny concentrations in Maryland, New York, and Pennsylvania, with almost no representation whatsoever in New England, and with no developed organizational network of parishes and institutions and few priests. Protestant political authorities, additionally, were not helpful in aiding the Catholic Church to grow in the New World; indeed, Catholics were forced to attempt to transcend legal discriminations of various sorts. As Fisher notes, for instance, "When Maryland's Protestants enacted laws against Catholic worship, they were settling old scores as well as indicating their continued hostility to 'popery' " (2000, 29).

The sixth theme is that early Catholic leadership in Maryland tended to be (1) accommodationist in style, consistent with the requirements for survival of a minority religion in a hostile environment, (2) quasi-aristocratic to middle class thus providing the Catholic community in Maryland a hearing in elite Protestant circles, and (3) dominated by British and French Catholic leadership. The accommodationist style of early American Catholic religion blended in a Protestant-like emphasis "on a personal relationship with Jesus Christ" and a combined Protestant and Enlightenment-like emphasis on "a faith in the power of reason to confirm Christian truths" (Fisher 2000, 34).

A seventh theme argues that, in addition to being quite sedate and mellow in its presentation, the religious belief and practice of many of the earliest Catholics in America ranged from the state of being unchurched, to manifesting highly irregular and syncretic versions of the faith, to being Catholic in a highly privatized and compartmentalized manner with many Catholics eventually converting to some form of Protestant religion. However, as an eighth theme notes, and despite the almost uniform rejection of the Catholic religion by the various Protestant groups in early America, the fact that no one Protestant group could dominate the early Republic aided the eventual establishment of the principle of religious freedom—a principle that was favorable to the welfare of the Catholic religion—and to any other minority group—in the new land (Corbett 2001). Put another way, in early America, Catholics represented an insignificant religious, cultural, and political force. The fights over power and religious prestige during this period took place, then, between groups like the Calvinists in Massachusetts and the Anglicans in Virginia.

A ninth theme points out, happily, for the Catholic immigrants at least, that a not insignificant segment of the Catholic community sided with the winning Patriot side in the American Revolution, thus reducing somewhat and temporarily, anti-Catholic legal, cultural, and social discrimination. For one thing, the single richest American colonist of the time—Charles Carroll of Carrollton, Maryland—was a signer of the Declaration of Independence. There was also a natural tendency for the Irish Catholics living in the colonies—given their historic animosity with England—to take the rebel side in the conflict. As James T. Fisher observes:

> When the Revolution began in 1776, the Catholic population of the 13 colonies was estimated at 25,000 in a total population of 2.5 million. Many Catholics supported the patriot cause and a few contributed greatly to the struggle for independence from England. Charles Carroll, a wealthy landowner from Maryland, became an outspoken opponent of unfair colonial taxation in the early 1770s. . . . Carroll, who was called by one advocate of independence "a most flaming patriot," attended the First Continental Congress in Philadelphia, was a delegate to the Continental Congress two years later (where he signed the Declaration of Independence) and later helped write a new constitution for Maryland that ended discrimination against Catholics. The work of Carroll and others—including John Barry, the Irish-born "father of the American Navy," who commanded the first battleship commissioned by the Continental Congress—led George Washington to proclaim that American Catholics played their "patriot part" in helping the colonies achieve their independence. (2000, 30)

John T. McGreevy adds yet another consideration: that the alliance with Catholic France during the Revolutionary War and the heroism of the Marquis de Lafayette also reduced somewhat anti-Catholic feelings (2003, 11). McGreevy also notes the palpable loyalty extended to the new nation by Catholics quieted fears of disloyalty. He notes, for instance, that John Carroll, the first American Catholic bishop and the aforementioned Charles Carroll, "delivered two heartfelt tributes upon the death of George Washington" (2003, 11).

Finally, a tenth theme suggests two movements in dialectical tension with each other, one increasing anti-Catholic sentiment, the other strengthening the Catholic community. The first is that the massive influx of poor, uneducated, but quite devout Irish Catholics to American shores increased dramatically anti-Catholic bias and bigotry. As McGreevy states: "hostility to Catholicism began to swell in the 1830s on both sides of the Atlantic as German, and, especially, Irish Catholic immigrants made their way to Liverpool, Glasgow, New York, Philadelphia, and Boston" (2003, 11). The Anglo-Catholic accommodation with Protestant America ended with the influx of the Irish to America. As Fisher states:

> In 1826 there were approximately 250,000 Roman Catholics in the United States out of a total population of more than 11 million. . . . The Catholic community was then small and shared too much in common with the dominant Protestant majority to become a focal point of great national concern. Over the next three decades, however, the Catholic population would skyrocket to total more than 3 million, with the increase due largely to massive immigration from Europe. And if the numerical increase was not startling enough in itself, these new Americans were "different": most were impoverished, and many spoke an unfamiliar language. They also practiced their religion in a fashion different from American Catholics and Protestants alike. (2000, 49)

The second dialectically related movement involves the reality that this immigration also marked a new stage starting the process by which Catholicism, given its new numbers and genius in building organizations and institutions, gained some religious, cultural, and political strength that would last until the later part of the twentieth century (Morris 1997). Speaking of the bold, in-your-face type of Catholic leadership represented by Archbishop John "Dagger" Hughes, James T. Fisher observed that "in the 1940s and 1850s immigrant Catholics may have been unpopular, but an increasingly organized Church ensured that they were not entirely powerless. John Hughes, the Irish-born bishop of New York, was the most flamboyant of a new generation of leaders for an immigrant church bearing little resemblance to the church of Bishop John Carroll" (2000, 56).

Suggested Readings

Corbett, Julia Mitchell. *Religion in America*. 4th ed. Englewood Cliffs, NJ: Prentice Hall, 2001.

D'Elia, Donald J. *The Spirits of '76: A Catholic Inquiry*. Front Royal, VA: Christendom College Press, 1983.

Fisher, James T. *Catholics in America*. Oxford: Oxford University Press, 2000.

Hennesey, Father James. *American Catholics: A History of the Roman Catholic Community in the United States*. Oxford: Oxford University Press, 1981.

McGreevy, John T. *Catholicism and American Freedom: A History*. New York: W. W. Norton and Company, 2003.

Morris, Charles R. *American Catholics: The Saints and Sinners Who Built America's Most Powerful Church*. New York: Times Books, 1997.

Chapter 5

"Brick by Brick and by the Grace of God": The Construction of a Catholic Subculture

The broad middle period of Catholic history in the United States from the early mid-1800s to the convening of the Second Vatican Council in 1962 is dominated by one overriding religious and sociological reality: the construction of a partially self-contained Catholic universe that simultaneously served as a mechanism that successfully socialized Catholics into their faith and also served as a vehicle to represent, protect, and promote Catholic political interests in the midst of a non-Catholic hostile, environment. Catholicism proved especially vital during this period because the Catholic religion was embedded in a Catholic cultural milieu and set of institutional arrangements that surrounded the Catholic individual in his/her round of daily existence, hence constantly reinforcing and reasserting the reality and imperatives of that faith.

The cohesiveness and effectiveness of the Catholic subculture or Catholic plausibility structure was partially the result of a conscious design, as laid out in the seven provincial councils and three national plenary councils of Baltimore that spanned the years from 1829 to 1884. The blueprint for what its detractors called the "Catholic ghetto" took on life as doctrine was standardized; renegade clergy were disciplined; and churches, schools, hospitals, and other infrastructural requirements were built. Bishop Gerald Shaughnessy could legitimately quip that the bishops during this period "built the Church in the United States better than they knew" (Kelly 1995, 39). This structure grew and strengthened itself, jelling after World War I. The Orthodox Jewish scholar Will Herberg, speaking of the year 1957, observed that "the Catholic Church in America operates a vast network of institutions of almost every type and variety. . . . This immense system constitutes at one and the same time a self-contained Catholic world with its own complex interior economy and American Catholicism's resources for participation in the larger American community" (1960, 153–54). As Monsignor George A. Kelly puts it, "as a *tour de force* by a religious group, the institutional and community accomplishments of the American Church are unsurpassed in Catholic history" (1979, 456). Monsignor Kelly continues, listing five positive benefits for the Catholic community that were manifest between the post–World War II and pre–Vatican II era. For Monsignor Kelly:

- The overwhelming majority of the Catholic people had been effectively reached by the Church's manifold structures. They were practicing Catholics.

- The Church through its family life and school systems became the instrument of Americanization and upward social mobility.

- The leaders of the Church—Bishops, priests, religious, lay apostles—won the loyalty of the vast numbers of Catholics in major matters involving Church doctrine and Church policy.

- Catholic parishes for the most part were important local communities. Sometimes they were solely ethnic, most often neighborhood centers for Catholics, and occasionally social communities that related successfully to indigenous non-Catholics and to custodians of municipal affairs.

- The institutional Church also presided over the emergence of a Catholic elite—mainly through its colleges, seminaries, and lay apostolic movements for social justice, international peace, family life, and spiritual perfection. These movements owed their existence to the impetus given them by the Holy See from Leo XIII onward. Even the loyal opposition (typified by John Courtney Murray and Dorothy Day) proposed new approaches and new accommodations within the framework of the Church structure. (1979, 456)

The following set of themes play their important roles in this overall development. The first is that American civilization witnessed massive Catholic immigration from Europe, from both Ireland (largely a result of the potato famine) and Germany, and then later from southeastern Europe. The multitudes of Catholic immigrants—once orga-

The Catholic Church grows with the city of Chicago and the expansion of the American nation.
Courtesy of the Library of Congress Prints and Photographs Division.

nized—would eventually form the basis of a certain formidable amount of Catholic cultural and political influence that was absent in the colonial and early republican eras.

A second theme is that Catholic immigrants during this period *were*, indeed, to be eventually and to a significant degree, organized—and organized under a common religious banner, that of the Catholic Church. This existed despite the very real ethnic Catholic differences that existed— and today may exist to some degree in some highly attenuated fashion— between the Irish, Germans, Poles, Italians, and other nationality groups.

A third theme is that the one Catholic group that clearly dominated the others and essentially controlled most of the Catholic Church in America during this period were the Irish. What passed for an "official" Catholicism at this time and place, while no doubt consistent with the message of a universal Catholicism, was clearly colored by Irish attitudes and practices. This coloring was clearly a reflection of the Irish dominance of the Church institution. As, for instance, historian Jay P. Dolan points out:

Though the Irish did not account for more than 50 percent of the Catholic population in 1900, the percentage of Irish priests and bishops was much higher. Among the hierarchy, for example, 62 percent of the bishops in the United States were Irish, and more than half of them had been born in Ireland. A similar though lesser dominance could be found among the parish clergy. One of the few historical studies done on the Roman Catholic clergy found that 45 percent of all the clergy affiliated with the diocese of Saint Paul, Minnesota, from 1850–1930 were of Irish heritage. This Irish hegemony has remained consistent throughout the twentieth century, so that, by 1972, 37 percent of the American clergy and 48 percent of the hierarchy still identified themselves as Irish. (1985, 143–44)

The relationship of the other ethnic groups to the dominant Irish varied. The Germans and Poles, with their well-established European Catholic traditions, tried to fight the Irish while the Italians, Bohemians, and others from less established Catholic traditions were more likely to react to the Irish monopoly through indifference (Link 1975).

A fourth theme was that the clear orientation of the Church in this period, or at least after World War I, was simultaneously to be both "pro-Catholic" and "pro-American," "pro-Rome," and "pro-Washington, D.C." (Morris 1997). In order for this balancing act to be maintained, it required that the Church leadership reject *both* what Father Andrew M. Greeley has referred to as, respectively, the assimilationist (or "Americanist") wing led by Archbishop John Ireland and its more segregationist wing, led by Archbishop Michael A. Corrigan and Bishop Bernard McQuaid and the more radical German proponents of the "anti-Americanist" position (Greeley 1967). The end result of the titantic turn-of-the-century battle between the "Americanizers" and the "anti-Americanizers" was the adoption of the stance of being "in" but not "of" American society. In other words, the strategy was to "be American" by being devotedly, thoroughly, and unabashedly Catholic. This required, in turn, the policy of rejecting and criticizing certain key features of American society in the hopes of evangelizing the civilization, of making it Catholic. The successful implementation of this policy could keep Catholicism in the United States—in the words of Michael Zoller (1999), a "cultural improbability"—alive and thriving. It is interesting to note that it would take until the latter part of the twentieth century for some Catholics to try another approach termed

Archbishop John McCloskey of New York becomes the first American Cardinal. Archbishop James Roosevelt Bayley of Baltimore was a convert of English Protestant antecedents. The moving force behind the building of the magnificent St. Patrick's Cathedral on Fifth Avenue in New York City was Archbishop John Hughes who started construction in 1858. In their own respective ways, these three developments—the appointment of the first Cardinal in the history of the Catholic Church of the United States, the conversion of prominent Protestants, and building of an imposing religious edifice in one of America's great cities—was testimony to the growing importance of the Catholic faith as America moved toward the twentieth century. Here Archbishop Bayley of Baltimore Imposes the Cardinal's berretta upon Archbishop McCloskey of New York at St. Patrick's Cathedral, New York City, April 27, 1875.
Currier & Ives lithograph, c.1875, courtesy of the Library of Congress Prints and Photographs Division.

by sociologists as one of "cultural pluralism"—a certain form of "multiculturalism"—in which ethnic Catholic groups were encouraged simultaneously to respect the language, culture, and customs of their original ancestry while simultaneously and structurally taking their rightful place in the great body of American citizens. The contemporary Hispanic Catholic groupings represent the test case for this experiment in trying to balance ethnicity, religion, and national identity.

A fifth theme is that the plan for constructing the Catholic subculture was laid out in the series of Baltimore provincial and plenary councils starting in 1829 and ending in 1884. However, it is important to

Mount Saint Mary's College and Seminary is one of the Church's earliest institutions of Catholic Higher Education, founded in 1808.
Courtesy of the Library of Congress Prints and Photographs Division.

note that the 1928 campaign of America's first presidential candidate, Al Smith, marked as it was by a rabid anti-Catholicism that had deep roots in the nineteenth century, energized the building and proliferation of a host of Catholic parallel institutions and the making of a partially self-contained Catholic social universe. The Catholic subculture reached its peak, in terms of influence and effort, in the post–World War II era.

Theme six involves the nature of the subcultural reality created. Examples of the institutions that comprised the Catholic subculture or plausibility structure included parishes, seminaries, convents, schools and colleges, newspapers and mass media outlets, professional and academic organizations, unions, hospitals and health care units, and cultural, recreational, and retirement organizations. Many neighborhoods, also, represented more or less de facto Catholic enclaves (Carlin 2003).

The dialectically related developments of a cohesive and ever larger Catholic subculture and increasing political and cultural achievements points to a seventh theme: This was a period for the Church that earned both a grudging respect as well as incurred increased resentment and opposition from the non-Catholic American population. During the course of this middle period, there were many conversions to the Catholic faith. Eventually, however, the nature of the primary opposition to Catholicism changed, from that of Protestantism to that of secularism (Varacalli 2001; Carlin 2003). Indeed, as Protestantism started to lose its hegemonic and culturally defining status in American society, secularists started to utilize, very effectively, narrow interpretations of the First Amendment to deny public funds to Catholic schools and other agencies (Hamburger 2002).

By the 1950s, one could make a respectable argument, following an eighth theme, that precisely because of the successful implementation of the strategy to construct a Catholic subculture, America was on its way to becoming, if not a Catholic country, a country with a powerful and united Catholic presence (Kelly 1990). All of this changed radically and suddenly in the turbulent wake of the Second Vatican Council and the social forces intertwined with it (Kelly 1995; Varacalli 2001; Carlin 2003).

Suggested Readings

Carlin, David R. *The Decline and Fall of the Catholic Church in America*. Manchester, NH: Sofia Institute Press, 2003.

Greeley, Father Andrew M. *The Catholic Experience: An Interpretation of the History of American Catholicism*. Garden City, NY: Doubleday, 1967.

Kelly, Monsignor George A. *Keeping the Church Catholic with John Paul II*. Garden City, NY: Doubleday, 1990.

———. *The Battle for the American Church Revisited*. San Francisco: Ignatius Press, 1995.

Morris, Charles R. *American Catholics: The Saints and Sinners Who Built America's Most Powerful Church*. New York: Times Books, 1997.

Zoller, Michael. *Washington and Rome: Catholicism and American Culture*. Notre Dame, IN: University of Notre Dame Press, 1999.

Chapter 6

Contemporary Catholicism in the United States: A Case of Maturation, Cleansing, and Revitalization or Decomposition, Domestication, and Internal Secularization?

Due to a combination of both external societal and internal religious developments, the immediate post–World War II era (1945–62) of the Catholic Church in the United States that the orthodox Catholic scholar, Monsignor George A. Kelly (1989) has referred to as one of "gold status," suddenly disappeared in the mid-1960s. As David R. Carlin states:

> Given the(se) three factors . . . Vatican II, the end of the Catholic "ghetto," and the American cultural revolution that began in the mid-1960s—it is plain that Catholics were emerging from the Trent era and becoming full participants in American mainstream culture at precisely the moment when the culture was being revolutionized by a generalized rebellion against authority. The convergence of all three factors was a piece of great historical bad luck for the Catholic Church in the United States. It meant that American Catholicism was bound to undergo a sudden and rapid upheavel. (2003, 105)

From a traditional, conservative, or magisterial perspective, the Catholic Church suffered—and still to this day, suffers—from what, variously, has been referred to as a "decomposition," "domestication," and "secularization" (Woods 2004; Carlin 2003; Varacalli 2001; Kelly

1990; Morrissey 1985; Hitchcock 1972). Conversely put, from a liberal or progressive viewpoint, the last fifty years of Catholic Church history in the United States has, on balance, represented a blessing in the form of a "maturing," a cleansing of antiquated ideas and traditions, and a move to reason, science, and individual conscience (Greeley 1976, 1977; Dolan 1985).

The magisterial argument is that Catholicism in the United States started to decompose in the sense that, during the most recent period, there has occurred a successful revolt and rejection of the authority of the pope's central teaching authority of the Church. The result of this contestation of papal authority was, in a sense, the "Protestantization" of the Catholic Church with various groups and individuals within the institution "doing their own thing" and deciding for themselves what parts of the Catholic heritage to accept (if any), what parts they would change, and what new philosophies, both non-Catholic and nonreligious, they would embrace to the detriment of Catholic orthodoxy.

The decomposition of Catholicism took many varied forms. Some Catholics left the Church and religion altogether converting to some secular alternative (e.g., feminism, Marxism/socialism, Freudianism, libertarian capitalism, etc.). Others left the Church to find a home in either liberal Protestantism (e.g., the dominant progressive wings of the Episcopal, Presbyterian, or Congregational churches) or conservative Protestant options (e.g., evangelical or other small sect-like religious groups). Others found some new religions attractive (new age, scientology, transcendental meditation, etc.) or perceived that the grass was greener from the East (e.g., Hinduism, Buddhism, other Asiatic religions). Rejecting the Second Vatican Council, some schismatic Catholic "traditionalists" founded their own churches in an attempt to "go back" to an earlier variation of Catholicism not contaminated, in their minds, with modern influences.

Most Catholics *physically* stayed within the institution during this period of decomposition. However, many of these started to migrate *mentally* to other worldviews and philosophies, internally transforming the meaning of their Catholic faith. This internal transformation naturally had consequences for behavior and activity as these "communal Catholics," to use a phrase made famous by Father Andrew M. Greeley (1976, 1977), started to participate selectively in Church rituals (e.g., not participating in the sacrament of penance or "reconciliation" and reducing significantly their Sunday attendance in Mass, etc.). They proceeded to dissent from specific Church positions (e.g., on issues such as birth control, abortion, and human embryonic stem cell research) and felt less compelled to bring their Catholic faith into the public and civic sphere of American society (i.e., politically fighting for school vouchers for private schools or for a moment of silent private prayer in public schools, or attempting to ban legally or to reduce abortion, etc.). Over time, and with the ushering in of the next generation of Catholics socialized by such a "communal Catholicism," selective rebellion was transformed into apathy, indifference, and simple ignorance of the basic religious, intellectual, social, and political prerequisites of the Catholic faith (Davidson et al. 1991). This internal transformation in both thought and activity was aided, consciously or not, by a hierarchy reluctant, for whatever reasons, to discipline dissenters (Morrissey 1985) or at least to point out the reality and consequences of religious dissent to the unity and presence of the Catholic Church.

Other Catholics weathered the religious and cultural storms of the era with a religious commitment to the historic Catholic faith that became not only stronger but better thought out and more consciously held, an example of what Harvard psychologist Gordon Allport (1960), referred to as the "mature religious commitment." In many instances, these Catholics came from families with a long history of attachment to the Catholic faith. In other cases, some of these Catholics "backed into" a mature appreciation of their faith as they started to reject consciously the non-Catholic options surrounding them during this era of accelerated social change. And, finally and relatedly, not a few serious Catholics of this era of choice and pluralism represent converts from other faiths, who, in their searching, had discovered the Catholic tradition.

Concomitant with the "decomposing" of Catholicism, from the magisterial perspective, in this era was its "domestication." By domestication is meant the process by which a church starts less to challenge the host culture and society and more and more mirror its values and accept its activities. Decomposition and domestication are not synonomous; the former is a more inclusive reality than the latter. Put another way, the domestication of the Catholic Church was the single greatest consequence of its decomposition. This is so for the simple reason that the majority in any society, contemporary American society or otherwise, are conformists. As the classical sociologist Emile Durkheim noted in *The Elementary Forms of the Religious Life* (1965), the central religious commitment of the majority in any society is the "worship" of that society's central value system or what he called its "collective conscience." With the decomposition of the Church commencing in earnest in the mid-1960s, it was a predictable reality that the majority (not all) of Catholics, now "freed" of the demands of their once integrated and internally consistent subculture, would start to assimilate quickly into an American society emphasizing such values as autonomous individualism, materialism, moral and religious relativism, and utilitarianism. With the destruction of the Catholic "plausibility structure," it was almost a certainty, orthodox Catholic thinkers argued, that individual Catholics would start to define "success" not in Catholic religious terms, but in terms dictated and articulated in a society that was quickly losing its original Protestant cast and becoming ever more secular.

Intimately related to the domestication of the Catholic Church is a sociological phenomenon variously termed an "internal secularization" or "secularization from within." Sociologist Peter L. Berger, in his analysis of modern religion, *The Sacred Canopy* (1967), makes the distinction between two processes both weakening the impact of traditional religion on the institutions of society and on individual human consciousness. The first process, more obviously a reality in contemporary Western European society, he termed a "secularization from without." This can also be referred to as an "external" or simple form of secularization. In this form, secularism or out and out nonreligious ideas, simply fills the void, either socially or individually, vacated by traditional symbols and modes of thought. As previously acknowledged, there are more than a few ex-Catholics who have opted for the simple secular alternative. The second process, relatively speaking, more typical in the United States and within the American Catholic community and while no less corrosive to authentic religion, is much more subtle and subdued. Berger refers to the latter as a "secularization from within" or, conversely, an internal secularization. In this form, traditional religion remains, albeit as a hollowed-out, ineffective reality, providing little more than a thin veneer for what is in actuality and effectively nonreligious belief and practice. Put another way, Catholicism has tended, in recent history, to be interpreted in a way as to conform to progressivist and secular thought.

Examples of how an internal secularization operates today within the Church are abundant. In terms of a general theological worldview, certain statements are taken out of their proper context within the documents of the Second Vatican Council (1962–65) and post–Vatican II official theology and used to transform radically what passes for the faith. For example, the Vatican II phrase, that the Church is "the People of God" is used to promote incorrectly the idea that the Church is, at base, a "democratic" institution. In a second example, the Vatican II stress on the importance of a properly formed Christian conscience (conscience as the "supreme subjective norm") is transformed into a defense of the present American movement toward an "autonomous individualism," that is, of the idea that there are no restrictions *whatsoever* in what a person can believe in and that, in the final analysis, it is the individual who is the ultimate locus of authority. In another example, it is made to appear the case that the constitutive and mandatory Catholic concern for individuals to assist to institutionalize justice in the world can only be implemented through the application of socialist and utopian modes of thought and programs. In another case, the Catholic concern for a realistic ecumenism based on discovering what Vatican II referred to as those "rays of truth" found in other religions and in the cross-cultural commonalities of natural law thinking is transfigured purposely into the common progressive argument for moral and religious relativism, or the idea that all moral and religious positions are, more or less, equal in dignity and truth content. One can also point to the blurring between the important distinction between the Catholic understanding of the infinite mercy of God and the uncritical acceptance of the modern day, self-centered "therapeutic mentality," a mentality that tends to deny the reality of sin itself and to eliminate personal responsibility for conscious decision-making. Such examples of an internal secularization can be multiplied and represents the consequence of the great desire of many Catholic bishops, priests, religious, and laity to conform to the ways of the world and to make their religion presentation "acceptable" to secular cultural elites. In terms of the great classificatory scheme of H. R. Niebuhr's *Christ and Culture* (1951), this represents a strong movement toward a "Christ of culture" stance, of the idea that the priorities of the Church should be the priorities of the world, a position strongly endorsed by progressive Catholics who view recent developments within the Church and society as salutary. Put another way, it is an acceptance of the claim of the liberal Baptist theologian, Harvey Cox, who in his *The Secular City* (1990) declared that the larger culture is "out in front" of the Churches and that the churches must catch up to the world.

Could this modern situation for Catholics vis-à-vis a secular society be otherwise than it is? Progressive Catholics basically answer "no" as they view modern, secular developments as inevitable, irreversible, and positive. Others, however, believe that the present situation can be changed and altered significantly. The key issue, for orthodox Catholics, is whether or not present-day Catholic leadership has the will and the ability to rebuild a set of institutions capable of generating a Catholic belief system that can be perceived to be "real," that possesses what the pyschologist William James ([1902] 1994) refers to as a necessary "accent on reality."

Rooted in the work of the sociologist Charles H. Cooley (1909), such commentators point out that individuals need not be merely socialized by the messages of the mainstream culture; rather they are capable simultaneously of being shaped also by what is termed primary groups, whether the primary group formation crystallizes into what sociologists term subcultures or countercultures. Going back to our previous chapter, the relevant point is that at the midpoint of the twentieth century, the Catholic Church had established a coherent and impressive set of institutional arrangements (a "plausibility structure") that afforded its members an effective break and alternative to the dominant society message. As we have learned, the Catholic plausibility structure had reached its historical maximum effectiveness during the post–World War II period but is now in a state of severe disarray, damaged by the widespread internal dissent allowed to fester in the post–Vatican II period. The end result of this organizational *hari kari* has been that, without an effective and authentic mode of Catholic mediation, the dominant and now secular mainstream culture has had an almost uncontested ability to shape the minds and hearts of the younger generations of American Catholics. The decomposition, domestication, and internal secularization of Catholicism in modern American life is intimately associated with the collapse of the very Catholic plausibility structure built so steadfastly and painfully during the immediately preceding era of American Catholic history by bishop and immigrant alike in communal solidarity.

Progressive Catholics would agree only with the proposition that the Catholic plausibility structure has been weakened; they see that weakening as something quite positive. They assert that the destruction of what they invidiously refer to as the "Catholic ghetto" was both necessary and inevitable. It was inevitable, progressivists claim, because such a deinstitutionalization would have happened with or without the

occurrence of Vatican II due to the overpowering and liberating movement toward individualism, freedom, democracy, and other modern
values. Indeed, if anything, Vatican II was viewed by many progressives
as the Church's belated response to the themes of secular life. That Vatican II occurred when it did only speeded up, so this logic goes, an inevitable Americanization and modernization process. Progressive
Catholics also argue that the destruction of the Catholic ghetto or, more
neutrally termed, "plausibility structure" was necessary and called for
by at least the spirit of Vatican II. This is so given the progressive belief that the Catholic ghetto created a Catholic mentality and stance to
the world at odds with the necessary modern, ecumenical, worldview.
More traditional thinkers, of course, demure from this logic, arguing
that the construction of an intact and internally consistent plausibility
structure is a necessary, although not sufficient, condition to keep an
authentic Catholicism alive in the hearts and minds of the Catholic population and to evangelize throughout the rest of American civilization.

For better or worse, the progressive Catholic forces were able to
deconstruct quite successfully a good deal of the Catholic plausibility
structure in the post–Vatican II period of the Catholic Church in the
United States with a thorough Americanization, Protestantization, and
secularization the logical results. The Catholic restorationists, at the
moment of this writing, are in a heated battle with liberal Catholicism
over who controls the infrastructure of Catholic organizational life.

Suggested Readings

Berger, Peter L. *The Sacred Canopy: Elements of a Sociological Theory of Religion.* Garden City, NY: Doubleday, 1967.
Carlin, David R. *The Decline and Fall of the Catholic Church in America.* Man-
chester, NH: Sofia Institute Press, 2003.
Cox, Harvey. *The Secular City: Secularization and Urbanization in Theologi-
cal Perspective.* 25th Anniversary ed. New York: Simon and Schuster,
1990.
Greeley, Father Andrew M. *The Communal Catholic.* New York: Seabury,
1976.
———. *The American Catholic.* New York: Basic Books, 1977.
Hitchcock, James. *The Decline and Fall of Radical Catholicism.* New York:
Image Books, 1972.

Morrissey, Gerard. *The Crisis of Dissent.* Front Royal, VA: Christendom College, 1985.

Niebuhr, H. R. *Christ and Culture.* New York: Harper and Row, 1951.

Varacalli, Joseph A. *Bright Promise, Failed Community: Catholics and the American Public Order.* Lanham, MD: Lexington Books, 2001.

Woods, Thomas E., Jr. *The Church Confronts Modernity: Catholic Intellectuals and the Progressive Era.* New York: Columbia University Press, 2004.

Chapter 7

Too Little, Too Late? John Paul II, Benedict XVI, and the Catholic Restorationist Movement

When Karol Wojtyla ascended to the papacy in 1978, the progressivist revolt against Catholic orthodoxy was well underway, especially in the area of moral theology. Some progressive thinkers claimed that the pontificate of John Paul II signaled, to their chagrin, a return to a "pre–Vatican II" Church or, worse, to a medieval Catholicism. Other progressive thinkers gave him some credit for his development of Catholic social thought, which they see as basically progressive and for his ecumenical outreach to other religions which, if still too tepid for their tastes, still is viewed as fundamentally positive. All in all, however, progressive Catholicism has been in opposition to his papacy and his vision.

In some real ways, the pontificate of John Paul II, from a more orthodox or traditional perspective, *did* start to reverse or, at least, slow the progressive tide set in motion by a liberal interpretation of the significance of the Second Vatican Council, rekindling their hope for a bright promise for the Catholic faith in America (Johnson 1981). In other ways, his pontificate, from the orthodox perspective, witnessed the further decomposition, secularization, and domestication of the faith. Indeed, from an orthodox perspective, talk of a "Catholic moment" (Neuhaus 1987) in American history was just as premature as it was in 1978 with ensuing positive and negative developments representing more or less a "wash."

Some Catholic conservatives would contend that these contradictory movements can be explained, perhaps at least in part, as a function of John Paul II's philosophy and managerial style. John Paul II preferred to emphasize the future and to encourage the development of *new* movements, apostolates, and religious orders. Those who tend to defend the pope unqualifiedly argue that, practically speaking, this is all that he could do; the pope is, sociologically speaking, an "expressive leader" who can basically only suggest, guide, and inspire through his words, actions, and respected holiness. While not denying all the wonderously positive aspects of his pontificate, other orthodox Catholic commentators argued that the pope did have a juridical role in governing the Church. Such individuals claimed that he did not do well as a disciplinarian and did not do much in the form of active intervention to stop either the heterodoxy, at worst, or the poor management, at best, occurring within the long-standing structures and traditions within the Church (e.g., dioceses, religious orders, semi-autonomous organizations like Catholic colleges and universities, and social movements). Excommunication, for instance, was rarely exercised. Nor was there much in terms of the replacement, while in office, of bishops who were less than faithful or ineffective in maintaining the faith. This has led to the charge made by a not insignificant number of devout and orthodox Catholics that "the Pope disappointed us." These Catholics, it must be emphasized, are not to be confused with those "heterodox, right wing" Catholics who deny the validity of the Second Vatican Council and who have even argued that the See of Peter has been "vacant" since the death of Pope Pius XII.

On the other hand, there is no question that the papacy of John Paul II (1978–2005) energized the minority orthodox community within the contemporary Catholic Church of the United States to some significant degree. The term "restorationists" has been applied to this group. The term is neither completely accurate nor fair insofar as it is used to imply that the goal of the restorationists is to bring back into being some form of Catholic theocracy or the alleged "good old days" of a medieval Catholicism or even of the relatively golden era of a "1950s" American Catholicism. The term is useful, however, in pointing out the restorationist goals of bringing a dynamic orthodoxy back into the Church and of having it serve as a leaven in the larger society. The restorationists are concerned with institutionalizing a strong Catholic/Christian presence in the American public square and of co-opting and strengthening whatever is useful in modern life to promote Catholic/Christian goals (e.g., scientific or technological advances; cultural and political ideas such as democracy and the separation of Church and State, properly understood; rational systems to provide mass education and health care services; etc.). The term restorationist is being used in this volume in this latter sense.

Since 1978, restorationists *have* made some progress—albeit slow, uneven, and with many setbacks and complications—in laying the groundwork for the institutionalization of their vision. Many (although certainly not all) of the new bishops appointed by John Paul II are more orthodox and obvious in their allegiance to the historic faith. Newer cohorts of priests, sisters, and seminarians are likewise more serious, traditional, and sophisticated in their faith; furthermore, seminary recruitment is increasing under bishops who are orthodox. Not only are the religious orders that are traditional thriving, but new orthodox organizations, like the Legionaries of Christ, have recently come into existence. Opus Dei has become a major religious force on the American Catholic scene. Lay-based organizations like Catholics United for the Faith, the Wanderer Forum, Women for Faith and Family, and the Catholic League for Religious and Civil Rights are both growing in numbers and in their effectiveness as evangelizers and defenders of the faith. More than a few new orthodox Catholic colleges, albeit small ones, have been created. A few more like Franciscan University in Steubenville, Ohio, and the University of Dallas, Texas, have turned the corner back to orthodoxy. There has also been an explosion in ortho-

Pope John Paul II visits the United States in 1979. John Paul II also came to America in 1987, 1993, and 1995 visiting many cities.
Courtesy of the Library of Congress Prints and Photographs Division.

dox Catholic publishing ventures led by Ignatius Press. Mother Angelica's EWTN television and radio and computer highway ventures make the Catholic faith available across all the sectors of American society. Catholic websites and "bloggers" abound. Another innovation made possible in today's sophisticated world of communications is the creation of the International Catholic University, which offers, through the medium of electronics, the possibility of earning a college degree under the tutelage of nationally prominent orthodox Catholic scholars. Professional organizations of intellectuals such as the Fellowship of Catholic Scholars, the Cardinal Newman Society for the Preservation of Catholic Higher Education, and the Society of Catholic Social Scientists and other professional organizations of lawyers, businessmen, and medical personnel are on the rise once again (Varacalli 2001). Justified by the present popularity of the educational and societywide philosophy of multiculturalism, Catholic studies programs are now starting to appear even within public institutions of higher education such as the University of Illinois at two of its campuses, Urbana-Champlain and Chicago, and also at Nassau Community College in the SUNY system.

Catholic restorationists have been both creative and busy in their assorted religious, intellectual, and organizational activities. And these activities will no doubt generate newer and perhaps more effective apostolates. Within the internal Catholic community, the results have been far from satisfactory even in the larger dioceses led by overtly orthodox leadership, the result of forty years of neglect and active dissent. Indeed, one of Pope John Paul's strongest supporters, Bernard Cardinal Law, recently resigned in disgrace over his failure, over a prolonged period of time, to address the widespread priests' sex scandal. Overall, knowledge of and commitment to the Catholic religion on the part of the Catholic population continues to erode, albeit at different paces in different sectors of the Church, notable countertrends notwithstanding. Regarding the larger society, the matrix of restorationist activities has only recently registered any serious recognition on the part of the cultural gatekeepers of mainstream American life. Perhaps only two discernible dents into the secular monopoly existing within the American public sphere have been made recently by the restorationists: their political assistance in helping to re-elect George W. Bush to the American presidency and the hugh religious/cultural success represented by Mel Gibson's movie, *The Passion of the Christ*. However, humanly speaking, the efforts of the Catholic restorationists probably represent a case of "too little, too late." One thing is clear, however, Catholic restorationists, boosted by the recent election of an even stronger restorationist to head the Catholic Church, Pope Benedict XVI, and by their belief that the "gates of Hell" shall not prevail against the Church will continue to sacrifice and fight for a cause that is for them holy, if perhaps, forlorn.

Suggested Readings

Johnson, Paul. *Pope John Paul II and the Catholic Restoration.* New York: St. Martin's Press, 1981.

Varacalli, Joseph A. *Bright Promise, Failed Community: Catholics and the American Public Order.* Lanham, MD: Lexington Books, 2001.

PART III

AMERICA'S BEST KEPT SECRET: CATHOLIC SOCIAL THOUGHT

atholic social thought is the body of ideas promulgated by legitimate authorities within the Catholic Church on the issues of how, ideally, society and specific social arrangements (e.g., politics, economics, marriage, and family) ought to be constructed and how individuals ought to live moral lives. Contained within Catholic social thought is also a cognitive or social scientific component that analyzes empirically just how and why civilizations, social arrangements, and individuals fail to meet what the Church considers universal standards of conduct. Implicit, in many cases, is also a social policy aspect offering suggestions to public officials, scholarly and educational elites, and citizens about the creation of just laws and social programs promoting what the Church views as the "common good." Official Catholic social thought is derived from a variety of sources: from papal encyclicals and other papal statements, from the teachings of the Church fathers (e.g., Augustine, Aquinas), and later intellectual figures (e.g., John Henry Cardinal Newman, Heinrich Pesch), from the deliberations of the Second Vatican Council and worldwide synods of bishops convened by the popes, and, since the midsixties, from the documents produced by various national conferences of Catholic bishops.

In general, Catholic social thought has not made much of an impact on either world or American civilization. Probably its greatest impact has been in post–World War II Europe and Latin America in the wake of the destruction of the Second World War and through the creation of various Christian Democratic political parties. There are a variety of reasons for the failure of Catholic social thought to shape American civilization. They include, among others, (1) the dominance of a common and unsympathetic Protestant culture early in the history of the American Republic; (2) the contemporary monopoly held by an equally unsympathetic secular (nonreligious) worldview in the contemporary public square; (3) the practical limitations imposed on a poor, impoverished, immigrant Catholic Church early in American history; and (4) the contemporary assimilationist tendency of American Catholics to blend into an increasingly less-Christianized American civilization.

That Catholic social thought has not made much of an impact on American society does not mean either that it cannot or it should not make the attempt. The contemporary influence in American society of the philosophy of multiculturalism, for one thing, invites such an attempt. Multiculturalism precisely provides a vehicle for traditions hitherto ignored or belittled to present their ideas, ideally to be accepted or rejected based on the merit, or lack thereof, of their potential contribution to the making of a just and humane society. Advocates of Catholic social thought, while acknowledging the many positive features of American society (e.g., a high standard of living; significant scientific, technological, and medical advances; a legal system that, relatively speaking, defends the dignity of the otherwise disenfranchised) feel strongly that within its intellectual corpus lies a treasure chest of important ideas and suggestions that can enrich American civilization. More specifically, they argue, Catholic social thought can serve as a counterbalance to what are perceived to be the weaknesses and excesses of American society. From a Catholic eye, it is one dominated by the materialism generated by American corporate capitalism, by the dependency and loss of freedom concomitant with the general growth in the role of government power in the lives of American citizens, by the selfishness and "me-orientedness" produced by the continued trajectory of the key American value of individualism away from any concern for the common good of society, and the indifference to issues of ultimate truth that is part and parcel of the increased acceptance of the philosophy of religious and moral relativism.

Chapter 8, "Rome Has Spoken: Enough Said!" will provide the reader, among other contributions, with a brief introduction to some of the key ideas and claims of some of the major encyclicals written by Catholic popes of the nineteenth and twentieth centuries, with a special focus on the contributions of the recently deceased pontiff, John Paul II who reigned from 1978 until 2005. Chapter 9, "Four Responses of American Catholics to Catholic Doctrine," will give evidence of four distinctive reactions on the part of the American Catholic community to the official papal vision on Catholic social thinking: those of indifference, rejection, acceptance, and, finally, the attempt to carve out a "via media" between official church and other American traditions.

Chapter 8

"Rome Has Spoken: Enough Said!"

It was the saint/bishop of Hippo, Augustine, who made clear, theoretically at least, who has the final say in determining the doctrine, including the social doctrine, of the Catholic Church when he declared, "Rome has spoken: enough said!" As we shall learn from the next chapter and throughout the volume, getting Catholics—in the United States and elsewhere—to accept willingly and follow the Church's stated theology and vision for society is much easier said than done. In this chapter, however, the concern is with the *ideal,* not with the reality of the situation. Put another way, the focus of this chapter is with the vision of society that the Catholic Church propounds and through which it claims to help, both spiritually and materially, the lot of all mankind, the Catholic American community in the United States included. Given its complexity, only a representative sample of the logic and vision of Catholic social teaching can be presented in this chapter.

The Catholic Church claims that it perennially offers mankind a bright promise of eternal salvation resting with the Lord in the next life and a balanced, purposeful life in this world serving God, and through God, oneself, one's family, one's local community, and one's society. The Catholic vision enriches both world civilization and American culture primarily in two overlapping ways. The first is as the standard bearer and ultimate interpreter of the natural law, that is, conceptions of right and wrong that are embedded into the very constitution of the human being or, as Saint Paul put it, "written into the human heart." The natural law assumes that there is an objective morality structured into the very essence of nature, society, and the individual; furthermore, human reason can comprehend this objective morality. Through the natural law, the Church defends the existence of purpose in the world and the ability to comprehend truth, exemplify holiness, appreciate beauty, and exercise discernment and prudence in the utilization of the various goods of the earth. The natural law tradition, for the Church, is also the primary vehicle for legitimate ecumenical relations between individuals and civilizations given its belief in the common reasoning ability of human beings. It also serves as the primary antidote to the prevailing *subjectivist* (i.e., morality is socially constructed), and *therapeutic* (i.e., "me-oriented"), philosophies that are so popular today in Western civilization and which the Church claims bring so much social pathology and human destruction in their wake.

Second and overlapping with the natural law, the Church contributes culturally to civilization through her constant presentation and organic development of Catholic social doctrine or, more commonly referred to as Catholic social teaching. As the Commonweal Foundation Report, *American Catholics in the Public Square,* states:

> Catholicism is one of the few world religions with a highly developed system of social teaching because it has had to grapple with the political, social, and economic conditions of the modern world. Popes from Leo XIII to John Paul II, along with Catholics around the world, have addressed public square issues, such as the conditions of labor and the right to organize unions, the situation of the poor, the rights of families to bear, rear, and educate their offspring, the right of the church to teach in secular societies, and the rights of indigenous and ethnic cultures to maintain their languages and ways of life. . . . Compelling theological and philosophical reflection on globalization, the maldistribution of the world's goods, and the growing gap between rich and poor nations has been one of the major contributions of John Paul II to civic life around the globe. (2004, 2)

John Paul II's *Veritatis Splendor* affirms, among many other points, that the only valid understanding of freedom involves fidelity to truth. In his *Fides et Ratio* (1998), he analyzes the complementary and noncontradictory relationship between faith and reason. The fundamental importance of the family as the basic cell of society is analyzed in encyclicals that range from Pius XI's *Casti Connubii* (1930) to Pope Paul VI's *Humanae Vitae* (1968) to John Paul II's *Familiaris Consortio* (1981). In *Mulieris Dignitatem* (1988), John Paul II pronounces on the fundamental dignity of and equality between men and women. In Pius

XI's *Divini Redemptoris* (1937), the pernicious nature of atheistic communism is exposed, with *Non Abbiamo Bisogno* (1931) and *Mit Brennender Sorge* (1937) doing the same for Italian fascism and German national socialism. In *Divini Illius Magistri* (1929), Pius XI notes the foundational rights of parents to educate their children and the necessarily religious and moral nature of all education. In *Pacem in Terris* (1963), Pope John XXIII restates the Catholic principle that the purpose of government is to promote the common good which itself involves furthering the total person, both body and soul. *Centesimus Annus,* authored by John Paul II in 1991, provides a powerful Catholic critique of both capitalism and socialism, defending, in a qualified manner, the right to private property, profit, and the free market but cautioning against the consumerism and superficial gratifications found especially in the West. In *Evangelium Vitae* (1994), John Paul II calls on the laity to support and further central Catholic teachings to promote life at every stage of the life cycle, from the moment of conception until natural death. Creative, dignified work, he stated, is a constitutive element in the anthropology of mankind, and a prerequisite for a just social order is the key message of John Paul's 1981 encyclical, *Laborem Exercens.* The fundamental rights of workers to organize and fight for a decent material and spiritual existence is laid out in what many consider the first great modern social encyclical, *Rerum Novarum,* authored by Pope Leo XIII in 1891. *Quadragesimo Anno* (1931), written by Pope Pius XI, followed Leo's encyclical, laying out the proper organizational principle of society, that is, that of "subsidiarity" and the requirement of the Good Society to have vital mediating structures and intermediate social institutions to actively incorporate the citizenry into the dealings of civil society. Such mediating structures protect against both the abuses and ineffectiveness of statism and other forms of societal monopolization, including corporate capitalism. That the creation of an international world order demands the assistance of modern, more developed industrialized societies to those more traditional and least industrialized in nature and that "true development" entails the recognition of more than just economic considerations (cultural, social, moral concerns), is analyzed by Pope Paul VI in *Populorum Progressio* (1967).

Defenders of the role that Catholicism can play for society claim that, empirically speaking, there is simply no other agency on earth that has produced such a wealth of insight on how the world does, and should, operate. For believing Catholics, what the contemporary Catholic scholar, Father Richard J. Neuhaus (1995) says of the recent encyclicals of Pope John Paul II holds true for the ever developing, ever more sophisticated, and ever more useful tradition of Catholic social teaching: that it presents "the world with an ensemble of reasons to hope, of reasons to believe, of reasons to act, of reasons not to be afraid. There is nothing even remotely like this teaching in the whole of the world." These teachings, furthermore, as pointed out by Stephen M. Krason (1991, 1998, 2003), are both consistent with each other and organically related. And, again, the comprehensiveness and awe-inspiring scope of the social doctrine of the Church has only been lightly touched on here.

It should be pointed out, in concluding this brief introduction to Catholic social teaching, that the Church aids society and civilization in other ways. One is through its elaborate set of organizations and institutions, which can serve potentially as a powerful set of "mediating structures" in society. Another is the Church's ability to shape the character and personality of individuals, both Catholic and otherwise. Indeed, the Catholic Church has always evinced, as intrinsic to its very nature, a fundamental concern for the disenfranchised and those others in suffering and in need, for the building up of a vital community life, and for the construction of a well-ordered polity and society. Put another way, the Catholic concern for the dignity of the individual and for the institutionalization of justice in the world is not merely a contemporary phenomenon. James Hitchcock, for one, makes clear that the social dimension of the Gospel was not an entirely modern discovery: "traditional Catholicism was never indifferent to the social dimensions of religion, as manifested for example in the countless hospitals, orphanages, homes for the aged, and other institutions operated by the Church" (1984, 125–26).

The contributions to the individual and society, both actual and potential, of the Catholic Church in America will be explored in upcoming chapters. Also discussed will be the many controversies that surround these contributions.

Suggested Readings

American Catholics in the Public Square: A Report to the Catholic Community. Foreword by Margaret O'Brien Steinfels. New York: The Commonweal Foundation, 2004.

Hitchcock, James. *The Pope and the Jesuits: John Paul II and the New Order in the Society of Jesus.* New York: The National Committee of Catholic Laymen, Inc., 1984.

Krason, Stephen M. *Liberalism, Conservatism, and Catholicism: An Evaluation of Contemporary Political Ideologies in Light of Catholic Social Teachings.* New Hope, KY: Catholics United for the Faith, 1991.

———. *Preserving a Good Political Order and a Democratic Republic: Reflections from Philosophy, Great Thinkers, Popes, and America's Founding Era.* Lewiston, NY: Edward Mellen Press, 1998.

———. *The Public Order and the Sacred Order.* Portage, MI: Page Free Publishing, 2003.

Neuhaus, Reverend Richard J. "The Catholic Moment in America." In *Catholics in the Public Square*, edited by Thomas Patrick Melady. Huntington, IN: Our Sunday Visitor, 1995.

Chapter 9

Four Responses of American Catholics to Catholic Doctrine: Indifference, Rejection, Acceptance, or the Carving out of "La Via Media"

Regarding Catholic doctrine, including the social doctrine of the Church, when Rome speaks, American Catholics may or may not listen, care, learn, or obey. Sociological studies, conducted by James Davidson and colleagues, have demonstrated that successive generations (pre–Vatican II, Vatican II, and post–Vatican II) of Catholics in the United States manifest increasingly less knowledge of, and assent to, the teachings of the Catholic Church (Davidson et al. 1997; *American Catholics in the Public Square* 2004). More simply put, over the past forty years it is clearly the case that fewer and fewer American Catholics are listening to, caring about, learning from, or obeying the Catholic religious tradition. To take just two prominent examples, no more than half of American Catholics fully accept the Church's teaching about the intrinsic evil of abortion, as discussed in *Evangelium Vitae* (1994), among many other Church documents, and no more than a fifth appear overall to accept the Church's teaching banning artificial means of birth control as presented in *Humanae Vitae* (1968), again among many other Church pronouncements. The situation, from an orthodox Catholic perspective, is actually worse given demographic trends in the attitudes and practices of the Catholic faith with perhaps no more than 10 percent of Catholics of child-bearing age heeding the Church's advice on the issue.

Indeed, the prospects for an authentic Catholic presence in the

United States in the immediate future are extraordinarily bleak, at least based on recent social scientific findings. As the *American Catholics in the Public Square* report states (hereafter *Report*):

> The trajectory of . . . generational tendencies . . . [is] . . . summed up by political scientist David Leege: succeeding generations of Catholics are less likely to expose themselves to religious information or cues about faith and life, in part, because Mass attendance is down. That means less exposure to the church's teaching and far less group reinforcement in church settings among the young adult generation. (2004, 10)

The *Report* also makes good use of the sociological studies conducted by sociologist James D. Davidson (1999; Davidson et al. 1997), which compared "pre–Vatican II Catholics" (born before 1940), with "Vatican II Catholics" (born between 1941 and 1960) and with "post–Vatican II Catholics" (born between 1961 and the present). A few of the most salient conclusions about "post–Vatican II Catholics" are presented in the *Report* as follows:

- They are less involved in the Catholic community than their parents and grandparents. Forty-nine percent of young adult Catholics almost never go to church: 51 percent do go to church but only 21 percent go every week or more.
- The post–Vatican II generation is least involved in parish life and other religious activities. For Davidson, these findings suggest that Catholic rates of religious participation are likely to decline even further as the Vatican II and post–Vatican II generations replace the pre–Vatican II generation.
- Young Catholics . . . increasingly are marrying non-Catholics. (2004, 9–10)

The *Report* summarizes the social-scientific and other forms of evidence about the withering knowledge of and commitment to the Catholic faith on the part of most post–Vatican II Catholics as follows:

> Polling data, anecdotal evidence, and widespread observation make clear that coming generations of Catholics do not share their parents'

and grandparents' commitment to the institutional church, nor do they affirm their faith with equal, or sometimes any, intensity. Whether measured by Mass attendance, parish registration, or knowledge of Catholic teaching, at least half of those born after 1960 have an attenuated attachment to the core beliefs and practices that mark older generations of Catholics. (2004, 10)

How can this lack of knowledge and acceptance of the Church's teachings be explained? For one thing, human beings are, by their very nature, "free" to make choices, for good or for ill. No human organization can fully guarantee that its message, even when backed up by coercive force, will ever be accepted fully. Probably a more important explanation lies within what sociologists refer to as the processes of "socialization." This theory asserts that all human beings are born into the world "instinctually deprived," and hence, in a sense, "incomplete"; what "completes" the human being is the substitution of culture for instincts. In other words, all human beings, in order to become functioning members of society, must be "socialized." Furthermore, in a pluralistic society like that of the modern United States, there are a multitude of differing socializing agents (Luckmann 1961), of which the Catholic faith is only one. The Catholic faith, in other words, must compete for the hearts and minds of individuals baptized into the Catholic faith (as well as outside of the faith) with a host of other agents, many of whom present a message to the individual that is quite at odds with the Catholic vision. As we have already learned, for instance, America was, historically, a society dominated by Protestantism, much of it hostile to Catholicism. While Protestantism has lost much of its society-defining ability in modern America, what has replaced it as key to American culture—that is, various forms of secular thought—is arguably even more antithetical to the Catholic faith (scientism, capitalism, socialism, moral relativism, autonomous individualism, materialism, utilitarianism, etc.). Given the fact that most people in any society "worship" and consider "sacred" the key values of that society's central value system—what the classical sociologist, Emile Durkheim (1965) termed the societal "collective conscience"—it should come as little surprise that most (but again, not all) contemporary American Catholics are "nominally Catholic," with some other set of socializing agents more fundamentally shaping their worldview, character, personality, and social and personal priorities. Certainly it is the case that, by definition, to become a societal "elite" assumes acceptance of what the particular society in question considers crucially important. Add to all of this that the contemporary Catholic Church's "plausibility structure" has been so battered and defiled over the past forty years—and hence so weakened in its ability to provide an alternative worldview considered attractive and compelling—it explains the reality of the limited ability of Catholicism to evangelize successfully among its own population and the American population at large.

There are four major theoretical and empirical options that are open to members of the Catholic community regarding the issue of the reception of Catholic doctrine. In this regard, the distinguished sociologist of religion, Peter L. Berger, would refer to the situation that the Catholic Church in a pluralistic setting like the United States is one of facing various "options in social engineering" (1967).

Given the increasing assimilation of the Catholic population at large into a progressively more secular society, one major response is simply "indifference." This response reflects neither anger nor philosophical disagreement but the perception that the Catholic tradition is simply a "foreign," "alien" reality, a reality of no real consequence in the lives of everyday individuals who may or may not have been baptized into the Catholic faith but are, at least sociologically, outside the Catholic community. These are the nominal Catholics who rarely or at best occasionally participate in the life of the Church, perhaps at a baptism, or wedding, or funeral involving some family member or friend.

A second response is that of "rejection." This is the response of those who subjectively define themselves as "Catholic" and, at the same time, quite consciously disagree with a religious heritage they perceive to be "obsolete" and simply wrongheaded, and one that officially refuses to change. Those who take the rejection response basically have one of two options to embrace. On the one hand, they can leave the Catholic institution and accept some other worldview as their "ultimate concern," to refer to the definition of religion as espoused by the Protestant theologian, Paul Tillich (1957), or they "can stay and fight." The responses of those who choose the former vary. Some accept some type of secular philosophy. Others move to some version of Protestantism that better incorporates the modern values of individualism, freedom, and this-worldliness. Still others convert to some form of fundamentalist religious "sect" or schismatic "Catholic" traditionalist group because of their doctrinal and moral clarity and firmness vis-à-vis a more liberalized, pluralistic Catholic Church.

Another form of "rejection" is when one refuses to leave the Catholic Church and attempts to transform internally the Church into a different and preferred image, along a far more progressive (to refer to H. R. Niebuhr's 1951 phrase) "Christ of culture" version fostering Marxist, feminist, Freudian, anarchistic, or simply more individualistic visions. The purpose here is actually *to transform by redefinition* the meaning of Catholic doctrine. The previous discussion of an "internal secularization" or a "secularization from within" is relevant as such nonreligious ideas as a this-worldly salvation, autonomous individualism, class consciousness and class conflict, "conscientization," the therapeutic mentality, and moral and religious relativism are attempted to be incorporated into the Catholic faith.

A third response is that of the acceptance of the official teachings of the Church. This response, again, has become progressively smaller despite the fact that some young people have been attracted to the orthodox option (Carroll 2002), and conversely, have been rejecting the consequences of a secular world. They represent a cause of hope for orthodox Catholicism. The orthodox option takes two routes. For many among the older generation whose beliefs were formed prior to the Second Vatican Council, the orthodox embrace may be of a taken-for-granted nature, the end result of successful parental and Catholic socialization. For many younger Catholics who have embraced the orthodox option in the face of contemporary radical pluralism, the embrace may be more one of self-conscious awareness, of more self-conscious choice. For the latter, these individuals have gone through the "fiery brook" of sociological relativity and have concluded—after a period of experimentation, reflection, and comparison—that the Catholic Church provides the truest and most useful depiction of the "ends of man" and how to live a life devoted to God and, through God, to society, one's family, one's friends, and oneself.

The final reaction of some of the Catholic community to Roman exhortations of orthodoxy is to attempt consciously to carve out some "middle ground" between the Catholic religious tradition and modern secular life, between "Rome and Washington"—to refer to the title of a recent volume by the German Catholic scholar, Michael Zoller (1999). This response would see Catholic orthodoxy as an important option, but only an "option" in the life of modern Catholics. It is different from the second form of "rejection" discussed in its stated advocacy in defense of a Catholic pluralism, or the idea that there are many legitimate ways to be Catholic with none, theoretically, being granted any superior status. It would be a vision that grants a great deal of freedom to participate in the Catholic faith on radically individualistic terms or via the vision of some "sect-like" wing of the Catholic tradition, be it those who emphasize social justice concerns, liturgical issues, personal fulfillment as the religious goal, or the creation of human community as the essence of religion. In all of this, the official version of the Catholic heritage would be seen as an important resource, but *only* a resource, from which one "picks and chooses." Such a scenario, if it were to come about, would be consistent with the prediction of the ascendency of highly individuated forms of religiosity as predicted by the liberal Protestant sociologist, Ernest Troeltsch (1931), and his contemporary student, Peter L. Berger (1969, 1979).

Suggested Readings

American Catholics in the Public Square: A Report to the Catholic Community. Foreword by Margaret O'Brien Steinfels. New York: The Commonweal Foundation, 2004; also an insert in *Commonweal,* July 16, 2004.

Berger, Peter L. *The Sacred Canopy: Elements of a Sociological Theory of Religion.* Garden City, NY: Doubleday, 1967.

———. *A Rumor of Angels: Modern Society and the Rediscovery of the Supernatural.* New York: Doubleday, 1969.

———. *The Heretical Imperative.* New York: Doubleday, 1979.

Carroll, Colleen. *The New Faithful: Why Young Adults Are Embracing Christian Orthodoxy.* Chicago: Loyola University Press, 2002.

Davidson, James, et al. *The Search for Common Ground: What Unites and Divides American Catholics.* Huntington, IN: Our Sunday Visitor, 1997.

Tillich, Paul. *Dynamics of Faith.* New York: Harper and Row, 1957.

Troeltsch, Ernest. *The Social Teachings of the Christian Churches.* London: George Allen and Unwin, Ltd., 1931.

Zoller, Michael. *Washington and Rome: Catholicism and American Culture.* Notre Dame, IN: University of Notre Dame Press, 1999.

PART IV

DIVERSITY WITHIN UNITY?
THE SOCIAL GEOGRAPHY OF
THE CONTEMPORARY
AMERICAN CATHOLIC
COMMUNITY

Part IV (Chapters 10–19) raises issues of both the reality and the consequences of pluralism for the Catholic Church of the United States. It discusses what types of pluralism exist and how much of this pluralism represents a vivifying "diversity within unity." It seeks to explain how much of this pluralism, conversely, has furthered the doctrinal decomposition of the Catholic religion into competing factions who are only unified nominally, that is, "in name only." Both external social sources (Chapters 10–16) and internal religious sources (Chapters 17–18) are analyzed to see how they have produced differing theological and philosophical worldviews among the Catholic population (Chapter 19)—views that range from being compatible with each other to those representing incommensurate worldviews.

Chapter 10 discusses the successive waves of different ethnic groups into the Catholic Church of this country (e.g., English, French, Irish, German, Italian, Slav, Hispanic, Asiatic, African, Indian, Arab, Filipino)—all of whom have brought distinctive traditions with them. Chapter 11 makes the case that the original Catholic immigrants were basically poor, powerless, and with little prestige but that today's Church is typified as one strongly upper-middle class in orientation yet still represented by a wide spectrum of socioeconomic backgrounds. This chapter will also discuss just how these differing socioeconomic backgrounds tend to appropriate and interpret the faith differently. The implications of the fact that the Catholic population and the institutional presence of the Church varies from one region of the country to another is explored in Chapter 12.

That different generations of Catholics in America have been subject, for all sorts of historical, cultural, and structural reasons, to differential socialization is the focus of Chapter 13. Over the last three generations, there has been a steady decline in both knowledge about and commitment to the Catholic faith. Chapter 14 chronicles what sociological and psychological research says about how and why attachment to the Catholic faith typically waxes and wanes across the different stages of the individual life cycle.

Chapter 15 addresses the issues associated with gender within the Catholic Church. Do men and women actualize their faith differently, with women interpreting the Catholic message from a more "expressive," "nurturing," and "soft" manner than do men? Do single women interpret the faith at variance with the way that married women do? Do women, and men for that matter, accept the philosophical anthropological vision of Catholicism positing men and women as "equal but different" and in a necessarily complementary (i.e., not conflicting or independent) relationship? What type of Catholic women see the Church's official understanding of gender relationships as fundamentally sexist and oppressive to women? For those women who accept the latter interpretation, what options do such Catholic women take vis-à-vis Catholic leadership? Some believe they should they leave the Church and find some alternative religion or philosophy. Others think they should stay in the Church and try to change it from within. While the significant majority of Catholics in the United States are and have been historically defined as, in some sense and to some degree "white," there is the question of the relationship between the institution of the Church and non-white Catholics (e.g., African and Asiatic). Chapter 16 deals with the many times unhappy experience—although not universally so—of nonwhite racial minorities relating to the Church.

Many non-Catholics (and Catholics, too) are unaware of the fact that not all Catholics in the United States are Roman rite (or Latin or Western) Catholics. Chapter 17 presents a brief discussion of Eastern Catholicism, focusing on its genesis, emphases, and differences from the majority Roman branch of the Church Universal. Chapter 18 discusses other internal sources of differentiation within the Catholic faith, with its rich history of different religious orders, apostolates, ministries, and devotional styles. Chapter 19, the final chapter within this section, shows how these external and internal considerations have produced a multitude of theologies, philosophies, and methodologies all claiming, some not legitimately so from a magisterial framework, the title of being authentically Catholic.

Chapter 10

Varying Ethnic Traditions

The noted American historian, Oscar Handlin (1951), is famous for his insight in to the effect that the "history of America is the history of her immigrant groups." This is especially true for the Catholic American subculture, which consists of numerous nationality groups who have come in successive waves to American shores from all over the world.

In speaking of the possible prototypical responses of any new ethnic group to its host society, sociologists have identified basically four: the *out-group* (conforming to the new society), the *in-group* (rejecting the new society by maintaining a posture of withdrawal and segregation), the *ambivalent* (caught in a, at times, paralyzing tension between the worlds of the outside civilization and one's ethnic group), and the *indifferent* (emotionally and socially withdrawing from any tension resulting from "being members of two worlds" where the reaction here is simply "I don't want to deal with these issues, period." The first two reactions are the most prevalent. While the in-group reaction is not unusual, especially but not exclusively, in the first generation, the modal movement across generations and especially in light of an ever increasing powerful American mass culture, is the out-group response, that is, toward conformity with the larger society. Historically, many Catholic groups coming into the United States created or tried to create "national parishes," whether officially designated as such or de facto, which served temporarily as a "half-way" house between segregationist and assimilationist postures.

During the colonial and early republican eras, many of the relatively few Catholics who were in what is now the United States came from England and France (and a few from Ireland) and were most likely to reside in Maryland, Pennsylvania, and New York. Other Catholics could be found in French Louisana and in Spanish Florida and the southwestern rim of America.

Many of the English Catholics and French Catholics came to America to escape, respectively, Anglican/Calvinist hostility and the secular terror of the French Revolution. Despite being on the receiving end of discrimination in the colonies because of their non-Protestant faith commitment, the early British and French population was mostly able to blend in with Protestant America. They were both culturally similar and from the same socioeconomic background as that of the surrounding Protestant community (Fisher 2000, 34).

During the early to mid–nineteenth century, many Irish Catholics, spurred by the horrible "potato famine," and German Catholics immigrated to this country looking for gainful employment with anti-Catholic nativist movements starting to emerge as one consequence. Speaking of the Irish, Fisher observes that "in cities from Boston to Butte, Montana to San Francisco, Irish Catholics become the chief suppliers of unskilled labor for the rapidly expanding national economy" (2000, 52). Regarding the "approximately 1.7 million German Catholics . . . [who] . . . migrated to the United States between 1820 and 1920," Fisher continues:

> Between 1820 and the 1880s, Germans made up by far the second-largest Catholic immigrant group in America. . . . They tended to come from more prosperous backgrounds . . . [than the Irish] . . . and often boasted vocational skills that were highly desired in an industrializing American where they might find work as carpenters, bakers, brewers, or tailors. The German Catholic immigrant communities were most heavily concentrated in a region within a triangle from Cincinnati to Milwaukee to Saint Louis and back, cities that were not well established as their counterparts in the East and were therefore somewhat less susceptible to outbreaks of nativism. . . . German Americans were quite clear in their desire to maintain the customs and language of their native land. Their determination to establish "national" parishes eventually produced a conflict with the Irish-dominated leadership of the Catholic Church in America. (2000, 58–59)

Initiating a particularly massive nativist response, the turn into the twentieth century saw millions of Catholics mostly from southeastern Europe migrate to America primarily for economic reasons as they came from rural economies that offered less than subsistence living with resulting poverty and starvation.

Between 1870 and 1920, over 2 million Poles came to the United States, the great majority of whom were both Catholic and farmers. Like the Germans they too fought with the predominant Irish leadership over the issue of establishing their own national parishes led by their own Polish-born priests. The Catholic historian Monsignor John Tracy Ellis reports that one Irish-Polish conflict actually led to a group of Poles leaving the Catholic Church and forming their own group. He speaks of a "quarrel over control of church property and ecclesiastical jurisdiction which broke out among a group of Catholics of Polish birth and descent at the end of the . . . [nineteenth] century. By 1907 these differences had developed into the only sizable and enduring schism in the history of American Catholicism, in what came to be called the Polish National Church" (1969, 129). According to the Ellis account, as of 1969, the Polish National Church numbered about a quarter of a million adherents and is to be found principally in the areas of New England, the Middle Atlantic states, Wisconsin, and Chicago, Illinois with its chief bishop residing in Scranton, Pennsylvania (1969, 130).

Like many other Catholic immigrant groups, the southern Italian migration during this period was characterized by its poverty and peasant farmer base. By the end of the migration period the Italian American population numbered around 4 million, primarily located in the larger industrial cities of America. Southern Italian religiosity, however, was both village-centered and heavily infused with folk elements and, as such, was scorned by the more official interpreters of that Catholic faith, which, practically, meant the Irish bishops and priests (Vecoli 1969; Varacalli 1999, 2004).

Speaking of another major Catholic immigrant group, Fisher notes the migration of nearly 1 million French Canadians, between 1865 and 1920, who were "attracted by the growing labor market in the textile mills and shoe factories located in such New England towns as Nashua, New Hampshire, and Lowell, Massachusettes" (2000, 82). Mentioning "other predominantly Catholic immigrant groups of the late 19th and early 20th century," Fisher states that these included Slovaks, Czechs (commonly referred to as Bohemians), and Ukrainians who originated "almost entirely from either rural areas or small towns . . . and usually became urban-dwelling Americans . . . [creating] . . . 'urban villages' in the midst of large cities" (2000, 82).

On the one hand, American capitalists welcomed the cheap hard labor provided by the immigrants who worked the low-end jobs associated with the industrial revolution taking place especially in the urban areas of the country. On the other hand, many rank-and-file Protestants disapproved of the large Catholic immigration of this era. This negative response can be traced to two sources: (1) the numbers of Catholic immigrants were large, and hence, were viewed as a political threat to Protestant hegemony and (2) these immigrants were, for the most part, poor, uneducated, and came from sections of Europe considered less civilized and represented, not only a religious but also a cultural affront to Protestant sensibilities. Indeed, as but one example of this reaction, the noted sociologist Joseph Gusfield, in his volume *Symbolic Crusade* (1976), argued that the Prohibition amendment banning alcohol consumption in this country was not only motivated by "medical"/"health" concerns over alcoholism but just as much by cultural bigotry. "Morally inferior" Catholic immigrants were much more likely to consume beer, wine, and hard liquor as part of their everyday way of life. David R. Carlin notes the nativist sentiments of the Protestant majority toward the Catholic immigrant groups as follows:

> No sooner had the nation begun gradually to assimilate the Irish Catholics than a newer, bigger, and even more exotic flow of immigrants came into the United States. Beginning in the 1880s and continuing for thirty years, until the outbreak of World War I, Catholics from Italy and the Slavic countries . . . flooded into America. The earlier Irish may have looked strange to American eyes, but at least they spoke English (almost all of them), and in their homeland they had some experience of popular government and the common law. But look at these people from southern and eastern Europe—no English language; no common law; scant, if any, experience with democracy. (2003, 130)

No sooner had the nativist fear that America was being overwhelmed by religiously "pagan" and culturally inferior Catholic immigrants taken hold, it actually led the Protestant majority to pass restrictive immigration laws in the early part of the twentieth century which, in effect, stopped immigration into this country from southeastern Europe. The result, intended or not, of Americanizing the various Catholic immigrant groups was that they were now "cut off" from

Members of the Durazzano Society march down Post Avenue, the main street of
Westbury, New York, in honor of the Dell' Assunta observance, August 15, 1935.
The Assumption of the Virgin Mary is, in the Catholic religion, a "Holy Day of
Obligation" with required attendance at mass. Italian Americans have historically
had a very strong veneration of the Blessed Mother and celebrate many feasts outside of the parish to honor the mother of Jesus Christ, many times including a mass
service. The members of the Durazzano Society consist of descendants who immigrated from Durazzano, Italy (outside of Naples) at the turn of the twentieth century. They continue, to this day, their religious practices in Westbury, New York.
Many of the original immigrants who found a home in Westbury served as land-
scapers for the more prosperous Protestant elites living in nearby "Old Westbury,"
part of the so-called North Shore "Gold Coast" of Long Island.
Courtesy of Salvatore J. LaGumina.

their religious and cultural homelands. In 1965, then President Lyndon
B. Johnson opened up the floodgates to immigration once again. However, by now the European countries that had earlier provided a massive Catholic immigration to the United States were better off in terms
of a basic standard of living, so that immigration from European
Catholics did not resume with great numbers. Predictably, in hindsight,
the "new immigration" came from what is now variously called "Third
World" or "least Industrialized" societies (Henslin 2004). Certainly, not
all of these new immigrants are Catholic, but many are, at least nominally. The post-1965 immigration has seen a massive influx of "His-

panic" Catholic immigrants (i.e., those from Mexico, Central and South America, and the Caribbean), not all of whom identify politically with each other but who have come to these American shores to escape either economic deprivation or political tyranny. The new Catholic immigration also comes from India, Haiti, Arab nations such as Lebanon, and the only Asian Catholic country, the Philippines. Noting that "Asian-American Catholics . . . represent a diverse array of cultural traditions," Fisher follows that:

> Filipinos did not migrate to the U.S. mainland in large numbers . . . until the years after World War II. . . . Filipino-American Catholicism has made an important impact not only in the area of southern California but in Jersey City, New Jersey and other eastern urban areas. . . . Filipinos make up the only Asian American community that is predominantly Roman Catholic. (2000, 157)

Some immigrants have come from Vietnam with its French Catholic heritage, a result of the chaos ensuing from the Vietnam War. As Fisher observes, "the decade following the end of the Vietnam War in 1975 saw a massive exodus of refugees . . . especially to the U.S., where more than one million Vietnamese resided by the 1990s. The Vietnamese-American Catholic community, more than 250,000 strong, quickly organized tightly knit parishes in such locations as Orange County, California; New Orleans, Louisiana; and in the Houston, Texas area" (2000, 157).

While, during the early colonial period of American history, Catholics represented less than 1 percent of the total American population, today the figure is approximately 23 percent. Because of their vast numbers and historic presence, the Catholic Hispanic presence in the United States is worthy of special attention. As S. G. Liaugminas reports:

> Hispanics are now America's largest minority, with a population of more than 35 million, according to figures from Census 2000. An estimated 70 percent of them are Roman Catholics. That means that at least one out of every four Catholics in America is of Hispanic origin. A 1999 report by the National Conference of Catholic Bishops (N.C.C.B.) noted that the number of Hispanic Catholics in the United States had grown by 71 percent since 1960. The bishops projected by

the year 2050, Hispanics will constitute 24 percent of the U.S. population and more than 50 percent of U.S. Catholics. (2001, 3)

Liaugminas continues:

America's Hispanics come from 19 different Latin-American republics, as well as Puerto Rico and Spain. Mexican-Americans . . . [are] . . . the largest groups, accounting for 60 percent of the total, followed by Puerto Ricans at 17 percent and Cubans at 8 percent. In terms of looks, America's Latinos are as diverse as the countries they come from, ranging from blond Argentines to dark-skinned Dominicans and others of predominantly African origin. They are united by their Spanish language, their Spanish-influenced cultures, and their Catholic faith. (2001, 3)

Liaugminas adds the crucial historical point, however, that the Hispanic presence in the United States is by no means merely a post-1965 phenomenon. As he states:

The Hispanic presence in America is hardly new. Spanish-speaking Catholics arrived in what is now New Mexico during the late 16th century, decades before the first English colonies were established at Jamestown and Plymouth. During the 17th and 18th centuries, the Spanish crown claimed a swath of territory stretching from California to Florida. As late as 1848, New Mexico was considered part of Mexico, as were large parts of California, Arizona, Colorado, and Texas. . . . But after Spain lost its fragile hold on the American Southeast during the 18th century, and Mexico ceded the Southwest in 1849, the Hispanic presence in America went into severe demographic decline. During the 19th century, waves of settlers and gold-seekers from the East turned much of the Hispanic Southwest into Anglo-Saxon Protestant territory. Waves of Irish immigration to America turned the Catholic Church in the United States into an Irish-dominated church. (2001, 4)

There are many important issues associated with the significant Catholic pluralism that presently exists and is represented by the various ethnic traditions in our country. One is the dominant status—historically, and still, to a lesser degree today—of the Irish ethnic group.

However, the present trend within the Catholic Church seems to be putting a certain lid on just how distinctively Irish the institution is presently and will be on the future American scene. This is certainly the case given the demographic trends heavily favoring Hispanic Catholics and other members of the "new migration." It is also the case, to perhaps a slightly lesser degree, in terms of episcopal appointments and the ethnic composition of the clergy. Another issue involves how the various Catholic groups have related to each other, politically and culturally. In earlier historical periods, first the British and French Catholic and later, the German and Polish communities tended to fight the Irish monopoly while the less-well organized and affluent Catholic immigrant groups like the southern Italians and Czechs/Bohemians tended to manifest indifference to Irish control and just tried to live a Catholic life outside of official Church institutions in their own cultural and ethnic ways (Link 1975).

Regarding the contemporary situation, on the one hand, it is true that the present distinctively Hispanic Catholic population tends to reject, and is "turned off" by, the current dominance of an "Anglo-Catholic" version of the faith. Many present-day Hispanic Catholics see the present Anglicized version of the Catholic faith as too distant, cold, and abstract and is all too reminiscent of Italian-Catholic complaints about the Irish Catholicism of the late nineteenth century through to the better half of the twentieth century (Vecoli 1969; Varacalli 1999). Indeed, a significant percentage of contemporary Hispanics have left the faith for the more emotional and devotionally demanding forms of conservative Protestantism. On the other hand, Catholic authorities in the United States seem to be (finally) manifesting a more current openness to cultural pluralism within the Church in light of the Hispanic exodus. It remains to be seen whether this openness is superficial in nature or authentically held by contemporary Church leaders.

Another crucial consideration is how the various ethnic traditions have mediated or interpreted the Catholic faith. Is it one in which one's cultural and ethnic heritage subsumes the Catholic religious component? Or will the religious commitment trump in importance the cultural/ethnic component although still giving a healthy recognition to the latter? Another perennially important concern involves the nature and type of assimilation. As the ethnic Catholic assimilates, does he/she lose the Catholic faith? Or does he/she simply transfer the cultural "carrier" of the Catholic faith from his nationality group or ethnic background to that of the American nation or cultural system (as was predicted by and advocated for, by the American Catholic thinker, Orestes Brownson)? Related to this issue is whether or not one's socioeconomic class is a greater predictor than ethnic heritage of Catholic attitudes and behavior, especially after the immigrant/ethnic group in question has lived several generations in the American social context. Or is it, perhaps, possible to see the development of an authentic and realistic Catholic multiculturalism that allows one to incorporate both a live sense of one's Americanness and ethnicity/cultural heritage but within an ever broader orthodox Catholic worldview (Varacalli 1994, 1999)?

Suggested Readings

Brownson, Orestes. "Native Americanism." *Brownson Quarterly Review* (July 1854).

Fisher, James T. *Catholics in America.* Oxford: Oxford University Press, 2000.

Gusfield, Joseph. *Symbolic Crusade.* Chicago: University of Illinois Press, 1976.

Handlin, Oscar. *The Uprooted: The Epic Story of the Great Migrations that Made the American People.* Boston: Little, Brown, 1951.

Liaugminas, S. G. "Catholicism with a Latin Beat." *Crisis* (September 2001); www.crisismagazine.com/september2001/cover.htm.

Link, Richard. *American Catholicism and European Immigrants.* Staten Island, NY: Center for Migration Studies, 1975.

Varacalli, Joseph A. "Multiculturism, Catholicism, and American Civilization." *Homiletic and Pastoral Review* 94, no. 6 (March 1994).

———. "The Saints in the Lives of Italian-Americans: Toward a Realistic Multiculturalism." In *The Saints in the Lives of Italian-Americans: An Interdisciplinary Investigation,* edited by Joseph A. Varacalli, Salvatore Primeggia, Salvatore J. LaGumina, and Donald J. D'Elia. Stony Brook, NY: Forum Italicum of the Center for Italian Studies, 1999.

———. "Catholicism, Italian Style: A Reflection on the Relationship Between the Catholic and Italian Worldviews." In *Models and Images of Catholicism in Italian Americana: Academy and Society,* edited by Joseph A. Varacalli, Salvatore Primeggia, Salvatore J. LaGumina, and Donald J. D'Elia. Stony Brook, NY: Forum Italicum of the Center for Italian Studies, 2004.

Vecoli, Rudolph. "Prelates and Peasants: Italian Immigration and the Catholic Church." *Journal of Social History* 2, no. 3 (spring 1969).

Chapter 11

Differing Socioeconomic Class Backgrounds

Sociologists have well documented empirically just how one's socioeconomic class background tends to shape the way individuals and groups think and act as well as set the broad outlines for what they refer to as their respective "life chances." Indeed, some sociologists go as far as to argue that social class is the *key* predictor of attitudes, behaviors, and opportunities in social life. Without necessarily deciding if the latter claim is true, it is clearly the case that socioeconomic class background profoundly affects religious participation.

Social scientists have documented that, for instance, there is a much higher chance that an individual in America embraces atheism or agnosticism if he/she comes from the upper, especially professional, classes. This is a reality that should surprise no one in a society in which secularism and scientism is a well-entrenched reality in the American public sphere of life (i.e., in government, corporations, education, the arts, and the mass media). Furthermore, while the majority of those perched up high on the social ladder *do* accept religion, the *way* they embrace it is distinctive. It is more intellectual in nature and salvation tends to be seen in this-worldly social-justice oriented terms (i.e., in the attempt to make "heaven here on earth"). Religious rituals tend to be more sedate, "Apollonian," and "socially respectable" (Greeley 1972). Worldly success tends to produce an optimistic religion, one in which individuals perceive that they have control of their own and society's destiny. They are believers in the late President John F. Kennedy's claim that "God's work must truly be our own." Conversely put, social scientists have confirmed the claim of the Protestant theologian H. R. Niebuhr (1957) that there is a distinct "religion of the disinherited," that is, not only do the majority of individuals from the lower classes embrace religion but the way they do so is more emotional or "Dionysian" in ritual, and other-worldly in terms of salvation (Greeley 1972). Their religion is a religion of "the heart and not of the head" and, for Christians, it is one that stresses that ultimate justice will be meted out in terms of either otherworldly salvation or damnation or in terms of either heaven or hell. Their lack of worldly success tends to breed a religious style of pessimism, fatalism, cynicism, realism, and lack of confidence that they will see justice during their earthly existence; indeed, God and the problematic issue of eternal salvation is seen as the ultimate equalizer. One of the defining characteristics of a broad middle-class religiosity, in contradistinction to lower-class religiosity, is active involvement in religious organizations; the middle class is the group most likely to be "joiners," civic oriented, and to become involved actively in voluntary associations, American religious denominational life definitely included (*American Catholics in the Public Square* 2004).

How, then, does socioeconomic background play itself out in Catholic life, both historically and in the present era? Historically, the early Catholic Church in this country—sans some of the aristocratic Maryland founders—was an immigrant Church consisting of poor and formally uneducated individuals. These were individuals who relied on their bishops for not only religious, but also for cultural and political direction. These were individuals whose Catholic religiosity was non-intellectual, deeply devotional, and whose social justice–oriented activities were limited, for the most part, to providing help to neighbors, local villagers, and members of their home communities. These were individuals whose religiosity was also simultaneously wrapped up intimately with their European heritages or American ethnic attachments.

With the development of an intact Catholic plausibility structure, the fruits of the organizational revolution devised by the Baltimore provincial and plenary councils from 1829 to 1884, the possibility and reality of fostering a distinctive Catholic intellectual and social life appeared. Consistent with the opportunities for upward socioeconomic advance provided by the Industrial Revolution and an expanding nation, Catholics were now simultaneously "moving up the ladder" of this-worldly success in America *and* becoming more deeply and seriously Catholic. With the weakening of the Catholic plausibility structure in the 1960s onward and the subsequent assimilation of Catholics into an ever more secular America, the increasingly upper-middle-class cast of the Catholic Church produced what Andrew Greeley (1976, 1977) has referred to as a widespread "communal Catholicism" or what the Protestant theologian and sociologist Ernest Troeltsch (1931) called the "mystical" form of religious expression. This is a form of religious commitment in which the religious locus of authority is no longer with the religious tradition but resides within the consciousness of the individual. For the most part this communal Catholicism has translated into either a Protestantization or secularization of the faith on the part of bourgeois Catholics. Some might suggest, however, that the formula that increased upward social mobility and secularization go hand in hand is true *only* when the surrounding religious tradition has become weakened as, some believe, is the case in post–Vatican II America.

Studies by Gerhard Lenski (*The Religious Factor* 1961), Nathan Glazer and Daniel Patrick Moynihan (*Beyond the Melting Pot* 1960), and Bishop Silvano Tomasi (*Piety and Power* 1975) have made the argument that, at least during the immediate post–World War II period, it was the case that upward social mobility and political power actually was correlated with a deepening of religious orthodoxy. While no longer true in the American Catholic case, the latter relationship is an accurate description of reality for the fast-growing contemporary Mormon movement (Zellner 2001) in the United States, and as such calling into question the claim that a widespread secularization is inexorable.

Suggested Readings

Glazer, Nathan, and Daniel Patrick Moynihan. *Beyond the Melting Pot: The Negroes, Puerto Ricans, Jews, Italians, and Irish of New York City.* Cambridge, MA: M.I.T. Press, 1970.

Greeley, Father Andrew M. *The Denominational Society.* Glencoe, IL: Scott, Foresman, and Company, 1972.

Lenski, Gerhard. *The Religious Factor.* New York: Doubleday, 1961.

Niebuhr, H. R. *The Social Sources of Denominationalism.* Cleveland and New York: Meridian Books, 1957.

Tomasi, Bishop Silvano. *Piety and Power.* Staten Island, NY: Center for Migration Studies, 1975.

Troeltsch, Ernest. *The Social Teachings of the Christian Churches.* London: George Allen and Unwin, Ltd., 1931.

Chapter 12

Regional Variations

Social scientists and other scholars have documented how the local ecology or region of an area affects the nature of social life, including religious belief and activity. As Chester Gillis observes:

> There are . . . regional differences in the church that are tied to history and post–World War II migration. Catholicism in the Northeast, where there are generally enough clergy to staff parishes, and churches are abundant and in close proximity to each other, is different from Catholicism in the plains states where one priest may be serving a church and several missions, and all are fifty to a hundred miles away from each other. This is different still from Catholicism in some areas of the South where Protestants outnumber Catholics, and being Catholic is a minority status. . . . These differences color people's experiences of the church. (1999, 33)

The classic "urban," "rural," and "suburban" distinction is one important ecological and regional consideration. The classical French sociologist, Gustav LeBon (2002), once quipped that the average French rural peasant lost his Catholic faith the moment he stepped foot off the train at the Paris train station. The sociological point here follows the thought of sociologists such as Max Weber (1946, 1947) and Georg Simmel (Levine 1971). For Weber, cities "breathe free air" thus encouraging skeptical and independent modes of thought that are assumed to be antithetical to traditional religious belief. Similarly, Simmel's "geometric sociology" posited that urban life, vis-à-vis rural living, was characterized by an expansion in the number and size of the "social circles" one moves in, thus encouraging pluralism and a certain freedom in choosing among options. There is certainly more than a grain of truth to this contention; all things being equal, the social context of New York City is not as conducive to maintaining a strong sense of the Catholic faith as is one emanating from Peoria, Illinois.

However, all things are never equal. As noted by sociologists such as Andrew Greeley (1972) and Herbert Gans (1982), all major cities or urban areas contain "urban villages" or, to use the phrase of the classical sociologist, Ferdinand Tönnies (1957), traditional-like or "gemeinschaft" settings. In fusing ethnic or racial identity with religious identity, they tend to perpetuate the latter. Put another way, and especially starting with the Irish immigration, the early Catholic immigrants tended to congregate in great urban areas of America (e.g., New York, Boston, Philadephia, Chicago) and which, at least until World War II, became strong enclaves of the Catholic faith.

After World War II, however, and encouraged by government programs such as the G.I. Bill, moved by the crystallizing of an essentially materialistic and individualistic conception of the good life (what is commonly referred to as the "American Dream"), and driven by the desire for upward social mobility (in terms of the sociological trilogy of economics, status, and power), many urban Catholics moved to the suburbs (Carlin 2003). While not intrinsically antireligious in nature, the post–World War II suburbs provided locations in which many formally educated and aspiring middle-class Americans from different religious traditions converged. Catholics *did* confront a more advanced degree of pluralism in the suburbs than in their old parish-centered inner-city neighborhoods, but it should be pointed out that the organizational building genius of the Catholic Church quickly manifested itself in the suburbs where parishes and schools quickly dotted the landscape, providing enough of a Catholic environment, theoretically at least, to keep the faith vibrant. Empirically, however, the emphasis in religion started to shift *for cultural and religious reasons*—from a, more or less, exclusive participation in one's own religion, be it Catholicism, Protestantism, or Judaism, to a tacit acceptance of a biblically based common denominator religion, distilling the commonalities of the great world religions existing prominently in the United States at the time. This common denominator religion has been termed variously, by Will Herberg as the "American Way of Life" (1960) and by Robert Bellah as the "American Civil Religion" (1991). This general movement toward religious inclusiveness and abstraction—which, for religious conservatives, was viewed as indifferentism and religious and cultural relativism—was somewhat, again, partially but not completely, checked by the attempts of some of the leadership of the three great religious traditions to try to re-establish their own ethnic-religious collectivities in what at the time was the new frontier of suburban life. The reality of what sociologists call "chain migration" also helped to slow the blurring of religious and cultural lines to some degree. In Long Island, as with many other regions for instance, there are communities that are recognized as significantly "Catholic" or "Jewish" or "Italian" or "Irish," and so forth.

The urban, rural, and suburban distinction does not exhaust the way that ecological or regional considerations play themselves out religiously. One can divide usefully American civilization into such regions as "Northeast," "South," "Midwest," "Southwest," "Rocky Mountain," and "Far West." Historically, the "East Coast" and "Midwest" regions have demographically been considered Catholic strongholds. Regarding the East Coast, for instance, Chester Gillis (1999, 24–25) reports that, as of 1997, the Catholic population of Massachusetts was 2,968,041 or 49.3 percent of the state total. In New Jersey, the respective figures are 3,308,989 or 41.7 percent; in Connecticut, 1,359,910 or 41.6 percent; in New York, 7,309,228 or 39.5 percent; and in Rhode Island, 637,554 or 63.6 percent. Regarding the Midwest, the figures for Illinois are 3,650,022 or 31 percent of the state population; for Michigan, 2,191,854 or 23.2 percent; for Ohio, 2,228,085 or 20.1 percent; and for Pennsylvania, 3,552,569 or 29.6 percent. The styles of Catholicism has varied somewhat, with the Northeast presenting, at least up until the 1960s, a more traditional Catholicism with its Midwest analogue affected by a more populist touch.

The South and Rocky Mountain areas have been historically both less Catholic, with the Rocky Mountain area more imbued with a "frontier" mentality breeding a more selective Catholicism, and a Southern Catholicism historically having to contend with a strong, conservative Protestant presence. (However, there are indications that the generally more conservative and traditional milieu of the contemporary American South might actually be fertile soil for those serious Catholics that this volume refers to as the "restorationists.") Only Louisana has a strong Catholic presence with 1,336,072 or 31 percent of the state population. Over the past thirty or so years, however, many Catholics have followed the development of jobs and businesses to the South, Southwest, and Far West. A factor of tremendous importance in understanding the Catholic situation in the United States is the tremendous migration of Mexicans and other Hispanic Catholic groups to this country, especially in the Far West (California has no less than 8,053,296 Catholics representing 24.2 percent of the state population) and the Southwest (Texas has 4,317,171 Catholics and 23.1 percent of the state population). In Florida, one must take note of the impressive Cuban migration there as well as the large numbers of retired ex–East Coast Catholics, which have now given the state a significant Catholic presence of 1,982,676 or 13.8 percent of the state population). These Hispanic groups and individuals, notable exceptions recognized, tend to be poorer vis-à-vis the now predominately middle-class Catholic Church and tend to be attracted to the more devotional and emotive versions of the Catholic faith which, earlier, had been attractive to the white Catholic European groups. Indeed, the fact that the Catholic Church in the United States has since the 1960s been taking on a more "Anglo-Catholic," upper–middle-class look, feel, and style has led to an exodus of not a few Hispanic Catholics to various Protestant groups who provide, sociologically, a more vital expressive form of religion. Whether or not the Catholic Church in the United States can develop a "realistic multicultural" (Varacalli 1994) outlook more conducive to Hispanic Catholics and black Catholics and others with more traditional Catholic sensibilities remains to be seen.

Suggested Readings

Bellah, Robert. "Civil Religion in America." In *Beyond Belief: Essays on Religion in a Post-Traditional World*. Reprint ed. Berkeley: University of California Press, 1991.

Carlin, David. *The Decline and Fall of the Catholic Church in America*. Manchester, NH: Sophia Institute Press, 2003.

Gans, Herbert. *The Urban Villagers*. 2nd ed. New York: The Free Press, 1982.

Gillis, Chester. *Roman Catholicism in America*. New York: Columbia University Press, 1999.

Greeley, Father Andrew M. *The Denominational Society*. Glencoe, IL: Scott, Foresman, and Company, 1972.

Herberg, Will. *Protestant, Catholic, Jew: An Essay in Religious Sociology.* Garden City, NY: Anchor Books, 1960.

LeBon, Gustave. *The Crowd.* Mineola, NY: Dover Publications, 2002.

Levine, Donald N., ed. *Georg Simmel on Individuality and Social Forms.* Chicago: University of Chicago Press, 1971.

Tönnies, Ferdinand. *Community and Society.* East Lansing: Michigan State University Press, 1957.

Varacalli, Joseph A. "Multiculturalism, Catholicism, and American Civilization." *Homiletic and Pastoral Review* 94, no. 6 (March 1994).

Chapter 13

Generational Changes

There is much contemporary discussion in our present society of the
idea of a "generation gap." Under present situations of accelerated
social change, this discussion, with qualifications, is justified. This is so
because the cultural, social, economic, political, and religious context in
which one generation is raised or, more sociologically put, "socialized,"
can be significantly different from that of succeeding generations. To be
raised as a young person of ten years of age in the 1930s is not the same
thing as being socialized at that same age during the mid-1960s, which
is qualitatively different from being raised as a ten-year old in the mid-
2000s. The qualifications to any discussion of a "generation gap" are basically twofold: (1) it is not a universal phenomenon in all societies and
(2) there is a tendency to ignore continuities, subtle or not, that may exist
between the generations. Regarding the first qualification, traditional or
"premodern" societies characterized by modest amounts and degrees of
social change do not suffer generation gaps (since the social world experienced by one generation is basically replicated by the next). Simply put,
in these societies the life experiences of grandparents, parents, and their
children are essentially the same as they all live under the same set of religious ideas, political arrangements, types of work, and moral understandings. Regarding the second qualification, even under social
situations in which generation gaps are real, several factors must be taken
into account. The first is not to ignore the ability of parents and the original "family of orientation" to influence still their children, that is, the
next generation. To be sure, parents must deal with the many competing
agents of socialization whose messages may often be different (e.g.,
school, mass media, peer group influences, etc.). However, there is sociological evidence that many times, for instance, young people *are* influ-

enced, for better or worse, by their parents and their parents' generation of friends and relatives. Another consideration is more philosophical in nature and assumes that there is an underlying constancy to being human, that "people are people," a factor that transcends social and generational change, "the more things change, the more they stay the same."

Qualifications aside, the fundamental point is that a generational gap does exist today and therefore has implications for our study of the Catholic experience in America. Indeed, historians, sociologists, and other social scientists have quite convincingly documented that there are significant generational differences in the way that Catholicism has been appropriated by the Catholic population. An historian, for instance, might make reference to the classic question posed by Bishop Gerard Shaughnessy regarding the orthodoxy of the earliest Catholics in America: "Has the immigrant kept the faith?" For Shaughnessy the answer to his question was mostly "no" as Catholics were either converting to the religiously and culturally dominant Protestantism of the era, developing quite irregular and highly idiosyncratic forms of Catholic attachment, or were simply becoming unchurched. This unsatisfactory state of Catholic belief and practice, as least as gauged against norms of Catholic orthodoxy, could be compared historically to the much higher conformity to Catholic beliefs and practices forged in the immediate post–World War I era of the Church. This was an era in which Catholicism was protected by a "Catholic plausibility structure," or subcultural set of institutional arrangements, that was capable of successfully socializing Catholics and constituted the fruit of the organizational revolution ushered in by the Baltimore provincial and plenary councils commencing in 1829 and ending in 1884. This era, in turn, could be contrasted to the present situation characterized by a weakening of the Catholic plausibility structure and its capitulation to a prevailing secularism, in a sense marking a return to the earlier immigrant period.

Sociologists, for their part, have conducted more quantitative studies analyzing the last three major generations of Catholics in America: the immediate pre–Vatican II, Vatican II, and post–Vatican II generation. A major study completed by a team of Purdue University social scientists (Davidson et al. 1991) has provided convincing evidence documenting a major slide toward ignorance of, and dissent from, Catholic teachings on the part of these three successive generations. In other words, the immediate pre–Vatican II generation evinced both knowledge of and agreement with Catholic teachings. The Vatican II genera-

Children march in procession during confirmation ceremonies at Holy Rosary Parish, Washington, D.C., in 1915.
Courtesy of Salvatore J. LaGumina.

tion still provided evidence of knowledge of the tenets of the faith but started to disagree with some of the central positions of the Church, especially on issues of sexual morality. The post–Vatican II generation, now two generations removed from the historical (not theoretical) ideal of a "1950's Catholicism," gives significant indications of a widespread fundamental religious illiteracy and ignorance of the logic and rationale of the Catholic worldview and, as such, has substituted a secular worldview for one previously Catholic. This slide, it should be noted, follows the logic predicted by the progressive weakening of the Catholic plausibility structure or subculture necessary to mediate a civilization that has been predominately either Protestant or secular in nature.

The situation for those sympathetic to a restoration of Catholicism in the United States, however, is not completely bleak. There are fragmentary pieces of evidence that some young Catholics—together with other young Americans—reject unqualified pluralism, freedom, and individualism or, conversely, the nihilism, cynicism, and negativity of the past forty years of American life and are looking precisely for a worldview that is comprehensive and traditional yet sophisticated and also communal (Carroll 2002). And some have found that worldview in the Catholic religion. The conversion of the younger generation of Ameri-

Pope John Paul II blessing children during World Youth Day, Denver, Colorado, 1993. Sociologists note the decreasing ability of Church leaders to effectively socialize the younger generations of American Catholics into the tenets of the Catholic religion.

cans to the Catholic faith involves two considerations: the continuing delegitimation of the secular order and a Catholic Church organization well integrated and willing to offer the searchers, the ambivalent, and the open-minded a clear philosophical alternative. For orthodox Catholic sympathizers, there is little doubt that the former continues unabated; the issue is whether or not Catholic leadership has the ability to put its house back in order once again. Paul Johnson (1981), for one, believed that John Paul II would lead a "restoration" movement in the Catholic Church. Almost twenty-five years later, one can see some fragmentary movement in that direction but it is clear that the question of the future nature of Catholicism in the contemporary American context is still very much an open one.

Suggested Readings

Carroll, Colleen. *The New Faithful: Why Young Adults Are Embracing Christian Orthodoxy*. Chicago: Loyola University Press, 2002.

Davidson, James D., Andrea S. Williams, Richard A. LaManna, Jan Stenfte-nagel, Kathleen Mass Weigert, William F. Whalen, and Patricia Wittburg. *The Search for Common Ground: What Unites and Divides Catholic Americans*. Huntington, IN: Our Sunday Visitor, 1997.

Johnson, Paul. *Pope John Paul II and the Catholic Restoration*. New York: St. Martin's Press, 1981.

Chapter 14

Across the Life Course

Sociologists have identified five, more or less, distinct social stages that most individuals go through in their lives in society. Each stage has a set of distinctive socialization experiences and expectations that affect the way individuals feel and think at that particular moment in their biographical evolution. One's life course, then, continually affects the individual's approach to all aspects of life and sectors of society, religion included. An important point to make immediately is that certain stages are, more and others less, open to authentic religious involvement.

These five stages are (1) *childhood* (age up to age 12), (2) *adolescence* (ages 12–17), (3) *youth* (ages 18–35), (4) *adulthood* (ages 35–65), and (5) *old age* (65 and older) (Henslin 2004, chap. 3). During childhood children are obviously most capable of being influenced by their parents and family life. Indeed, for most children, the "world" is more or less synonomous with the "family" as the family holds a (temporary) near-monopoly over socialization. Regarding the issue of maintaining the vitality of religion and Catholicism in social life, this can be either good or bad depending on whether parents are religious believers and whether they make a concerted effort to pass on their religious tradition to their children through saying prayers, taking children to religious services, providing catechetical instruction, explaining social and familial events in a religious framework, and living an ethical life in accord with the religious tradition in question. As sociologists Peter L. Berger and Thomas Luckmann point out in their magisterial treatise, *The Social Construction of Reality* (1966), given the plasticity of the human being, the most precarious moment in maintaining any tradition is when the next generation emerges. No tradition, religious or otherwise, is guaranteed permanence over time; it must be reapprehended continuously by successive generations. Keeping a religion alive, especially under modern conditions of secularism and pluralism, requires a great deal of work.

During the later stages of childhood, a key issue emerges: whether or not the child will attend a religiously oriented school. The Catholic system of parochial education is quite extensive and for serious Catholic parents who can afford the tuition—not always modest—the grammar school experience serves to reinforce the family's attempt to pass on the faith. Those serious Catholic parents, for whatever reason, who send their children to secular public schools will obviously have a more difficult time in religious socialization. Those nominal Catholic parents who send their children to Catholic schools, not specifically for religious instruction, but for educational and disciplinary reasons, are at least introducing their children to Catholic ideas and sensibilities and are setting up the possibility for a later conversion to the faith. Those nominal Catholic parents who send their children to secular public schools should expect, all things being equal, that their children will not grow up with any functional understanding of the Catholic religion. While later conversion is always possible, it would usually require some wrenching event, sometimes of a tragic nature, to force the individual to a fundamental rethinking of his/her philosophy and an openness to Catholicism.

The adolescent stage, usually, but not always, is marked by periods of rebellion and experimentation on the part of teenagers usually centrally focused on carving out their own identities apart from parental and familial (and religious) influence. Theoretically this doesn't necessarily entail a knee-jerk rejection of the value system developed to date by the young person, but often it does just that. During the period of adolescence, the young person usually relies more heavily on the ideas of peers who are similarly trying to assert their independence. It is quite usual in this period to see young Catholics question the fundamentals of their faith; the behavioral correlate is a sharp downturn in faithful Mass attendance and other parish and Church-related activities. A key question here is whether the young person has had a previous and serious introduction into the Catholic faith. If the answer is yes, there is the possibility that later in the life cycle he/she will come back to the faith in one manner or another. If the answer is no, the possibilities of such a return are lessened considerably, although certainly not completely.

Some young people from the working and minority communities, after completing their period of adolescence, which is usually coterminous with graduation from high school, start their period of early adulthood by going to work full time and getting married and starting their families. However, it is more and more the case—and almost always the case, among the middle and upper-middle classes, that the end of adolescence marks the beginning of the "youth" period in the life cycle. This is the period that goes hand in hand with the completion of one's college education which varies from a two-year community college degree up to the twelve or more years required to complete medical and other professional degree requirements. This period is easily the most antithetical to the maintenance of any traditional religious commitment like that of the Catholic religion. Students are expected to bask in the presence of a cornucopia of ideas—many of them utopian and challenging to the societal status quo. The more the college student is divorced from practical day-to-day responsibilities—that is, the more the student is less grounded in his earlier allegiances to such things as family, neighborhood, job, and church—the greater is the chance that the student will conceive of anything that smacks of tradition to be obsolete and to be rejected. Conversely, the more the college experience is layered within the student's hitherto familiar world of family, neighborhood, and older friendship ties, the less radical and disruptive will be the college years from the frame of reference of his/her previous socialization into the Catholic faith.

The one major exception to the oppositional nature of the youth period vis-à-vis religion is with those more utopian forms of religious commitment that stress opposition to the existing authority structure of society, traditional religious authorities included, and that, further, claim to promote a worldwide social justice movement through the promotion of left-wing ideologies like socialism, feminism, and sexual liberation, among others (Carlin 2003). These forms of religious commitment that, empirically speaking, found to exist among Catholics, are dedicated to a radical reinterpretation of what stands for the faith (Varacalli 2001). Our previous discussion of a "secularization from within" is relevant here.

On the one hand, the "early" period of adulthood (35–50) can be conducive to traditional religion as the ex-student has typically "come down to earth" and is grounded to practical moral and financial commitments to one's spouse, children, community. Sociologically, it is not surprising to see a young married couple start to take, once again, their Catholicism more seriously, especially with the birth of their first child. Many originally are attracted, once again, to the religious institution not so much out of some reconversion to religious doctrine but to the belief that one's child requires a sound morality that is transmitted by the religious institution. Over time, some of these couples slowly start to reappropriate willingly the religious message. On the other hand, the early period of adulthood is *not* conducive to a serious commitment to religion given that this is the period when the young adult is trying to make a mark in his/her professional career. In a society in which, at least until recently, following philosopher-sociologists Auguste Comte (Lenzer 1983) and Max Scheler (1980), economics tends to trump the spiritual, it is not surprising, therefore, that many career-oriented individuals will regard their commitments to Catholicism as a decidedly secondary consideration.

There is, oftentimes, though not always, a shift to a more religious emphasis as the late period of adulthood starts to set in. For many, "one

Young Catholics carrying the cross during outdoor mass at World Youth Day, Denver, Colorado, 1993. One of the many accomplishments attributed to the reign of Pope John Paul II from 1978 to 2005 was his ability to connect with young people and reawaken their interest in religion and the Catholic faith.

is now able to clearly smell the coffee," and understand more fully the extent to which their professional careers and marriages have been successful and in which ways they have not. A period of "retrenchment" and tying up loose ends may start to emerge as one focuses more and more on the prospects of one's children, grandchildren, and other "significant others" and how one can help them. There is often a mental migration here: from the idea of "time since birth" to "time left to live" (Henslin 2004, 75). This period is usually one in which there is a greater role for reflection and thoughts of the past and of what might, or might not be, on the "other side" of the great divide. "Having done whatever one has done" now frees the individual to be more altruistic which, many times, translates into being more religious.

To be "old" in America today is different than forty years ago. Seniors today are in better health, have more money, are more formally educated, and live more vigorous lives than in previous generations. Nonetheless, this is the period when one sees one's spouse, close friends, peers, and familiar faces either die or struggle with serious illness or other misfortunes. It is clearly, for many, a period in which some considerable time is spent thinking about the possibility of an afterlife, asking forgiveness for past sins, and trying to make amends for one's failures. God is, most probably, on the minds of many in this last worldly stage of life—a life that traditional Catholics refer to as a "vale of tears."

Suggested Readings

Berger, Peter L., and Thomas Luckmann. *The Social Construction of Reality: A Treatise in the Sociology of Knowledge*. Garden City, NY: Doubleday, 1966.

Henslin, James. *Essentials of Sociology: A Down-to-Earth Approach*. 5th ed. Boston: Allyn and Bacon, 2004.

Lenzer, Gertrud, ed. *Auguste Comte and Positivism: The Essential Writings*. Chicago: University of Chicago Press, 1983.

Scheler, Max. *Problems in the Sociology of Knowledge*. London: Routledge and Kegan Paul, 1980.

Chapter 15

Women and the Church

Gender makes a difference in all social relations, including the way one apprehends and practices religion. Women tend to be more nurturing, cooperative, and social than men and tend to be peacemakers. They not only participate more than men in the sacramental system of the Church but also tend to have a softer, more "therapeutic" understanding of God. Women apparently read the Gospel of Jesus Christ and Church tradition through somewhat softer eyes. Men tend to be more aggressive, competitive, solitary, and concerned with the implementation of abstract conceptions of justice. Men, relatively more unchurched and perhaps, intuitively, more natural law practitioners tend to accept conservative and traditional social postures. Women tend to be more sympathetic to individuals who suffer tragedy in their lives due to unfortunate circumstances that are felt to be out of the control of the individuals involved. Men tend to stress individual responsibility and take what they consider to be a more realistic, that is, "harder," understanding of the causes of poverty and failure in life.

One result of these differences is that women are more likely to vote for the quasi socialist policies of the Democratic Party while men tend to cast their ballots for the quasi capitalist policies of the Republican Party (Varacalli 1995). Concerning the 1980 and 1984 presidential elections, for instance, Rinehardt and Perkins (1989, 53) observed that "despite their greater religiosity, women as a whole were demonstrably less supportive than men of Ronald Reagan in either of his elections." Relatedly, the Commonweal Foundation Report, *American Catholics in the Public Square,* sees this gender gap increasing in the post–Vatican II era of the Church in the United States. As it states: "an emerging generational shift among younger Catholics (those born after 1960) is it-

African American nuns at a Catholic Church service on the south side of Chicago, 1944.
Courtesy of the Library of Congress Prints and Photographs Division.

self divided along gender lines, with men favoring reduction in taxes and social spending (hence favoring Republicans), and younger women—who are also pro-choice—tending not to favor such reductions (hence favoring the Democrats)" (2004, 6). It is important to note, however, the qualification to the gender gap argument made by Bryce Christensen who argues that a good deal of the "gender gap" vanishes when one divides women into the categories of "married" and "single." Married women tend to vote more along conservative and traditional lines than do single women, the latter who tend to be "married," as Christensen puts it, to the government and its welfare state. While gender differences do persist, some of the gender gap differences can be better conceptualized, for Christensen, as a "marriage gap" (1990, 51).

Just *why* gender matters, however, is a subject of much heated dispute. Some theorists posit differences by virtue of *nature* and others by *nurture*, and many see male-female differences as a combination of both (Henslin 2004, chap. 3). The nature-nurture debate, of course, cannot be settled here. The point, however, is that gender does make an impact on our discussion of Catholicism in the United States.

Parish Life

One often commented on difference between men and women is the far greater participation in the rituals and organizations of the Catholic Church by women. Just about any Catholic parish in the United States contains a seemingly infinite number of committees and organizations devoted to a wide range of issues that include education and catechetics, social justice, liturgy, and sacramental life. And almost all of these are dominated by women with the only men usually participating being either older, retired citizens or young men who are employed by the parish. While theoretically it is the pastor, always male, that has the "final say" in parish affairs, women tend to have a "practical" power over many decisions as overworked pastors—many with no associate pastors to assist in the administration of the parish given a drastic drop in priestly vocations since the late 1960s—are only typically too happy to grant. That the lack of formal authority infuriates many Catholic women, especially upper-middle-class, professional, career-oriented women, is a point that will be addressed presently (Varacalli 1983).

The Sisterhood

During the early to mid–twentieth century, the Catholic Church was abundantly blessed with thousands of religious women, that is, sisters and nuns. Many Catholic families, especially the Irish, considered it an honor that one of their daughters would forgo traditional marriage and children to dedicate their lives to serving Christ through the Church. It should be pointed out that a vocation to the religious life also entailed educational and career opportunities that were absent for many working-class Catholic women of the era. Sisters or nuns were crucial in the running of schools, orphanages, hospitals, and other elements of the social apostolate. Their "children" were the hundreds of thousands of individuals who were helped through their selfless devotion. John T. McGreevy speaks of the devotion in addressing the "social question" on the part of so many Catholic sisters and nuns as follows:

The number of women joining religious communities jumped dramatically in the last decades of the nineteenth century and by 1920
ninety thousand women, many of them foreign born, served American religious orders. The massive American Catholic investment in
parochial schools staffed by nuns exhausted much of these women's
energy, but American nuns also developed expertise in areas closely
connected to social welfare. Nuns provided training and skills for
young women, sometimes in institutions founded prior to Jane Ad-
dams's far better known efforts at Hull House in Chicago, and Catholic laywomen began a modest settlement house movement in various
locations in the country. Most remarkably, Catholic nuns ran almost
all of the four hundred Catholic hospitals located in urban areas and
near large populations of Catholic immigrants. . . . Catholic nuns also
built the country's most extensive orphanage network. (2003, 129)

In the wake of the Second Vatican Council, according to the typical liberal interpretation, changing conceptions about the social roles
of women in society made religious life a far less attractive option for
Catholic women. For one thing, one liberal interpretation of the Second Vatican Council was that the only "religious action" that really
counted was "in the world"; this made a commitment to the religious
life seem, to some, obsolete and wasteful of human potential. On the
other hand, those whose commitment, qua professional woman, remained within the institutional Church started to argue for the ordination of women. The secular version of equality led many religious
women and other Catholic women to feel that the refusal to ordain
women to the priesthood was not only theologically incorrect but a reflection of a culturally specific patriarchal and sexist attitude on the part
of male clergy and Catholic men. Concurrently, the second wave of feminism, ushered in with books such as Betty Friedan's *The Feminine Mystique* (1963), led to a profound change in the fundamental "identity"
of women and in the way many modern woman interpreted the traditional religious or familial calling. Simply put, the argument was now
that men and women were interchangeable units, at least in the economic sphere, and that all "successful" women would have access to
professional careers as defined by secular elites. As a result, today religious life is in an aging state with many of its members quite progressive and liberal in orientation.

A countermovement, however, is noticeable as new neotraditionalist religious orders of women, like the Sisters of Life, founded by the late John Cardinal O'Connor of New York, are now on the rise and constitute an important element of the restorationist or "neo-orthodox" movement in the Church. The restoration argument is that there are countless women in society who would dedicate themselves to the religious life if only the Church would make a strong invitation to them. The restorationists argue, in effect, that the shortage of sisters and nuns is an artificial one, caused by progressive Catholics in charge of religious life. The causes, for the restorationists, are various: the lack of a fundamental commitment to recruitment, a constant disparagement of the importance of religious life, and the liberalization that has occurred within female orders that has made the call far less distinctive, challenging, and well defined. It remains an open empirical question as to whether the liberal or restorationist interpretation of the nature of religious life is more correct and whether, as such, the significant growth of these new traditional religious orders of women will continue unabated into the future.

The Fundamental Options

There are three basic positions that women can take vis-à-vis the Catholic (and Judaic-Christian-Islamic) tradition (Corbett 2001). They are: (1) total rejection of the institution and the tradition, (2) fomenting internal revolution (their advocates would say, "reform") within the institution, and (3) basic acceptance of the religious institution and tradition. The first position argues that the Catholic tradition is inherently sexist and harshly patriarchal and hence incapable of any satisfactory movement away from this alleged posture. The second position agrees that the Church is thoroughly infused with sexist attitudes and practices, but the belief here is that the Church can be changed, especially if women "stay and fight." The response of Rosemary Radford Ruether to the question as to why she stays in a Catholic Church that she views inherently sexist is relevant: "I stay because the Church has the xerox machines and you need the xerox machines in order to win the revolution." The last position accepts the philosophical anthropological understanding of Catholicism that men and women are "equal but different" and play, by virtue of nature, a complementary role to each other. It is one that accepts, from a orthodox Catholic worldview, the rationale regarding the theological impossibility of ordaining women, to wit: that the religious tradition demands this be the case given that, historically, all of Christ's apostles were men and that Christ understood the significance of this fact. Put another way, Catholic women in this third option fully accept the official teaching of the Catholic Church; conversely, they do not see the issue in the secular terms of a fight over power and prestige.

Suggested Readings

Corbett, Julia Mitchell. *Religion in America.* 4th ed. Englewood Cliffs, NJ: Prentice Hall, 2001.

Friedan, Betty. *The Feminine Mystique.* New York: W. W. Norton and Company, 1963.

Henslin, James M. *Essentials of Sociology: A Down-to-Earth Approach.* 5th ed. Boston: Allyn and Bacon, 2004.

McGreevy, John T. *Catholicism and American Freedom: A History.* New York: W. W. Norton and Company, 2003.

Steichen, Donna. *Ungodly Rage: The Hidden Face of Catholic Feminism.* San Francisco: Ignatius Press, 1991.

Chapter 16

The Issue of Race

It can be argued reasonably that racism, or the belief that a group is culturally inferior to another group due to alleged biological factors, is an intractable social problem. It represents a virulent and extreme variation of a fundamental "ethnocentrism" structured into human existence by virtue of the anthropological necessity and inevitability of socialization. Put another way, the racist temptation is always a possibility because of the inevitability of humans developing an "us" versus "them" or "in-group" versus "out-group" posture.

Racism is not always a matter of "whites" feeling superior to "blacks," "reds," or "yellows." Many Japanese, just prior to the Second World War, felt racially superior to not only whites and blacks but also to their Asian neighbors (e.g., Chinese, Filippinos, etc.). To mention a more contemporary example, one has just to refer to the carnage and inhumanity foisted by one black African Rwandan tribe over another.

There certainly *were*, however, feelings of superiority on the part of Spanish and French Catholics toward the Native American population during the age of conquest and exploration. As historian James T. Fisher frankly admits, "the idea that Native American civilization could be considered valuable and complete in its present state was inconceivable to Catholics and Protestants alike" (2000, 12). It is important, however, to acknowledge that there were discernible differences in the attitudes toward and treatment of the Native American population between, on the one hand, the more nominally Catholic and sometimes simply ruthless and barbaric Spanish *conquistadores* and French fur traders and, on the other hand, the more religiously committed and morally consistent Franciscan and Jesuit missionaries who devoted

A large group of nuns from Daughters of Our Lady of the Snow, 1944. Saint Katharine Drexel stands third from the left. In her lifetime, she established many missions for Native Americans.
Courtesy of the Department of Special Collections and University Archives, Marquette University Libraries.

themselves, in the words of Pope Paul III in 1537, to instructing the Native Indians so that they "should be converted to the faith of Jesus Christ by preaching the word of Jesus Christ and by example of good and holy living" (Fisher 2000, 16–17). Qualitative differences noted, many of the Catholic missionaries manifested toward Native Americans what would today be considered an unacceptable paternalism many times treating them in a childlike manner. The missionaries inadvertently also brought various diseases to the New World such as cholera and smallpox, which wrought incredible human misery for Native Americans. On a more positive side, James T. Fisher acknowledges that some Indians "were enticed by the spiritual and healing powers of the missionaries as well as by the promise of protection and the offer of such basic necessities as food and shelter. . . . At the same time, many Indians were attracted to the richly symbolic nature of the Roman Catholic faith" (2000, 17).

In his short historical essay, "The Catholic Church in the United

States of America," Father Robert J. Fox (2000) discusses the treatment of the Native American in a Protestant-dominated American civilization. He notes both that "the abuse of the Indians by the white man mars the pages of American history" (2000, 8) yet provides many examples of how the Catholic Church tries to ameliorate the horrible treatment afforded Native American tribes by the invading white civilization. Particularly noteworthy in this regard is the apostolate of Saint Katherine Drexel who founded a new order of nuns in 1891, the Sisters of the Blessed Sacrament for Indians and Colored People. This order devoted itself to trying to assist both the material and spiritual well-being of African and Native Americans. Regarding the latter, Saint Katherine established no less than fifty missions for Native Americans in sixteen states ("Saint Katherine Drexel" 2005).

Another major example of how racial prejudice and discrimination played itself out in American history is broached by Julia Mitchell Corbett in her volume, *Religion in America* (2001) in the egregious failure of American Christianity in its treatment and oppression of black African Americans. Certainly, the history of dominant white Christian denominations in America toward African Americans is one that exposes a great deal of hypocrisy and failure to live up to the tenets of Christianity itself.

Viewed from a worldwide perspective, racism is neither the only nor main reason for the institution of slavery. As Henslin states, "contrary to popular assumptions, slavery was not usually based on racism, but on one of three other factors: compensation for debt, for crime, and as a result of war and conquest" (2004, 166). On one hand, historically, the issue of white racism in the form of the acceptance of the institution of slavery toward blacks in America is more a Protestant than a Catholic issue. America, again, was almost generically a Protestant nation during the early years when slavery existed and flourished. Furthermore, slavery was mostly a reality in the southern states—to this day still a Protestant culture—in which Catholicism was not a major religious, cultural, or political force. Indeed, historians have noted the ability of many white Protestant Christian slaveholders to develop ideologies (Henslin 2004, 116) that argued that they, the slaveholders, were actually doing the slaves a favor by bringing them, chains notwithstanding, out of their native African tribal religions and into the "light" of a Christian and more "advanced" nation. Such ideologies, if successfully accepted by both slaveholder and slave, obviously served the function of maintaining this institutionalized evil in American history until President Lincoln's Emancipation Proclamation marked the beginning of the end of slavery in America.

Catholic hands, however, were far from clean regarding attitudes and practices toward blacks. Although some historians present the case that Catholicism protected slaves in certain ways (Caponnetto 1991), arguing, for one thing, that slaves, like freemen, were made in the image of God, the Catholicism of the era did not ban slavery, as is obviously evidenced by the many slaves taken by the Christian *conquistadores* in Central and South America. And it is important to make clear that there were certainly some American Catholics, especially among the Catholic elite, who themselves owned slaves.

The black Catholic scholar, Cyprian Davis, O.S.B., chronicles many important facts in what to him was the overall disappointing record of the Catholic Church in the United States toward both the black slaves prior to the Civil War and after the war, to the freed black American population. In his *The History of Black Catholics in the United States* (1991), he notes, for instance, that early in American Catholic history, many prominent Catholic families like the Carrolls, many religious orders of men and women, and even bishops were slaveowners (1991, 36–40). Indeed, for Cyprian Davis:

> By and large, the Catholic laity who were white accepted the condition of slavery. During the Civil War white Catholics fought on both sides. Yet even in the North the sentiment of the Catholic laity, most of whom were recent immigrants, was decidedly anti-black. This was especially so in regard to Irish immigrants. As many American Church historians have pointed out, this anti-black sentiment on the part of the Irish in the period prior to the Civil War was the result of resentment over "the competition of the Negro worker in the labor market." . . . Both the Irish and free black population in the North were on the bottom rung of the social and the economic ladders. (1991, 58)

According to Davis, the antipathy to blacks was a phenomenon at the time that united most white Americans, whether Protestant or Catholic. As he states:

> In the nineteenth century there were few white Americans who really believed that blacks were equal to whites. The assumption of black in-

feriority was an accepted part of the social and cultural landscape, a conclusion not to be questioned. On this point, the majority of Catholics differed little from their contemporaries, whether in the South or in the North. (1991, 59)

Interestingly enough, Davis argues that the Church Universal, in general, was way ahead of the Catholic Church in the United States regarding the racial question. As he noted, for one thing, Pope Gregory XVI condemned the slave trade in 1839 through the publication of his apostolic letter, *In Supremo Apostolatus Fastigo* (1991, 39). He follows:

Catholics outside of the United States, beginning with the papacy and including both clerics and lay, had developed a moral consciousness that by the middle of the nineteenth century could no longer tolerate slavery. But the Catholic Church in the United States found itself incapable of taking any decisive action or of enunciating clearly thought out principles regarding slavery. (1991, 61)

In the judgment of Cyprian Davis, the reaction of the institutional Catholic Church, in the second plenary council, to the needs of the newly emancipated 4 million slaves in post–Civil War America was hardly any better. As Davis concludes, "the Bishops did not bring credit to themselves in their failure to work for a unified and practical way to meet the crisis caused by the emancipation of the slaves. The large influx of European immigrants at this time can scarcely be sufficient reason for the lack of a national plan on behalf of the African Americans" (1991, 121). Despite concluding that "the history of the Catholic Church's efforts to evangelize the black people of the U.S. in the period following the Civil War is not a very glorious one . . . still there are . . . [Catholic] . . . individuals . . . who never dismissed black men and women in the United States as pathetic creatures without honor, without respect, and without resolve" (1991, 136).

Historian John T. McGreevy provides a complimentary, although somewhat more sympathetic and ambiguous, interpretation regarding the Catholic stance toward slavery and the African American population in the United States. For McGreevy:

Catholic opposition to abolition cannot be reduced to the particular racial dynamic. Many Catholic intellectuals around the world accepted slavery as a legitimate, if tragic, institution. This acceptance rested upon the pervasive fear of liberal individualism and social disorder that so shaped Catholic thought during the nineteenth century, along with the anti-Catholicism of many abolitionists. (2003, 52)

He continues:

Catholics insisted that slaves be permitted to marry and receive an education, frequently expressed doubts about the morality of slavery as it existed in the nineteenth century, and almost never defended slavery as an unqualified good. But most Catholics accepted slavery in principle . . . declaring slavery "not in itself intrinsically wrong." Fearful of social disorder and unwilling to distinguish the suffering of slaves from other human miseries, Catholics lumped immediate slave emancipation with a religious and political radicalism that threatened the foundations of society. (2003, 56)

Indeed, even Cyprian Davis himself notes more than a few bright spots in the history of the relationship between African Americans and the Catholic Church in the United States. Among these would be the attention that some Catholic religious orders gave to the African apostolate. Davis speaks of the "missions for black Catholics established by three religious communities—the Josephites, the Society for African missions, and the Society of the Divine Word" (1991, 200). Relatedly, in 1829, he notes that the first black religious congregation of women in the United States, the Oblate Sisters of Providence, was founded (1991, 261). Another would be the convening of a series of five black Catholic lay congresses running from 1889 through 1994. For Davis, "they demonstrated beyond a doubt not only that a black Catholic community existed but that it was active, devoted, articulate, and proud" (1991, 193). Yet another would be the founding, in 1900, of the Knights of Peter Claver, a fraternal and benevolent organization analogous to the Knights of Columbus. This association served the vital function of supplying insurance for the welfare of each member's family relatives after death. Other positive milestones would be the ordinations of James Augustine Healy and Harold Perry as the nation's first and second black bishops in the years, respectively, of 1875 and 1966. The year 1988 would see thirteen black bishops in the United States and the first black archbishop, Eugene Marino, appointed to the archdiocese of Atlanta.

Sunday mass at Saint Elizabeth's Catholic Church, Chicago, Illinois, 1942.
Courtesy of the Library of Congress Prints and Photographs Division.

And two organizational creations of significant importance were the founding of the Federated Colored Catholics of the United States in 1924 and, ten years later, of the first Catholic Interracial Council. Mention should also be made of an important turning point in the history of both American Catholicism and the American Civil Rights movement when, in 1947, Archbishop Joseph Ritter ended racial segregation in the Catholic school system in St. Louis.

Cyprian Davis concludes his important history by noting that "the last three decades of the twentieth century witnessed a momentous period of change within the black Catholic community. The number of black Catholics has grown to approximately 1.5 million, with the major centers still being southern Louisiana and the metropolitan areas of New York, Chicago, Washington, D.C., Miami, and Los Angeles" (1991, 260).

While racist attitudes and behavior on the part of some significant sectors of the American Catholic community manifested themselves throughout American history, one particularly serious eruption demanding some attention occurred during the post–World War II era in the urban North. African Americans had started to migrate from the South to the northern cities, beginning in the 1920s, in the hopes of finding employment, an escape from the overtly racist past of the American South, and, later, with the development of the welfare state, easier access to government assistance and programs. It was also a time when the Catholic base, still a working-class to lower-middle-class base, resided in those same urban cities. The enormous migration of southern blacks was perceived by many of the Catholic ethnics who lived in the urban neighborhoods of the North to constitute a threat in many ways. Many Catholics saw blacks as economic threats and as carriers of crime and immoral behavior that would destroy the existing working-class Catholic neighborhoods that the white ethnics had worked so hard to build and maintain and at great personal expense. Along with "urban renewal" projects carried out by planners such as Robert Moses, which destroyed many functioning ethnic Catholic neighborhoods in the name of "progress," the introduction of the poor black population was seen as the vehicle by which white neighborhoods would experience rapidly declining property values, the introduction of public housing (bringing with it an "undesirable" clientele), deteriorating school systems, violence including riots, and an exodus to the suburbs. But it is important to add, following John T. McGreevy in his important treatise, *Parish Boundaries: The Catholic Encounter with Race in the Twentieth-Century Urban North* (1996), that the defense of ethnic neighborhoods was not just economic and material in nature. Rather, the Catholic ethnics saw their neighborhoods in essentially religious, moral, and communal terms with the focal point of life for many being the parish and the parish school. While many Protestants and Jews—less spatially and morally tied to their city neighborhoods— fled to the suburbs, many neighborhood-centered Catholic ethnics attempted to defend their home turf, thereby dramatically increasing the chances of conflict with the incoming black migration.

The eventual connection of millions of now urban blacks with the "civil rights" movement of the 1960s, and later the "black power" movement, and an increasingly closer association with the liberal wing of the Democratic Party in turn generated a countermovement: an "ethnic revival" movement involving many white ethnic Catholics that led them to migrate to the Republican Party under President Nixon and later President Ronald Reagan. The period of the 1960s through the

1980s was one of much unrest, hostility, ugliness, and confrontation between blacks and working-class ethnic white Catholics. It was also a period in which a growing "progressive" Catholic movement, spurred on by its active participation in the Civil Rights movement and its liberal interpretation of the Second Vatican Council equating the mission of the Church in terms of this-worldly justice issues, increasingly aligned themselves more and more with the African American side of the issues and with the leadership wing of an increasingly liberal Democratic Party propelled to power by the capturing of the Democratic presidential nomination by George McGovern in 1972. These "progressive" Catholics saw the Catholic ethnic versus African American conflict as a battle between, respectively, parochialism and racism on one hand, and, on the other, universalism and justice. Others—including other Catholics—saw the conflict as a more complex matter of competing rights and wondered out loud why it should be expected that relatively disadvantaged Catholic ethnics give up their neighborhoods to sacrifice for the perceived needs of another group, albeit in more objective need, when, for instance, more middle-class and privileged suburbanites of all religions were not being asked to make comparable sacrifices for the admittedly and undeniably laudable goal of African American advance.

In order to understand the historical and contemporary relationship between African American Protestants and Catholics and the institutional Catholic Church and the American Catholic population, the following additional seven themes of crucial significance must be addressed. Being brought over in chains as slaves, the *first* important theme is that the earliest African immigrants to America were converted from their tribal religions to Christianity. The conversion process was not completely successful initially as elements of Christian belief were syncretized with African tribal religion, a condition that to a certain degree, continues to exist today. A *second* theme is that the African American population today is overwhelmingly Protestant, with most African Americans affiliated with the Baptist and Methodist denominations or smaller sectlike Protestant groupings. Approximately 9 percent of the contemporary African American community is Catholic and a somewhat smaller percentage Black Muslim.

During the early part of American history, the *third* theme notes, there were small pockets of black Catholics in Florida, Maryland, and Louisiana. Around 1900, for instance, only about 2 percent of African Americans were Catholic, in part because of a residential disparity:

while the vast majority of black Americans at the time lived in the South, the Catholic population at the time was concentrated in the North. Catholic institutional life in the South, from parish existence to all other forms or organizational life, furthermore, following the Protestant and societywide pattern, was highly segregated. *Fourth*, the Catholic inability to attract African Americans to its fold, especially during the earlier period of American history, was the result of a combination of many factors. One was the meager presence of Catholicism in early American society. Another was the racist or at least unsympathetic attitudes that many Catholics shared with the American population at large toward blacks. Another was the perception that the Catholic Church had all that it could handle in trying to deal with its "own" people, that is, millions of impoverished and uneducated European immigrants. These Catholic immigrants, furthermore, also had their own hostile rivalries and resentments with each other, which compounded the organizational problems confronting Catholic leadership; dealing with the black-white divide constituted a further difficulty that some thought, unfortunately, best to avoid.

A *fifth* theme was that Catholicism was, relatively speaking, most attractive to the African American community and actually attracted a not insignificant number of converts to the faith between the period of the 1940s through to the mid-1960s. This was a period coinciding with the growth of an integrated and increasingly respected Catholic subculture. Some African Americans during this period, perhaps, saw a conversion to the Catholic faith as a vehicle for gaining status and upward social mobility. Especially attractive to many African American Catholics was the opportunity to send their children to Catholic schools. With the decline of the Catholic subculture starting in the tumultuous 1960s, concomitant with a rise in socioeconomic mobility and other factors such as the growth of the Black Pride movement and the increased status of the Baptist denomination, Catholicism would have been expected, sociologically, to have become a less attractive alternative for black Americans. Apparently, however, this was not the case. In 1990, 9.2 percent of the black American population call themselves Catholic. Perhaps, again, the key attraction of the Church lies with its school system, one even more important to many black Americans given the perceived failure of the public school establishment to meet properly the various educational and character developing needs of African American children and youth. Many contemporary African Americans are, to the consternation of their political allies in the Democratic Party, defenders of such social policy initiatives as school vouchers and tuition tax credits.

In order to understand the Catholic response to racism, a *sixth* theme emerges, to wit, that distinctions must be made between official Catholic social teaching, the stance of the institutional Church, and the attitudes and practices of the Catholic population. Official statements such as Pope Pius XI's 1937 encyclical, *Mit Brennender Sorge* ("With Burning Concern") which repudiated philosophies of racial superiority, are indicative of the Church's vision that all human beings are created in the image of God. However, in specific social situations, such as the Church's presence in the early American South, Church leadership, either due to prudential judgment, a failure in courage or character, or the corruption of racist ideas themselves into the individual psyche, did fail to fully implement the Church's vision on racial issues in her institutional life. Finally, the gap between the ideal Catholic depiction of race relations and the reality of the average Catholic or parish varied even more enormously depending on the knowledge and acceptance of Church teachings on the part of the individual or community in question.

The *seventh* theme is that one can discern three, more or less, distinct historical postures on the part of the African American Catholic community concerning the issue of racial integration versus segregation within the broader Catholic American community. The first period was segregationist/separatist as African Catholic leaders such as the black lawyer Thomas Wyatt Turner, who founded the Federated Colored Catholics Association, argued that it was best that black Catholics have their own distinctive parishes, neighborhoods, cultural life, and organizations. This position gave way to the integrationist response, popular in the 1940s through mid-1960s, that emphasized the commonality of humanity and the universalism of Catholicism, a position most forcibly put forth by Jesuit Fathers John La Farge, S.J., and William Markee, S.J. (1957), who created and advocated Catholic interracial councils. The integrationist model fell out of favor with many African American Catholics during the mid-1960s, due to either radical/pluralistic/segregationist/separatist visions that coincided with the rise of the Black Power movement or to more moderate versions of religious and cultural pluralism, the latter still popular today. The more moderate version of religious and cultural pluralism tries to tread a line between a radical rejection of American society/non-African religious institutions and an allegiance unmediated by the black African heritage to American society and religious organizations.

Suggested Readings

Caponnetto, Antonio. *The Black Legends and Catholic Hispanic Culture*. St. Louis, MO: Catholic Central Union, 1991.

Corbett, Julia Mitchell. *Religion in America*. 4th ed. Englewood Cliffs, NJ: Prentice Hall, 2001.

Davis, Cyprian. *The History of Black Catholics in the United States*. New York: Crossroad, 1991.

Fisher, James T. *Catholics in America*. Oxford: Oxford University Press, 2000.

Fox, Father Robert J. "The Catholic Church in the United States of America." In *A Catechism of the Catholic Church: 2,000 Years of Faith and Tradition*. Alexandria, VA: Park Press Quality Printing, 2000.

LaFarge, John. *The Manner Is Ordinary*. Garden City, NY: Image Books, 1957.

McGreevy, John T. *Parish Boundaries: The Catholic Encounter with Race in the Twentieth-Century Urban North*. Chicago: University of Chicago Press, 1996.

———. *Catholicism and American Freedom: A History*. New York: W. W. Norton and Company, 2003.

Pope Pius XI. *Mit Brennender Sorge*, 1937.

"Saint Katherine Drexel." *Catholic Culture*, March 3, 2005, www.catholic culture.org.

Chapter 17

Eastern Catholicism

Many Catholic Americans are either not aware or only dimly aware that the Catholic religion consists of two great branches of equal dignity and rank, Western and Eastern Catholicism, each with their own set of somewhat different liturgical practices, ecclesiastical disciplines, and spiritual traditions that are nonetheless united in their Catholic faith by a common set of essential beliefs and sacraments as well as agreement on the role of papal and magisterial authority. (It is important at the onset of our discussion to make clear that "Eastern Catholicism" is not the same thing as "Eastern Orthodoxy," a point that will be elaborated on subsequently.) As the Second Vatican Council's statement, *Orientalium Ecclesiarum* ("Decree on the Catholic Eastern Churches") declares: "The Catholic Church values highly the institutions of the Eastern Churches, their liturgical rites, ecclesiastical traditions and their ordering of Christian life. For in these Churches, which are distinguished by their venerable antiquity, there is clearly evident the tradition which has come from the Apostles through the Fathers and which is part of the divinely revealed, undivided heritage of the Universal Church" (1).

The Catholic Church actually consists of no less than twenty-three churches of which the Roman or Latin is only one. The twenty-two Eastern churches of the Catholic Church can be divided into those that are *Byzantine* (Albanian, Belarussian, Bulgarian, Croatian, Georgian, Greek, Hungarian, Italo-Greek-Albanian, Melkite, Romanian, Russian, Ruthenian, Slovak, Ukrainian); *Alexandrian* (Coptic, Ethiopic); *Antiochene* (Maronite, Syrian, Syro-Malankar); *Armenian*; and *Chaldean* (Chaldean, Syro-Malabar) (www.home.nyc.rr.com/mysticalrose/eastern.html).

Catholic Americans are mostly innocent of the Eastern Catholic tradition for the simple fact that, overwhelmingly, Catholic Americans come from lands in which the Western or Latin Church is established, with the result that Eastern Catholicism is a distinctly minority presence in Catholic America, although many Eastern Catholic Churches have *eparchies* (i.e., dioceses) and parishes in the United States that attempt to address the religious needs of those immigrants who have come from Eastern countries.

Eastern Catholics constitute a small statistical minority in the United States. Eastern Catholics who migrated to the United States mostly settled in the industrial Northeast, in Connecticut, New York, Pennsylvania, Ohio, Michigan, and Illinois. Originally they worked in factories, mines, and mills. A few (Maronites and Melchites) went to Birmingham, Alabama. Some adventurous Ruthenian souls even went as far west as Colorado to work in the mines. All of this initial wave of Eastern Catholics to America was part of the great period of immigration, circa 1880–1924. However, some came as refugees from communism after World War II. This migration provided Eastern Catholic religious culture with a new "shot in the arm" or vitality, whose long-term impact remains, at best, an open question.

Eastern Catholics, for the most part, originally immigrated to the United States from those lands once considered part of the Eastern Roman Empire, from what is now referred to as Eastern Europe, Asia, and Africa. Emperor Diocletian, who ruled between 285 and 305 A.D., divided the empire for administrative reasons between Rome and Byzantium (Saunders 2000; Crocker 2001). Later, when Constantine became emperor, Christianity was legalized with the issuing of the Edict of Milan and in 330 A.D. established Constantinople (present-day Istanbul, Turkey) as the capital of the Eastern part of the Roman Empire. Christianity, as such, grew with this basic dichotomy with the Western part of the empire under the influence of Latin culture and the Eastern part shaped by Hellenistic culture (Saunders 2000).

Cultural and linguistic particularities have produced somewhat different expressions of the Catholic faith between its Western and Eastern branches, but no basic differences in belief structure. For instance, in Eastern Catholicism the sacraments (or what Eastern Catholics prefer to term "the Mysteries of Initiation") of baptism, holy communion, and confirmation are administered simultaneously while, in the Western rite, they are separated and bestowed upon the individual at different stages of the maturation process. Furthermore, "confirmation" is referred to in the Eastern tradition as "chrismation." Additionally, the Eastern tradition developed the practice of the "veneration of icons" while in the West the use of statues was implemented as a mode to venerate the saints. While some Eastern Catholics do pray the "Holy Rosary of the Blessed Virgin Mary," a Western Catholic prayer, Eastern Catholics have their own prayer to the Mother of God called the Acathist Hymn, a hymn used, by the way, by Pope John Paul II to close the Marian year. Yet another difference resides in the issue of a married priesthood, which is allowed and often encouraged in the East, but is not permissible, except by special dispensation from mandatory celibacy, in the West. It is important to emphasize that attending a Divine Liturgy in an Eastern Catholic Church is equivalent to attending a Roman Catholic Mass and fulfills the Catholic's Sunday and Holy Day obligations.

Political, cultural, linguistic, and religious disputes had existed between the Western and Eastern branches early in the history of Christianity. Eventually this culminated in the mutual excommunications between the bishop of Rome and the patriarch of Constantinople in the year 1054 A.D. (Corbett 2001). As such, Christendom suffered its first major schism as the Churches of the West remained loyal to the bishop of Rome and continued to view him as the pope of all Christendom while the various ethnic and cultural branches of Christianity in the old Eastern Roman Empire stood firm in their belief that each branch should be led by its head bishop or *patriarch* with only a "primacy of honor" for the pope. (The only Eastern Churches that did not break off from Rome were the Maronite Rite Catholic Church whose patriarch resides in Lebanon and the Italo-Albanian Church.) Those Christian Churches from the East that have, over the years, maintained their dissident status in separation from the Catholic Church form the various branches of what is referred to as Eastern Orthodoxy. Those Eastern Churches with their special rites and traditions and that have since reunited with the Catholic Church together form the Eastern Catholic Church. All reunited Eastern Catholic groups have counterparts in the Eastern Orthodox Churches. It is important *not* to refer to Eastern Catholics as "uniates"; this is viewed by Eastern Catholics as a derogatory term utilized by the Eastern Orthodox to "put down" those groups who rejoined the Catholic Church. Fighting a two-front war, so to speak, minority Eastern Catholic Americans also resented the tendency, in the pre–Vatican II Catholic Church, of some Latin rite Catholic bishops to attempt *Latinization,* that is, to strongly suggest or even force Eastern Catholics to abandon their own practices and substitute in their places Roman practices. In more than a few cases, forced Latinization led to defections, either individual or in the form of mass movements, from Eastern Catholicism back to Eastern Orthodoxy. As a matter of fact, the largest schism in the history of American Catholicism occurred in the nineteenth century with the loss of 100,000 Carpatho-Rusyn Eastern rite Catholics to Eastern Orthodoxy in reaction to the stance taken by the famous leader of the "Americanist" faction of the Catholic Church in America, Archbishop John Ireland. Eastern Catholics, while sharing with the Eastern Orthodox similar culture and liturgy, more importantly (at least to those religiously centered) constitute a large part of the legitimate and indispensable theological mosaic and pluralism found in the Catholic Church. Indeed, as the Second Vatican Council's document, *Orientalium Ecclesiarum* ("Decree on the Catholic Eastern Churches") puts it:

> The holy Catholic Church, which is the Mystical Body of Christ, is made up of the faithful who are organically united in the Holy Spirit by the same faith, the same sacraments, and the same government. They combine into different groups, which are held together by their hierarchy, and so form particular churches or rites. Between those churches there is such a wonderful bond of union that this variety in the Universal Church, so far from diminishing its unity, rather serves to emphasize it. For the Catholic Church wishes the traditions of each particular or rite to remain whole and entire, and it likewise wishes to adapt its own way of life to the needs of different times and places. (2)

The Eastern Catholic tradition undoubtedly is liturgically rich and beautiful and has contributed much to the Church Universal as well as representing a salutary presence for the Catholic community of the United States. Empirically speaking, there are more than a few Roman Catholics in America who, "turned off" by the thinning out of the Latin liturgy by "progressive" Catholic clergy, are attending and participating in the longer, more demanding, and majestic Eastern liturgy. Theologically speaking, the Catholic Church is made up of both Western and Eastern Catholics with all Catholics subject to the bishop of Rome as the successor of Peter and visible head of the Church Universal.

Suggested Readings

Corbett, Julia Mitchell. "Ethnic Christianity." In *Religion in America*. 4th ed. Englewood Cliffs, NJ: Prentice Hall, 2001.

Crocker, Harry J. *Triumph: The Power and the Glory of the Catholic Church—A 2000-Year History*. Roseville, CA: Prima Publishing, 2001.

Orientalium Ecclesiarum. "Decree on the Catholic Eastern Churches." In *The Documents of Vatican II*, edited by Walter Abbott. Washington, DC: America Press, 1966.

Saunders, Father William. "The Eastern Rite Church." *Arlington Catholic Herald*. Three-part series, March 9, 16, and 23, 2000, www.catholicherald.com.

Chapter 18

Religious Orders, Devotional Styles, and Other Internal Sources of Catholic Differentiation

The purpose of this chapter is to discuss some of the various sources of differentiation within the Catholic faith, other than the previously addressed Roman/Latin/Western versus Eastern distinction. Indeed, the Catholic Church also has a rich and continually developing history of different religious orders, devotional styles, ministries, and apostolates.

This rich source of Catholic differentiation is the result of a complex interplay of theological, cultural, and historical factors. Theologically, in accepting what John Cardinal Newman meant by "development," the Catholic Church accepts the idea that the absolute truth of the Catholic faith can be mediated by a seemingly infinite number of cultural and historical applications, that is, philosophies, methodologies, customs, and rituals. Similarly, Catholicism believes that one evangelizes a constantly changing outside world through the process of inculturation. The key proviso is that it is the Catholic faith that is transforming the world and not vice versa.

In addition to a plethora of Catholicized philosophies, methodologies, customs, and rituals, the perennial Catholic engagement with culture and history also unearths and energizes the complete and exhaustive set of religiously possible expressions, expressions that have been posited usefully as dyadic opposites: reason and faith, nature and grace, authority and conscience, action on behalf of justice and contemplative prayer, Church doctrine and personal devotion/private religious experience, intellect and mysticism, and universalism and particularism (Varacalli 2001). In the felicitous phrase of Karl Adam, Catholicism represents "an infinitely various yet unitary thing" (1954, 9). Ideally, the perfect Catholic individual would blend, synthesize, and combine these cultural/historical and universal religious expressions in his/her daily life. In reality, different Catholic subcultures and different Catholic individuals tend to emphasize some expressions over others (while supposedly not denying the usefulness of all and, furthermore, with all expressions organically connected). This selective emphasis—across time, space, and individual personality—is what produces the rich variety of Catholic religious orders, devotional styles, ministries, and apostolates.

Religious Orders

Both the Church Universal and, only to a slightly lesser degree, the Catholic Church in the United States is blessed with a multitude of religious orders, which can include clergy (priests and deacons), religious (sisters/nuns and brothers), and laity (including both men and women). A religious order is an organization sanctioned at its founding by magisterial authority, that attempts to fulfill some specific set of religious mandates or imperatives. The Jesuits, Dominicans, and Augustinians, for instance, are known for their commitment to education. There are, for example, no less than twenty-eight Jesuit colleges and universities in the United States, including America's first Catholic college, Georgetown. The Franciscans and the Poor Clares are especially noted for the care of the poor. The Vincentians and Salesians are known for their central concern for all aspects of the social apostolate, with the Scalabrinians focusing on the needs of the immigrant. Benedictines and Carmelites are noted for their intense prayer and spiritual life. The Paulists are celebrated for their interest in the intellectual life and the Daughters of Saint Paul for their fidelity to the pope and the publishing of all the social encyclicals through their press, and so forth. Many times religious orders have more than one charism; the Vincentians and Salesians also having a central concern for education in addition to the social apostolate. In addition to education and intellectual concerns, the Jesuits were known for their heroic missionary work in Canada in the years before the American Revolution.

Religious orders are shaped by the specific charismatic gift given by God to its founder or founders. The founders, in turn, are to some de-

gree, influenced by the social and historical milieu that they found themselves immersed in and discovering the needs to be addressed. Saint Ignatius Loyola, the founder of the Jesuits or, more formally, the Society
of Jesus, was responding to the crisis in Christendom caused by the
Protestant Reformation in the sixteenth century. The early Jesuits were
militants, later popularly referred to as the "pope's marines," and were
crucial to the success of the Catholic Counter Reformation. St. Francis
and St. Clare, founders, respectively, of the Franciscans and the Poor
Clares, were responding to an overemphasis in the Church of Italy during the Middle Ages on materialism and political machinations.

Over time, however, and due to the changing sociocultural and historical factors that emerge after the death of the founder, the nature of
any specific order can evolve, sometimes in directions that meet the
needs of a changing world or that take it outside the parameters of religious orthodoxy. The Jesuits and the Congregation of the Sisters, Ser-
vants of the Immaculate Heart of Mary (I.H.M.) have moved, in their
own minds, in the direction of the former, of accepting and embracing
many contemporary philosophies such as individualism, self-expression,
Marxism, and feminism, which are viewed as liberating and elevating.
However, beliefs and practices may develop that contradict the
founder's intention and the logic and integrity of 2,000 years of organically developing Catholic tradition. James Hitchcock (1984) and
William Coulson (1996) have, respectively, made the latter case regarding the same religious orders of Jesuits and I.H.M. Sisters. For
Hitchcock and Coulson, these Catholic groups have fallen prey to the
contemporary "therapeutic mentality"—a soft, "me-oriented" philosophy devoted to the perceived emotional and physical needs of the individual—and other forms of secular thought that push the group outside
the orbit of Catholic thinking and acting (Varacalli 1997).

Sometimes revitalization movements occur in a religious order as a
reaction to secularism and materialism becoming dominant in a religious order. Recently, for instance, Father Benedict Groeschel has
founded his own stricter branch of the Franciscans. In other cases, new
religious orders emerge to replace the vitality and vigor that once characterized the more established religious orders. Two of the fasting growing and vibrant religious organizations devoted to orthodoxy in both
the Church Universal and the United States are Opus Dei and the Legionaries of Christ. Mention should also be made of new religious orders of women like that of the Sisters of Life, founded by the late John

Cardinal O'Connor of New York. Such new orders and organizations are replacing in importance the older religious orders of women which, generally speaking, have excessively liberalized, are losing their distinctiveness, demographically are aging, and are in danger of becoming defunct.

Devotional Styles

Given the fact that the Catholic Church understands itself as a 2,000-year-old institution that has successfully "spanned the ages," it should come as no surprise that it has accumulated a multiplicity of ways of expressing devotion to God. Serious Catholics frequently participate in the receiving of the Holy Eucharist while nominal Catholics do not, just one indication of a growing religious indifference on the part of many Catholics in an increasingly secular American civilization. Many contemporary Catholics exclusively pray directly to Jesus Christ, thus rejecting the Catholic belief in the saints as useful, if not required, intercessors. Many contemporary Catholics, conversely, consider Mary the "mediatrix of all graces" and pray to Christ through Mary, expressing great devotion to the Mother of God. A still sizable segment of the Catholic population utilize the mediation of the saints. The choice of saints depends on such factors as ethnicity/nationality, the match of the personal charism of the saint with the personality disposition of the individual who is praying, or the pairing of the "speciality" of the saint with the particular needs of the petitioner. Americans of Italian, Polish, Irish, etc., decent are more likely to be attracted to saints associated with their ethnicity in Catholic religious traditions. Spiritually oriented Catholics might prefer a Saint Francis of Assisi or a Saint Teresa of Lisieux; intellectually oriented Catholics might choose a Saint Thomas Aquinas or a Saint Augustine; believers in a muscular Catholicism might be attracted to a figure like Saint Michael the Archangel, or a Saint George or a Saint Joan of Arc or, perhaps, a William Wallace; while Catholic fathers might rely on their patron, Saint Joseph.

Some Catholics will manifest their devotion by attending and participating in the religious novenas that take place in the parish (especially popular, as historian Jay Dolan [1985] notes, during the mid–twentieth-century American century). Many Catholics argue that the majesty of the cathedral or elaborately decorated Church, in conjunction with long and splendid liturgical celebrations, enhances contact with God, while others prefer a simpler and, generally, more Protestant-like architecture and a shorter and simpler ritual. Some devotions are based on the Church's long tradition while others are more contemporaneous and Americanized. Some others will rely on activity that takes place outside of the parish such as the traditional neighborhood feast or in the familiar surrounding of the home or in the presence of the beauty of God's nature. Yet for others the "debarking location" to the Transcendent is the monastery or in the retreat house. Some devotions may contain a significant element of emotion as in either an African Catholic ritual or a Catholic charismatic setting involving the soliciting of the Holy Spirit or, in some cases, through singing and hymns. For others, the emptiness of silence is a precondition for union with the Divine. Some pray intermittently throughout each day, others only when they feel they need supernatural assistance, and yet others almost never feel the need for spiritual contact. For some, prayer life is directed to personal spiritual ends while for others it is tied to family, community, and national needs or to causes tied to the social and intellectual apostolates of the Catholic Church.

The Catholic Church seeks that religious devotion be orthodox ecclesiastically. Manifestations incorporating either pagan (premodern Christian) or neopagan (postmodern Christian) elements remain problematic for Church authorities. An example of a corrupting neopagan element would be the incorporation by some progressive Catholics of "new age" symbols in the Catholic liturgy. An example of a corrupting pagan element would be the "saint worship" (as compared to "veneration") still practiced by some Italian American Catholic ethnics in parish-sponsored feasts. As a matter of fact, a recent study conducted by Salvatore Primeggia and this author concluded that *both* paganistic and neopaganistic expressions co-exist alongside of religiously orthodox manifestations and sensibilities in the 100-year plus annual celebration of the famous Italian-American-Catholic "giglio" feast ("feast of the lillies") of Williamsburg, Brooklyn (1996). In addition to an orthodox Catholic veneration of the saints, this feast, the authors argued, provided abundant evidence of "old world" superstitions, magic, folk religiosity, and peasant southern Italian cultural beliefs (*"la via vecchia"* or "the old way") as well as contemporary secular ideological commitments to American patriotism, upward social mobility, and a general sense of "Italianita" (or of being Italian, upscale style).

The Giglio (Lillies) feast has been celebrated for over hundred years in Williamsburg, Brooklyn, and is considered perhaps America's most famous Italian American religious and cultural celebration. The feast has its roots in Nola, Italy, and honors the heroic activity of Saint Paulinus, who, according to legend, rescued villagers captured by Mediterranean pirates in the fourth century. The Brooklyn feast has been studied by sociologists Salvatore Primeggia and Joseph A. Varacalli who note that the feast has been an agent of Catholic evangelization while continuing to manifest both old world southern Italian and contemporary American allegiances.

Courtesy of Frank C. D'Amato.

Providing a microcosm for demonstrating the complex interrelationships between religion, culture, and ethnicity, the research on the giglio feast forced the authors to reconsider the relationship between the "sacred" and the "profane" as discussed, for instance, by Mircea Eliade (1959) and Emile Durkheim (1965). For observant Catholics, it was the sacramental activity within the walls of Our Lady of Mount Carmel Church associated with the feast that constituted sacred activity; for others, it was the feast itself, memories of family and friends, and the associated streets of the neighborhood and community that represented the "ultimate concern" (Tillich 1957) of the feast for participants and observers. In terms of the feast's relationship to an official Catholicism, it serves, for some, as an effective vehicle for evangelization into the faith. Yet, for many others, its represented a ritual celebrating some traditional nonreligious or modern form of attachment. Yet for still others, both the parish and streets were integrated holistically and imbued with a moderate sense of the sacred. For a remaining segment, nothing involving the religious and cultural activities of the feast warranted any designation other than that of an interesting, but little more than quaint, spectacle.

Ministries and Apostolates

In Catholicism, there is also a legitimate variety of ways by which one can serve God and through God both Church and society. As it is stated by Saint Paul in I Corinthians 12:4-7: "and now there are varieties of gifts, but the same Spirit; and there are varieties of service but the same Lord; and there are varieties of works but it is the same God who inspires them all in everyone. To each is given a manifestation of the Spirit for the common good."

Russell Shaw makes a relevant distinction between *lay ministry* and the *lay apostolate*. Technically, ministries is the proper term in relationship to some Church-related liturgical or ritualistic function while apostolate is the proper term for a nonliturgical endeavor or activity in the world outside of the Church in what can be referred to as the "temporal sphere" of society. More sociologically or commonly understood, the former involves those jobs and activities necessary for the Church, *qua institution,* to run effectively. Examples of such jobs and activities would be extraordinary eucharistic ministers, catechism instructors, lectors, teachers, parish council volunteers, administrators of one sort or another, and so on. The latter involves those commitments of Catholic individuals who are not tied contractually with any Church-related agency but, as Catholic Christian citizens and members of the People of God, see it as their duty to "Christianize the temporal sphere" through their everyday activities as parents, neighbors, community activists, and professionals in both the public and private sphere. There are many voluntary organizations not legally tied to the bishops but spiritually loyal to the Church such as Catholics United for the Faith (CUF), the Catholic League for Religious and Civil Rights, the Knights of Columbus, Human Life International, the Fellowship of Catholic Scholars, the Society of Catholic Social Scientists, the Cardinal Newman Society, and many organizations of Catholic lawyers, doctors, nurses, and scientists that attempt to promote a Catholic presence in American society and the public sphere.

Russell Shaw (2002) argues the absolute necessity of both the lay ministry and lay apostolate for the health and welfare of, respectively, the Church and American society. He bemoans, however, the present-day weakness of the lay apostolate, which is a result of both the general increasing secularization of the larger American society. Others analysts, like sociologist Monsignor George A. Kelly and historian James Hitchcock note a more subtle but still very real and enervating "secularization from within" that has occurred even within lay ministry, that is, within the Church organizations themselves.

In his statement, *Christifideles Laici* (1988), John Paul II noted another related issue, to wit, that an increasing "clericalization of the laity," that is, the cooptation of the laity into clerically run activities, is increasingly weakening the lay apostolate. These developments are both a reflection of and a cause for the general weakening of a Catholic presence in contemporary American civilization.

Suggested Readings

Adam, Karl. *The Spirit of Catholicism*. Garden City, NY: Image Books, 1954.

Dolan, Jay P. *The American Catholic Experience: A History from Colonial Times to the Present*. Garden City, NY: Doubleday, 1985.

Eliade, Mircea. *The Sacred and the Profane*. New York: Harcourt, Brace, and World, Inc., 1959.

Hitchcock, James. *The Pope and the Jesuits*. New York: The National Committee of Catholic Laymen, 1984.

John Paul II. *Christifideles Laici* (1988), www.vatican.va/holy_father_john_paul_ii/apost_exhortations/documents.

Primeggia, Salvatore, and Joseph A. Varacalli. "The Sacred and Profane Among Italian American Catholics: The Giglio Feast." *International Journal of Politics, Culture, and Society* 9, no. 3 (1996).

Shaw, Russell. *Ministry or Apostolate? What Should the Catholic Laity Be Doing?* Huntington, IN: Our Sunday Visitor, 2002.

Varacalli, Joseph A. "The Failure of the Therapeutic: Implications for Society and Church." *Faith and Reason* 23, no. 1 (spring 1997).

Chapter 19

Differing Theological and Philosophical Worldviews

The fact that the Catholic Church (1) is internally characterized by many religious subtraditions and (2) has encouraged/allowed these subtraditions to interact significantly with cultural currents in time and space has produced many different theological and philosophical worldviews that lay claim to the title of being Catholic. Religiously and juridically, the issue of which theologies and philosophies are orthodox and which are heterodox belongs to the magisterium, or teaching authority, of the Church. Analytically, such decisions are based on the consideration as to whether or not the ideational system in question is consistent with the Catholic religious tradition and philosophical anthropological understanding of the nature of the human being (or whether it can be modified to be made consistent). Religious and philosophical systems that are, for instance, radically *world-rejecting* (e.g., the Amish part of the Protestant Anabaptist wing of the Protestant Reformation, Hinduism, Buddhism), *magical* (e.g., premodern spiritualism), *materialist* (e.g., communism), *scientistic* (e.g., Comtean positivism), *individualistic* (e.g., libertarian), *sexual liberationist* (e.g., Freudianism), *deterministic* (e.g., behaviorism), *androgenist* (e.g., feminist), *utilitarian* (e.g., laissez-faire capitalism), or *reductionist* (e.g., antisupernaturalist) could never claim fundamental compatibility with Catholicism. Whether or not any of these options could be modified significantly to be made compatible with the faith yet without losing their internal logic and character is problematic and would have to be determined on a case by case basis. Relatedly, the decision to emphasize and employ a particular theological or philosophical approach at a certain juncture is based on the prudential judgment, made by the serious Catholic with final authority vested in magisterial authority, as to whether it is capable of mediating effectively the Catholic message to a particular community rooted in a specific sociohistorical context. Some might argue, for instance, that a phenomenological perspective that could be incorporated within a Thomistic framework is a potentially attractive possibility for the modern individual because it simultaneously builds upon yet corrects and transforms the subjectivist and experiential bias prevalent in the contemporary age.

Perhaps one useful (but not exclusively so) dichotomy is between pre- and post-Enlightenment worldviews, with most of the former and most of the latter representing worldviews, respectively, capable and incapable of being made compatible with the faith (Rowland 2003). Pre-Enlightenment worldviews tend to accept the classical idea of the existence of an objective moral order discernible by the reasoning power of the human being or, put another way, of the perennial reality and relevance of the natural law "written into the human heart." For this reason, the Greek philosophy of Plato and Aristotle can and has been adapted successfully by Catholic thinkers like Saint Thomas Aquinas who have demonstrated the compatibility of reason with faith. The Catholic worldview, similarly, accepts the Greek understanding of a constant and unchanging human nature but modifies its ironclad determinism and overwhelming sense of tragedy with the Christian belief in free will/choice and that the sacrifice of Jesus on the cross marks man's ultimate possible victory over death.

It is true that most post-Enlightenment (but not postmodern) worldviews *do* have a conception of the "Good Society" (e.g., Marxism, feminism, Freudianism, positivism, liberalism); however, their philosophical anthropological vision of mankind is opposed to the Catholic vision. The vision of Marxism is, at base, materialistic and economic. Radical feminism assumes a nonexistent androgyny that violates the reality and imperatives of nature. Freudianism posits as its ideal a therapeutic ceasefire in a meaningless world. Positivism envisions an all-embracing scientism beyond freedom, dignity, and responsibility. Liberalism erroneously assumes that something good can come out of a "society" of unfettered atoms, of the widespread emergence of "autonomous man." Furthermore all post-Enlightenment, postmodern philosophies (e.g., deconstructionism, existentialism) not only deny the existence of an objective moral order but also denigrate the role of human reason in the affairs of humankind. Put together, this points to the fact that there are severe limits to the useful conversational abilities between Catholic and modern non-Catholic worldviews and modalities which, in many cases, are simply incommensurate (MacIntyre 1984; Varacalli 1998).

However, empirically it is the case that there nonetheless remain many traditional, pre-Enlightenment theologies, philosophies, and worldviews that are pregnant with possibilities for fertile exchange with the Catholic religion (Varacalli 1994). During his recent reign, John Paul II, for instance, encouraged the development of distinctively African practices that he felt could be made consistent with the faith. Again, the Catholic logic is *integrationist, incarnational,* and *sacramental.* It is one that posits that one best evangelizes the faith through inculturation: that one builds and spreads Catholicism by accepting and transforming all that is truthful, holy, beautiful, and useful that can be discovered in non-Catholic sources and milieux.

Suggested Readings

MacIntyre, Alasdair. *After Virtue: A Study in Moral Theory.* Notre Dame, IN: University of Notre Dame Press, 1984.

Rowland, Tracey. *Culture and the Thomistic Tradition.* New York: Routledge, 2003.

Varacalli, Joseph A. "Multiculturalism, Catholicism, and American Civilization." *Homiletic and Pastoral Review* 94, no. 6 (March 1994).

———. "Symposium: Catholics and the Practice of Sociology and the Social Sciences." *The Catholic Social Science Review* 3 (1998).

PART V

CONTROVERSIES AND TURNING POINTS IN AMERICAN CATHOLIC HISTORY

"Historical Events Before Vatican II," Chapter 20, and "Contemporary Issues After Vatican II," Chapter 21, focus on specific historical events, developments, and social movements that have had a profound impact on the American Catholic experience. The division of intellectual labor between the two chapters can be roughly marked by the years of the Second Vatican Council (1962–65). The former chapter deals with historical material occurring before the Second Vatican Council and latter chapter addresses historical occurrences from the Second Vatican Council up until the present.

Chosen for analysis in Chapter 20 are the issues of the controversy over trusteeism, nativism and immigration, the provincial and plenary councils of Baltimore, 1828–84, the American culture war and the school controversy, the Cahensly affair, the heresy of Americanism, the origins of the national Catholic bureaucracy in the United States, the separation of Church and State, the Catholic attempt to restore academic scholarship in Christ, and finally, the presidential election of John F. Kennedy.

Topics chosen for study in Chapter 21 are Vatican II: the battle over its significance, the Bicentennial Program (1973–83) and movement (1973–), the new Catholic knowledge class and Catholic higher education, the theology of liberation: the American context, ecumenism, catholics and politics in the contemporary United States, the emergence of a "communal" Catholicism and the role of conscience, the birth control controversy, the ordination of women, intermarriage, abortion: a case of competing "rights," homosexuality, religious education, the controversy over Mel Gibson's *The Passion of the Christ*: the culture war at play in both American society and within the catholic community, and dissecting the sexual scandal in the contemporary Catholic Church.

Chapter 20

Historical Events before Vatican II

The Controversy over "Trusteeism"

During the early years of the American Republic, up until the advent of the Civil War, the Catholic Church was embroiled in the controversy over trusteeism. More specifically, the controversy entailed the issue of who was to control local parish property and make clergy parish appointments. Was the proper authority ecclesiastical in nature or should it reside with the local lay congregation in the form of elected trustees?

While the official answer of a basically hierarchal organization to this question was ecclesiastical authority, there were many early American Catholics who defended and attempted to implement what sociologists of religion call a congregational style of leadership in their local parishes. There were various reasons for the development of trusteeism, whether of a practical, sociohistorical, or philosophical nature. Practically, as has been noted previously, the early institutional Church in America was characterized by a dearth of solidly formed priests, financial resources, standardized doctrinal and ritualistic practices, and centralized authority. Given this, it was often the case that members of the early Catholic lay community rose to the needs of the situation and were involved centrally in the construction and maintenance of local parishes. Logically, such individuals possessed a sense of ownership over their own creations, including the right to shop around for the pastor of their liking. Additionally, the lay trustees were most likely to be from the most prominent sector of the Catholic community, in terms of wealth, prestige, and political influence, and, concomitantly, held a strong sense of their own worth and decision-making prowess. More theologically put, they had a strong belief in their own charismatic gifts. And, conversely put, as Michael Zoller points out, the upper-class population was more likely than those Catholics found on the lower rungs of society to harbor anticlerical attitudes (1999, 60). Indeed, as has been documented in other sections of this volume, socioeconomic class remains a potent variable in explaining the degrees and nature of attachment to the institutional Church in America.

Sociohistorically, the early Catholic community was, again, embedded in a cultural climate shaped by generic Protestant sensibilities and, for some elites, both Catholic and otherwise, by Enlightenment thought (Dolan 1985). Robert N. Bellah et al. (1985) has referred to these two competing foundational worldviews of the early nation as, respectively, "biblical individualism" and "republican individualism," with the former being much more widely accepted by the American (Protestant) population. The widespread acceptance, at the time, of biblical individualism had logical consequences for the typical form by which religion organized itself. As Michael Zoller put it, "Americans were naturally congregationalists and inclined to organize the church from below" (1999, 58). This cultural climate had legal and political consequences for the early Catholic Church as the Church, qua institution, was prohibited from owning its own property. In a report sent to the Roman Cardinal Leonardo Antonelli in 1785, America's first bishop, John Carroll who was consecrated in 1789, explained that "strictly speaking, there are no ecclesiastical foundations here" (quoted in Hennesey 1981, 76). At that time, James Hennesey elaborates, "property in the United States was held, either individually or corporatively, by civil title" (1981, 76). This legal and political reality, if unchanged, Bishop Carroll contended, could have simply destroyed the historic nature of the Catholic faith in the New World. For Carroll, "the unity and Catholicity of our Church would be at an end; and it would be formed into distinct and independent societies, nearly in the same manner as the Congregational Presbyterians of your neighboring New England States" (quoted in Hennesey 1981, 77). James Hennesey, S. J., summarizes well this dilemma for the Church in the early Republic: "the problem was how to conciliate historic Catholic polity, with its bias for hierarchial and clerical control, with a legal system and popular feeling strongly influenced by prevailing American democratic winds as well as by even older English antipathy—long antedating the Reformation of the sixteenth century—to the claims of Roman and canon law" (1981, 77). The defenders of an ecclesiastical or institutional Catholicism were eventually to win the day, at least in part given the increasing political power of a Church that was growing in size and centralizing its authority. As Michael Zoller stated, "not until the 1860s, after the high water mark of nativism and after the Civil War, when the mood has shifted and it became clear that Catholic bishops were a political force to be reckoned with, were individual states' regulations concerning incorporation gradually changed" (1999, 61). Bishops had gained firm control of both Church property and personnel appointments.

However, the root sociohistorical causes of trusteeism in the early Church involved not merely the cultural role that Protestantism and the Enlightenment fostered in terms of such values as democracy and individualism but, also, in a sense, its direct opposite: the primordial attachments engendered by nationality and ethnicity. As has been previously argued, one useful—if by itself incomplete—way to analyze the history of American Catholicism is through focusing on the successive waves of immigration from differing parts of the globe. As Andrew Greeley noted, trusteeism involved "internal problems . . . [with] . . . the Church . . . with schism or near schisms happening in New York, Philadelphia, Norfolk, and Charleston—schisms . . . in most cases . . . [based] . . . on ethnic lines" (1967, 68). Simply put, pre–Civil War battles over the local control of a parish occurred between the English, French, Germans, and Irish, all of whom wanted their parishes and priests to represent their own ethnic traditions. The partial, if far from complete, assimilation of immigrant Catholic groups into a common Catholicism and Americanism (Glazer and Moynihan 1970; Tomasi 1975), in conjunction with the growing strength of a centralized Church under the control of the bishops, were some of the reasons for the eventual tempering and taming of the ethnic impulse behind trusteeism.

One final reason for the growth and subsequent demise of trusteeism in the early American Catholic Church should be noted. It involves what Jay Dolan has referred to as the Catholic Enlightenment philosophy accepted by some elite English Catholic thinkers, which tried to reconcile a Catholic worldview with the social and intellectual traditions of the Enlightenment (1985, 108). As Dolan observed, an "important component in the Catholic Enlightenment movement in Europe was the active participation of the laity in the life of the Church. In the United States, this took its most concrete form through the democratization of local church government through the adoption

of the trustee system" (1985, 110). However, Dolan observes that
"after 1820 or so, the Catholic Enlightenment began to falter; the democratization of religion also started to wane, so that by mid-century,
religion in America was becoming once again more hierarchical in nature" (1985, 190). To whatever degree the Catholic Enlightenment
was a force within the early American Catholic community, it was
tied into a middle- to upper-class worldview, one that would attenu-
ate with the introduction of a mass of poor and working-class immigrants, many of them Irish, into the country. And so too would the
proletarian nature of the Church's base population weaken the at-
tractiveness of the trustee system in American Catholicism, at least
through most of the twentieth century. However, with the move into
a middle-class status of a sizable segment—the most powerful segment—of the Catholic population since the mid-1960s, various calls
for the democratization of Catholicism, reminiscent of the early calls
for lay control, or at least lay input into parish and Church life, have
appeared and give no evidence of disappearing. Indeed, to make matters more challenging for those who defend the historic ecclesiastical
understanding of the institution, the original "biblical individualism"
(Bellah et al. 1985) of the earliest advocates of trusteeism has secularized into something closer to the "autonomous individualism"
(Riesman, Glazer, and Denny 1961) of many modern-day nominal
Catholics, thus making it far less possible to carve out some common
religiously based common ground. A crucial question then arises: Will
the contemporary calls for democratization lead to schisms within the
Church or can democratic impulses be contained within and tamed to
actually energize the Church institution? In conclusion, it is perhaps
important to note that historian James Hennesey looked to the "substantial, although ultimately fruitless, contribution to church government on the local level" (1981, 114) attempted by Bishop John
England (d.1842). For Hennessey, "he was conscious both of the signs
of the times and of the Catholic need for continuity with the Church's
authentic tradition" (1981, 114). As Jay Dolan similarly stated,
Bishop England "sought to achieve a situation in which, he said, 'the
laity are empowered to cooperate but not to dominate'" (1985, 166).
For interested readers, Father Andrew Greeley devotes considerable
length to Bishop England's experiment in parish governance in his *The
Catholic Experience* (1967).

Nativism and Immigration

Nativism refers to the in-group reaction of prejudice and discrimination on the part of a nation's host group, that is, the "natives," toward immigrant newcomers whose life styles are perceived to be alien or foreign to the existing culture. Ironically, when applied to early American history, this term does not apply to the true "Native" Americans, the indigenous Indian tribes of the continent, who were conquered by elements of Protestant civilization and subsequently ignored because of their cultural and political impotence in the New World. There were, however, demonstrable outbreaks by the "new nativists," that is, elements of Protestant America. Protestant-inspired nativism emerged against such newcomer groups as Catholics, Orthodox Christians, Mormons, black Africans, and Jews who were viewed as, in some sense, biologically or culturally or religiously inferior pagans threatening a true Christian American way of life. A prominent example of an American nativist group, especially active during the beginning of the twentieth century, was the Ku Klux Klan whose malevolent activities included murder and mutilation.

A few introductory points should be made at the outset of our discussion of nativism. It is important to state that not all mainstream Protestants manifested bigotry toward non-Protestant immigrants. Many Protestant Americans had an innate sense of decency and fairness and supported, to varying degrees and at whatever level of self-conscious awareness, conceptions of religious liberty and universal human rights. Others subordinated their biases to the practical recognition that America needed the immigrants as a cheap source of labor to help build up the new nation.

It is also important to note that nativist uprisings against Catholics were not constantly manifested throughout American history. Rather they waxed and waned, more or less according to predictable sociological considerations. Nativist discrimination, for instance, almost always attenuated itself during periods of war where the need for comradeship and victory in battle tended to outweigh religious prejudice. The fact that many Catholics supported the revolutionary cause, assisted the nation in its war against Mexico in 1846, were needed by both sides in the Civil War with the majority of Catholics living and fighting for the North, and shed considerable blood for America in two world wars tended to abate, temporarily at least, anti-Catholic feelings in the nation.

On the other hand, the Spanish American War of 1898, waged against the Catholic nation of Spain and which saw the Philippines and Puerto Rico acquired by the American nation, aroused the ire of the dominant American Protestant majority. As James T. Fisher notes, the war "was viewed by many Americans as a triumph of Anglo-Saxon Protestantism over a decadent European nation" (2000, 90). Even more historically important, nativist sentiments tended to flare up when Catholic immigration to America increased. Many have concluded that the restrictive immigration laws passed by Congress and that started, as of May 1921, were aimed at keeping Protestant America safe from excessive Catholic influence. James Hennesey quotes the Protestant theologian Martin Marty who stated quite bluntly that, at the time, "moderates throughout the nation were no less disturbed than Ku Klux Klansmen about the threat that America would go Catholic by immigration" (1981, 237). Nativist sentiments also flared up during periods of economic downturn when the host population viewed immigrants as taking jobs away from "real Americans." And very important, nativism was resurgent during political elections when Catholics sought office, especially when the national stakes were high. There was clearly significant anti-Catholic animosity toward America's first Catholic presidential candidate, Alfred E. Smith, in 1928, and not inconsequential opposition to John F. Kennedy's successful bid in 1960.

A final introductory point to be made is that, ironically, all Catholics themselves were not completely innocent of nativist-like sentiments. For one thing, the various Catholic ethnic groups did not always respect each other's cultural way of life. Another instance would be the negative attitude that some Catholic working-class ethnics harbored periodically toward African Americans (with whom they were often in competition for jobs in the inner cities). The latter were somehow viewed as "outside of the American pale." And more recently, some Catholics, now comfortably "native," hold much the same attitudes toward the post-1965 "new immigration" from the Third World that had been held against their own Catholic forefathers by earlier American Protestants.

There were three major waves of Protestant-based nativism against Catholics during the nineteenth century in America. Ninety-four Protestant ministers formed the American Protestant Association in 1842 as an angry response to the petition of Bishop Francis Patrick Kenrick of Philadelphia to city officials in the city of brotherly love. Bishop Kenrick complained that it was abusive, in his opinion, for Catholic children in the public school system to be forced to use the "King James" version of the Bible, the Bible of choice for Protestants. According to Monsignor John Tracy Ellis, for this Protestant organization, "the principles of popery were 'subversive of civil and religious liberty' and they therefore were uniting to defend Protestant interests against what they called 'the great expectations now making to propagate that system in the United States'" (1969, 64). Monsignor Ellis believed that the constant fomenting of anti-Catholic sentiments by groups such as the American Protestant Association inflamed the tempers of many Protestant Americans at the time leading to outbreaks of violence. Particularly ugly during this period was the burning of the Ursuline Sisters convent at Charlestown, Massachusetts, in 1834 and three days of destructive rioting in Philadelphia. This was also the period in which the infamous lies about Catholic convent life were perpetuated through the sordid tales of "Maria Monk." According to Ellis, "the decline of the movement was hastened by the outbreak of war with Mexico in May, 1846" (1969, 69).

In 1854, the Know-Nothing or American Party was formed, which was very influential until the Civil War. According to Michael Zoller, "the Know Nothing Party's influence was at its peak in the 1850s, when it had more than 70 representatives in Congress" (1999, 83). In 1855, the Know Nothings accomplished a major, albeit temporary, victory— the passing of the Putnum Bill in New York forbidding Catholic bishops from holding property in their own name. The Know-Nothing Party had evolved from a secret patriotic association termed the "Order of the Star Spangled Banner." The association's statutes specified that "the Order's goal is to oppose the Church of Rome's underhanded political activities and other threats to Republican institutions, and to ensure that public offices come into the hands only of 'native born Protestant citizens'" (Zoller 1999, 80–81).

In 1887, the American Protective Association was created and represented a third wave of nativist sentiment during the century. The association was formed "in order to ensure 'true Americanism'; it demanded that citizenship be denied to anyone 'subject to any ecclesiastical power not created or controlled by American citizens'" (Zoller 1999, 139). Furthermore, "the growing strength and numbers of Catholics and their increasing prominence in business and government offered to the A.P.A. campaign a seeming plausibility that predecessors had lacked. . . . For the next decade every corner of America rang with cries of warning against the Church of Rome" (Ellis 1969, 109).

The fact that millions of poor and formally uneducated Catholic immigrants, along with Jewish and Eastern Orthodox immigrants with similar characteristics, came teeming into American shores around the turn into the twentieth century guaranteed that nativism, including nativism focused against Catholics, would not easily disappear. "The most blatantly anti-Catholic group in the country during the first half of the twenties was," for James Henessey, "the Ku Klux Klan, four to five million strong at its peak and spread throughout southern, mid-western, and middle Atlantic states. The Klansmen had a long enemies list but . . . Catholics stood at the top of it" (1981, 246).

As previously mentioned, by the end of World War II, Catholics were coming of age in the United States, moving up the American socioeconomic ladder yet maintaining a religious organization that was impressive and increasingly powerful. The Catholic presence in post–World War II America was so impressive and potentially powerful that there was a palpable fear on the part of now secularizing Protestant elites that American civilization might, indeed, be converted to Catholicism. Such a fear created organizations such as Protestants and Other Americans United for the Separation of Church and State, founded in 1947. According to Hennesey, "Paul Blanshard became a spokesman; his *American Freedom and Catholic Power*, issued in March, 1949, was in a sixth printing by August" (1981, 295).

The fear of Protestant and, now increasingly, secular elites about Catholic power was to extinguish quickly given the weakening of the institutional integrity of the Catholic Church during the post–Vatican II years and, concomitantly, the uncritical assimilation of the younger generations of Catholics into American secular life. Put crudely, as Catholics have become less "foreign" vis-à-vis what passes for conformity to American mainstream life, discrimination has decreased also. The startling exception to this, however, are for those Catholics who have attempted to maintain and live publicly an orthodox, now increasingly countercultural, Catholic life in a modern, secular America. For such Catholic Americans, "nativist" bigotry remains a dangerous (if not physically so) and ever present facet of daily life.

"The Propagation Society. More free than welcome." An anti-Catholic cartoon, reflecting the nativist perception of the threat posed by the Roman Catholic Church's influence in the United States through Irish immigration and Catholic education. *Lithograph, c.1855, courtesy of the Library of Congress Prints and Photographs Division.*

The Provincial and Plenary Councils of Baltimore, 1828–84

It is hard to comprehend fully all the obstacles the early Catholic Church in the United States had to confront and eventually surmount in establishing itself as a viable religious, cultural, and political entity. As just mentioned, the Church was embedded in a Protestant nation whose attitude toward Catholicism ranged from overt hostility at worst to a seemingly ingrained suspiciousness at best. The majority of Catholic immigrants, moreover, were poor and uneducated. Additionally, they came from diverse cultural and national backgrounds, and often fought each other over religious issues fraught with important symbolic significance such as control of local parish life and Church policies. There were few priests and many of them were of the rogue variety escaping religious discipline and civil punishment in Europe. The American Catholic Church, qua institution, was financially strapped with few parishes, seminaries, schools, and other organizations to construct its necessary "plausibility structure," promote a coherent philosophy, and protect an organized community life.

Church leadership, obviously, had its hands full and much planning had to be accomplished. That planning was executed basically through the holding of ten meetings starting in 1829 and ending in 1884. The Baltimore provincial and plenary councils would provide the blueprint for a Catholic Church in America that would, by the post–World War II period of American history, have no rival throughout the world (Kelly 1990, xiii). As the Commonweal Foundation Report, *American Catholics in the Public Square* cited:

> Over two centuries, U.S. Catholics built and supported a range of institutions—hospitals, social-welfare agencies, primary and secondary schools, colleges and universities—that have provided an infrastructure in which to practice and transmit Catholicism, including its social teachings. Those teachings, moreover, were made available not simply to a clerical or intellectual elite, but to ordinary Catholics. Furthermore, these institutions have been the vehicles by which millions of immigrant Catholics have moved into the mainstream of American society. (2004, 4)

The ensuing discussion of the Baltimore meetings, based on two entries in the 1912 *Catholic Encyclopedia*, is far from complete and perhaps mundane in its sometimes repetitive presentation but its necessary and crucial purpose is to offer a sense of the many types of issues that the bishops of the early Republic grappled with in the attempt to build up the Church, regularize and standardize the practice of the faith, and make its presence a dominant reality for the Catholic population and a respected institution in the American society at large.

James Hennesey notes the historical origin of the idea of such regional councils. For Hennesey,

> a reforming decree of the Council of Trent ordered that provincial councils—formal meetings of the Bishops of an ecclesiastical region— be held every three years. Nowhere was this better observed than in the United States during the middle years of the 19th century. Seven provincial councils of Baltimore were held between 1829 and 1849 and plenary national councils followed in 1852, 1866, and 1884.

Prime mover in initiating the series of Baltimore Councils was the 34 year old Cork priest John England, who arrived in Charleston, South Carolina in 1820 as its first Catholic Bishop. (1981, 113–14)

Attended by one archbishop and four bishops, the First Provincial Council was held in 1829. It dealt with such issues, among others, as the rules surrounding baptism; the purpose of financial contributions; the granting of absolution; the mastering of Christian doctrine as a prerequisite for marriage; rules regarding mixed marriages; the singing of hymns and saying of prayers at evening services; rules regarding holy days of obligation; the obligation of the rich to sustain pastors; the role of the bishop in refusing Christian burial; the requirement of using the Douay version of the Bible; warning against improper theaters, dances, and novels; the prohibition of Freemasons being admitted to the sacraments; the rights of bishops to assign priests their respective missions; the use of Latin in administering the sacraments and in the burial service; the building of Catholic schools; and also that parish ownership should ideally be consigned to the bishop. Regarding the latter, Jay Dolan considers the 1829 meeting the first serious move by the bishops against lay ownership of Church property; he states that by the 1884 meeting, the bishops' authority was absolute on this issue (1985, 172).

The Second Provincial Council was attended by one archbishop and nine bishops and held in 1833. It addressed, among other things, the method of selecting bishops, entrusting to the Society of Jesus the tasks of overseeing the Indian missions in the West and the missions among the former American slaves now repatriated to Liberia in Africa, and the erecting of seminaries.

The Third Provincial Council, held in 1837, was attended by one archbishop and eight bishops. Among the concerns it addressed were the obtaining of ecclesiastical property through civil law, the separation of ecclesiastical cases from civil tribunals, the prohibiting of priests from soliciting money outside of their own parishes, appropriate music at divine worship, and changes in both holy days of obligation and days of fast and abstinence.

In 1840, the Fourth Provincial Council of Baltimore issued statements by one archbishop and twelve bishops. Among them are the following: temperance societies are recommended to the faithful, the prohibiting of Catholics from attending public schools using the Protestant version of the Bible or singing sectarian hymns, and that all ecclesiastical property should be in the name of the bishop.

The Fifth Council was attended by one archbishop and sixteen bishops in 1843. Enacted, among other things, were the following: laymen may not deliver orations in churches, the bishops noted lack of expedience in extending the Tridentine decrees concerning clandestine matrimony to places where they have not already been promulgated, and the bishops prohibited priests from borrowing money for church uses without permission of the bishop.

One archbishop and twenty-two bishops attended the Sixth Provincial Council of Baltimore in 1846. Among its decrees were that the Blessed Virgin Mary was chosen as Patron of the United States, the canons concerning the proclamation of the banns of matrimony were to be followed, and that the bishops were to use a formula sanctioned by the Holy See in taking the oath at their consecration.

The last and seventh Provincial Council of Baltimore served, de facto, as a plenary council for the Catholic Church of the United States. It met in 1849 and was attended by two archbishops and twenty-three bishops. Among its declarations were that the American bishops will communicate to the Holy See that they think it opportune to define as a dogma the Immaculate Conception of the Blessed Virgin Mary, that priests are forbidden to assist at marriages of those who have already had a ceremony performed by a Protestant minister or attend such a ceremony, and that the Holy Father be petitioned to raise New Orleans, Cincinnati, and New York to metropolitan status.

When the whole American Republic was considered part of the ecclesiastical province of Baltimore, the first seven of ten provincial councils convened in that city provided the necessary vehicle to attempt to implement a common discipline throughout Catholic America. However, after several other ecclesiastical provinces were created by the Holy See, it became logically necessary to convene national or plenary councils to standardize and regularize the practice of the Catholic faith.

The First Plenary Council of Baltimore was held in 1852, presided over by Archbishop Kenrick of Baltimore and attended by six archbishops, thirty-five bishops, the abbot of T. Mary of La Trappe and the religious superiors of the Augustianians, Dominicans, Benedictines, Franciscans, Jesuits, Redemptorists, Vincentians, and Sulpicians. Among the most important legislation it passed was making of the decrees of the first seven provincial councils of Baltimore obligatory for all U.S. dioceses. Furthermore, the Roman ritual was to be observed in all dioceses; bishops were exhorted to consult the advice of their clergy in the governing of their dioceses; the office of chancellor should be instituted in each diocese; bishops should appoint censors for religion-related books; European priests desiring to be transferred to an American diocese must have the permission of the American bishop in question; bishops have the right to define parish boundaries, the jurisdiction and privileges of pastors, and the appointment of incumbents; there should be a Catholic school in every parish and an ecclesiastical seminary in each diocese; yearly accounting of the administration of church funds should be instituted; lay people are not to take any part in Church administration without the consent of the bishop; and a Society for the Propagation of the Faith should be established. For James Hennesey (1981, 160), the bishops of the First Plenary Council made clear that "not only have we to erect and maintain the Church, the Seminary, and the Schoolhouse, but have to found hospitals, orphanages, and provide for every want of suffering humanity which religion forbids us to neglect." Michael Zoller (1999, 92) notes the importance of this plenary session in proposing the creation of no less than ten new dioceses.

The Second Plenary Council, held in 1866, was presided over by Archbishop Spalding of Baltimore and attended by seven archbishops, thirty-nine bishops or their representatives, and two abbots. James Hennesey portrays the general thrust of this meeting as follows:

> As in previous American councils, the Bishops agree on a series of internal disciplinary decrees designed to harmonize Church procedures throughout the country. What was new in the 534 pages of legislation was a series of statements on theological topics: Revelation, the Church as custodian of Revelation, the doctrine of "outside the Church there is no salvation," the nature and necessity of Faith, Sacred Scripture, the mysteries of the Trinity, creation, redemption, sanctification, the future life, and veneration of the Blessed Virgin Mary. The text relied heavily on recent papal statements, including many of the same documents cited by Pope Pius IX in his 1864 *Syllabus of Errors*. But the tone was distinctively American and nowhere was the *Syllabus* mentioned. The Bishops tried to deal with the actual problems of the Church on their own side of the Atlantic. Their approach was for the most part a more positive one than has been accepted in Rome. (1981, 160)

Jay Dolan also notes the importance of this shift to a devotional Catholicism in the decrees of the Second Plenary Council:

> Considerable attention was given to the forty hours devotion to the Eucharist and benediction of the Blessed Sacrament and the need for processions associated with these devotions; legislation was enacted which encouraged the organization of confraternities associated with various popular devotions such as those of the Eucharist, the Sacred Heart of Jesus, Mary, St. Joseph and the Holy Angels, and others. Such extensive consideration of the Catholic devotional network was absent from previous and subsequent Church councils and suggests by the 1860s the importance as well as the newness of devotional Catholicism in the United States was very much in the forefront of episcopal consciousness. (1985, 213)

James Hennesey brings to light at least one major mistake of the 1866 meeting, "the failure to adopt a cohesive and vigorous program for evangelization of the four million freed black people" (1981, 161).

The Third Plenary Council was held in 1884 and was presided over by Archbishop James Gibbons of Baltimore and attended by fourteen archbishops, sixty-one bishops or their delegates, six abbots, and one general of a religious congregation. It is acknowledged widely by Catholic scholars (Hennesey 1981, 186; Dolan 1985, 353) that this council marked the end of the organizing or "blueprint" phase of Catholicism in the United States. As Dolan says:

> Between 1829 and 1866, the national Church councils met regularly; these councils gave some degree of unity to the Church by formulating a body of legislation to regulate Church life. The last national meeting, the Third Baltimore Council of 1884, was the culmination of this conciliar movement; it passed a body of legislation that surpassed all previous councils in terms of detail and inclusiveness. The legislation of Baltimore III remained the Magna Charta of American Catholic Church life for the next several decades. (1985, 352–53)

Dolan also notes that "about one-fourth of this legislation focused on education, the centerpiece of which was the decrees on the parochial school" (1985, 271). Relatedly, he observed a concern about the quality of education, teacher competency and education, and the establishment and enlargement of institutions of Catholic higher education to be funded primarily by wealthy Catholics (1985, 272). Dolan also points out that the Third Plenary Council, by making the authority of the bishop supreme in all local Church affairs, was mirroring centralizing developments in papal authority at the time (1985, 180, 190, 222–23). Another major consequence of the meeting was that it "produced the 'Baltimore Catechism,' the famous series of questions and answers that every American . . . [Catholic] . . . school child learned by heart for the next seventy-five years" (Morris 1997, 85).

James Hennesey notes, relatedly, the importance of this council authorizing *A Manual of Prayers* (1981, 177). Also of importance is that the "Third Plenary Council had urged greater devotion to the Third Person of the Trinity. The 'Americanists,' (i.e., progressive Catholics trying to harmonize the Catholic faith with American culture and society) stressed the correlation of this theological emphasis with their own stress on the importance of individual initiative" (Hennesey 1981, 197).

Something akin to the national planning role of the Baltimore councils was unsuccessfully attempted with the creation of the National Catholic Welfare Council in 1917. However, with the legitimation afforded the idea of national episcopal conferences of Catholic bishops by the Second Vatican Council, the Catholic Church in this country did witness a period, just ending now, where there was operative a strong national Catholic bureaucracy of a decidedly progressive bent. Conservative Catholic opposition to this liberal bureaucracy, which conservatives felt, was ofttimes out of step with the philosophy and program of John Paul II (1978–2005) and the Vatican has recently served, at least practically, to limit the activities of what was once called the National Conference of Catholic Bishops/United States Catholic Conference. As a matter of fact, dissatisfaction with their national bureaucracy has recently led some bishops of a more orthodox, traditional bent to call for the re-instituting of a national plenary council to deal with major issues confronting the Church, most prominently, the contemporary sexual scandals, as a way to check the progressive monopoly typical of national bureaucratic structures.

The American Culture War and the School Controversy

As James D. Hunter (1991, 1994) has correctly noted, American civilization has always experienced some significant degree of cultural warfare, although the combatants and, in some cases, the issues have changed from one sociohistorical context to another. One issue that has consistently remained a hotly debated issue throughout American history lies within the realm of education or, more specifically, over who should educate the population at large and, relatedly, who should receive public financial support for educational endeavors. As he cited in his *Culture Wars: The Struggle to Define America*:

> The reason that the contemporary culture war extends to the realm of education is not difficult to divine. . . . The education of the public at every level—from elementary school through college—is *not* a neutral process of imparting practical knowledge and technical skills. . . . The schools are the primary institutional means of reproducing community and national identity for succeeding generations of Americans . . . thus the conflict will inevitably reach the institutions that impart these collective understandings to children and young adults. (1991, 198)

Fundamental to James Hunter's overall thesis about cultural warfare in the United States is that the nature of the combatants have changed throughout time and context. During the early period of American history, the cultural line of demarcation was a generic and mainstream Protestantism versus all non-Protestant immigrant and new emerging groups on the American scene. The most numerically important of the latter groups by the mid–nineteenth century were Catholics, but also included Eastern Orthodox Christians, Jews, and Mormons. By the mid-to late-twentieth century, the line of demarcation in the culture wars had shifted to a coalition of secular groups and progressively oriented Catholics, Protestants, and Jews on the one hand, against, on the other hand, a coalition of traditional and conservative Catholics, evangelical Protestants, Orthodox Christians, Orthodox Jews, and most Mormons (the latter groups, empirically speaking, having been successful to date in resisting a significant internal secularization of their religion).

Regarding the issue of education, most nineteenth-century Catholics did not accept the argument that the then public school system, albeit literally nonsectarian, was religiously neutral; rather the Catholic contention was that, either consciously or unselfconsciously, the American public school system was a vehicle for the Protestantization of Catholic children and young adults. As Michael Zoller put it, most Catholics of the time felt that " 'nonsectarian' still did not mean 'nondenominational' but rather the lowest common denominator of Protestantism" (1999, 82). As our previous discussion of the Baltimore councils and plenary sessions makes clear, it was the desire of both Rome and the majority of Catholic bishops to establish private Catholic schools in as many parishes as possible as a way of guaranteeing the successful socialization, education, and evangelization of the Catholic population in the United States into the basics of the faith.

Not all Catholic leaders, however, were as suspicious of or as outright antagonistic toward the American public school system as was the majority of Catholic elite leadership. For instance, the leading Catholic "Americanist" of his time, Archbishop John Ireland, was "seen as a defender of American institutions, particularly public schools" (Zoller 1999, 103). As Michael Zoller cites:

> Ireland tried to find a compromise between the public schools' claim to monopolize education and the demand for separate Catholic schools. . . . On the one hand, he wanted the Church to be relieved of the financial and staffing burdens involved in establishing its own schools so that it could concentrate on its central mission. On the other hand, Ireland's American nationalism was reflected in his opinion that public schools were the epitome of "American institutions." . . . Ireland made clear, however, that this praise applied only to "secular instruction," and that church-approved religious instruction must be guaranteed before Catholics could forego having their own schools. (1999, 120)

There were two attempts at carving out an educational compromise between the Catholic Church and secular government. One took place in 1873 in Poughkeepsie, New York, and was initiated by Archbishop John McCloskey and the other in 1891 in Faribault and Stillwater, Minnesota, and was arranged by Archbishop Ireland himself. In both cases, Catholic parishes leased their school buildings to local public authorities for some nominal fee. For their part, the public schools assumed responsibility for hiring teachers and maintaining the buildings but agreed to allow Catholic religious instruction, under Church authority, in the same buildings but outside of regular school hours. Such compromise attempts were doomed to failure given that they did not satisfy key constituencies of the two respective parties. Many Protestants and secularists thought that the government had gone too far in accommodating the faith requirements of Catholics, while many Catholics thought that the Church had made too much of a concession to government, allowing nonsectarian instruction in secular subjects to lead Catholic youth away from their religion and self-identity as practitioners of the faith. As Jay Dolan observed, "the Catholic commitment to parochial schools got stronger just as the public school commitment to religion weakened. The walls separating Church and State in the area of education had steadily risen in the late nineteenth century; this development canceled out any attempt at compromise between Catholics and a state-supported system of education" (1985, 276). As such, Catholic parents were forced to use either the public school system or send, if they could afford the cost, their children to local parish and diocesan schools. Many Catholic parents, either out of financial consideration, lack of a local available Catholic school, or simply, indifference to religious commitment, sent their children though the public school system.

The Catholic school system, however, impressively did develop and expand, at least up until the advent of the Second Vatican Council, concomitant with the general strengthening of what has previously been referred to as the "Catholic plausibility structure." The anomie brought about by the combined effects of the exaggerated forces of the social change and social protest in the 1960s and the confusion over the significance of the Second Vatican Council (1962–66), however, led to a significant weakening in the commitment to a self-consciously specific form of an authentic Catholic education. While some small Catholic colleges closed, the typical Catholic response in higher education was to promote a "secularization from within" as Catholic administrators and faculty started to accept secular understandings of the purpose and nature of education. Regarding elementary schools, Jay Dolan highlights the "peculiarly Catholic" debate over its ultimate utility to both the society and the individual as "many people questioned the value of educating children in separate, denominational schools" (1985, 442). This Catholic self-doubt about the Catholic educational enterprise is expressed quintessentially by the title of a popular book published at the time by the progressive Catholic, Mary Perkins Ryan, titled *Are Parochial Schools the Answer? Catholic Education in Light of the Council*. Dolan lists other reasons for the 1960s onward decline of the parochial school. For Dolan, "another obvious reason was financial. As large numbers of women religious either left religious life altogether or abandoned teaching for other ministries, the need to hire more lay teachers and thus pay higher salaries became paramount" (1985, 442). Another reason for the weakening of the Catholic school system was demographic; the post–World War II "baby boom" (which the Lutheran thinker Allan Carlson [1993, 2003] viewed as almost purely a "Catholic" phenomenon) ended with many empty classroom seats the result. In the final analysis, the weakening of the Catholic plausibility structure and commitment to Catholic education proved to be dialectically related and mutually reinforcing.

In general and consistent with the revised lines of combat in the *contemporary* culture war, Catholic progressives tend toward the acceptance of a secular understanding of education that is viewed as "liberating" and superior to antiquated Catholic and classical education and, as such, are either not interested in promoting Catholic education or, at best, desire to redefine it along secularized lines. Catholic restorationists, traditionalists, and conservatives are more obvious in their belief in the essentialness of Catholic education and of the need to preserve, even while organically updating, what is, for them, the intellectual and moral treasure to be found incarnate within a 2,000-year-old tradition. Important debates ensue, among the latter camp, in terms of the correct means to rehabilitate Catholic education. Some are politically active in attempting to change the contemporary understanding of Church and State relations to one more open to funneling, either directly or indirectly, taxpayer monies to private and parochial schools through such policy proposals as vouchers and tuition tax credits. Other traditionists fear that *any* involvement with government, even indirect, will inevitably bring with them certain obligatory strings attached, strings with secularizing implications. For many with such sentiments, it is better for Catholic schools to adopt a policy of complete financial self-sufficiency. Other traditionalists, afraid that secularization has deeply eroded even Catholic elementary school education, are supportive of home schooling, believing that the only true guarantee to passing on an authentic Catholic education, during the early stages, is through parental education.

The Cahensly Affair

One of the more vexing problems faced by Catholics in the United States at the turn into the twentieth century was the issue of the nature and extent of the assimilation of Catholic ethnic groups into American culture and society. In Andrew Greeley's terminology, the Catholic Church was divided into two competing camps, the "Americanizers" and "anti-Americanizers" (1967). The former desired that the Catholic immigrant groups relinquish as quickly as possible their national heritages and substitute an American one, without losing their Catholicity. The Americanist position had been stated quintessentially in 1854 by Orestes Brownson. For Brownson, "The Americanization of the Catholic body does and will go on of itself, as rapidly as is desirable, and all we have to do with it is to take care that they do not imbibe of the notion that to Americanize is necessarily to Protestantize. The transition from one nationality to another is always a dangerous process, and all the Americanization I insist in is that our Catholic population shall feel and believe that a man may be a true American and good Catholic" (quoted in Dolan 1985, 296). The anti-Americanist position argued that it was precisely the original nationality of the immigrant that was the indispensable and non-negotiable carrier of his/her Catholic faith; to Americanize was to guarantee a significant amount of "leakage" of Catholic immigrants from their religious faith. This fundamental disagreement over the best way to maintain Catholic identity was and is still relevant to all American Catholic ethnic groups. However, it took on a particular salience at the turn of the century between two groups, the dominant and generally proassimilationist Irish American Catholic and a German American Catholic community generally antiassimilationist who were geographically concentrated in the Midwest, possessed their own long and distinguished Catholic pedigree, and who openly attempted to break the Irish monopoly in the American Catholic Church. It is very important to point out that this divide didn't fall completely around the issue of ethnicity as there were powerful Irish prelates, such as Archbishop Michael A. Corrigan and Bishop Bernard McQuaid, who supported the anti-Americanist position.

In the decade immediately prior to the beginning of the twentieth century, the debate turned into a raging controversy that involved leading Irish Catholic prelates, German Catholic clergy and laity, Pope Leo XIII, and even attracted the interest of the American president at the time, Benjamin Harrison. (Harrison's natural interest was to see the Americanization of European immigrant groups and also to guarantee that there was no undue foreign influence operating on American shores.) In 1890, anti-Americanist leaders met in Lucerne, Switzerland, where they drafted a memorial to Pope Leo XIII suggesting ways to protect the Catholicity of American immigrant groups by guarding against "religious leakage." According to Dolan, "the Lucerne Memorial made several recommendations for the care of immigrants in the United States. These included separate parishes for each nationality, administered by priests of 'the same nationality to which the faithful belonged,' catechetical instruction in the mother tongue, separate parochial schools for each nationality, equal rights for the clergy of each nationality, and representation within the hierarchy of each nationality'" (1985, 298). In 1891, a German Catholic layman, Peter Paul Cahensly, personally delivered the Lucerne Memorial to the pope and the controversy ensued when its contents were made public in America. The Americanists billed the memorial as a "German plot" in which the German Catholic community in the United States would become inextricably interwined with a foreign German Catholic Church. The Americanist leadership, led by such Irish Catholic bishops as James Cardinal Gibbons and Archbishop John Ireland, tended to portray the Lucerne Memorial as some kind of political conspiracy and, in any event, were able to convince Pope Leo XIII "that its proposals were 'neither opportune nor necessary'" (Dolan 1985, 298–99). The phrase, "Cahenslyism" was originally coined by America's leading Americanist of the era, Archbishop John Ireland, during the polemics; the label has now become a standard in American Catholic history.

The defeat of the German anti-Americanists probably sped up a bit for American Catholic ethnics an assimilation process into American culture and society that, to some significant degree and in certain ways, was inevitable. It also made it harder for nativists to argue that Catholicism represented a foreign threat to American civilization. It also served to provide some autonomy for American Catholic Church leaders from European affairs.

However, a few crucial questions from the Cahensly experience remain. Can the Catholic Church become "too American," especially with reference to a contemporary situation marked by an advanced degree of secularization? Can the American hierarchy and dominant middle-class Catholic population become too independent from Rome and oblivious to important developments in the worldwide Catholic Church? Regarding the first question, what are the advantages and limitations of the present "Anglo" domination in an American Catholic Church into which millions of non-Anglo Third World (e.g., Hispanic,

African, Asian) immigrants continue to pour? And, relatedly and second, what will be the consequences for a highly Anglo-like American Catholic Church surrounded by a non-Western world that is witnessing a significant resurgence of traditional, orthodox Catholicism? These issues are addressed centrally in a volume authored by Philip Jenkins, *The Next Christendom: The Coming of Global Christianity* (2002).

The Heresy of Americanism

The turn into the twentieth-century Catholic Church in the United States was marked by a titanic struggle between two factions that would erupt again in the post–Vatican II era. The first, or liberal/progressivist "Americanizer" faction, believed that Catholics ought not view American culture and society as in any significant way antithetical to the Catholic religion. The second, or conservative/traditional camp, argued that the full assimilation of Catholics into American ideas and life was fraught with dangers to the faith.

In 1899, Pope Leo XIII intervened by issuing his encyclical, *Testem benevolentiae*, which focused on the so-called "heresy of Americanism." In the encyclical, the pope admonished Catholics about certain attitudes and practices opposed to the faith. These included the tendencies to (1) assert the superiority of "natural" to "supernatural" reality; (2) posit the superiority of "active" (e.g., social activism) to "passive" (e.g., prayer) virtues; and (3) reduce the faith to surrounding culture. The latter danger included both external and internal considerations. By the former, the pope meant what today orthodox Catholics would call a false ecumenism in which the Catholic religion is co-opted or relativized by the visions of other religions and secular worldviews. By the latter, the pope meant the idea of a radical democratization within the Church that would, for all intents and purposes, eliminate the central guardian role performed by the Church's magisterium (Varacalli 1989).

According to Church historian Monsignor John Tracy Ellis, the pope "was not accusing the Catholics of the United States of holding these views; he was merely warning that if such doctrines were being taught, they were erroneous." To no one's surprise, the Americanizer and anti-Americanizer factions interpreted the significance of *Testem benevolen-*

tiae quite differently. As Monsignor Ellis continues: "Following the publication of the Pope's letter, the bishops of the Provinces of Milwaukee and New York thanked Leo XIII for saving the American Church from the threat of heresy. The more common reaction in the United States, however, was that embodied in the reply of Cardinal Gibbons to the pontiff on March 17, 1899, when he said, 'This doctrine, which I deliberately call extravagant and absurd, this Americanism as it had been called, had nothing in common with the views, aspirations, doctrine, and conduct of Americans'" (Ellis 1956, 533).

Whether Cardinal Gibbons, himself a moderate Americanist, was correct at the time in his assessment of the orthodoxy of those Catholics with Americanizer sentiments has been, and will continue to be, debated. The political and sociological reality, however, was that the issuing of *Testem benevolentiae* in 1899 and, later, *Lamentabili Sane* ("Syllabus Condemning the Errors of the Modernists") and *Pascendi Dominici Gregis* ("On the Doctrine of the Modernists") by Pope Pius X in 1907 clearly was a victory for the conservative/traditional camp.

This combined Roman intervention did not so much stop the engagement of Catholics with America as it encouraged the development of an acceptance of American culture and society that was contained within, and contoured to, the Catholic religion (Morris 1997). The consequences of the conservative/traditional victory, almost needless to say, was also hotly disputed. For progressivist Catholics, the period starting from World War I up to the Second Vatican Council was depicted as a religious, moral, and intellectual wasteland, with Catholics marginalizing themselves into a "Catholic ghetto." In 1955, for instance, the Catholic historian, Monsignor John Tracy Ellis published an influential essay, "American Catholics and the Intellectual Life," making the claim that Catholics had a dismal record in intellectual and scholarly activities in American society. To the contrary, for the conservative wing, this was a period, reaching an apogee in post–World War II America, in which American society was slowly but steadily being transformed into one consonant with Catholic Christian principles. Monsignor George A. Kelly (1989), for one, has labeled this period one of "gold status," not only for the Church in America but also for the Church Universal, that is, across all time and space. The "Americanist" program may have been stalled but it erupted with a vengeance in the post–Vatican II period.

The Origins of the National Catholic Bureaucracy in the United States: From the National Catholic War Council to the United States Conference of Catholic Bishops

The last council of Baltimore was held in 1884 and no permanent national Catholic agency was established in the wake of the series of plenary and provincial councils held throughout the century. This fact was a great disappointment to the "progressive" wing of the Catholic Church. As Robert Cross pointed out in his *The Emergence of Liberal Catholicism in America*, "the liberals of the 1890s were eager to limit diocesan autonomies in order to obtain effective national action" (1958, 214). Historical accident, however, would intervene in the liberals' favor with the outbreak of World War I. The war required a national Catholic coordinating agency to be created in order to coordinate the Catholic community's contribution to the war effort. In 1917, the bishops created that agency in the National Catholic War Council, headed by Monsignor John Burke. As James Hennesey put it, "formation of the War Council was a major organizational step for the Catholic Church of the United States. For the first time in its history an institutional commitment was being made to social and political action" (1981, 227).

Predictably enough, when the war was successfully concluded, the incipient national bureaucracy did not dissolve but found other reasons to exist and even expand, a perfect example of what sociologists refer to as "goal displacement." The liberals were successful, at least in a formal sense, in transforming the goals of the organization from those concerned with the war effort to those attempting to promote elements of a distinctly liberal "socially conscious" Catholic agenda for the era.

In 1919, a National Catholic Welfare Council was set up, along with an administrative committee, to assist in the Church's social justice apostolate in the United States, in dealing with issues such as education, immigration, and social action. In 1922, the word "conference" replaced the word "council" to indicate that the now National Catholic Welfare Conference was "consultative" and not "legislative," thereby not challenging the authority of the bishops heading a local diocese. This change was considered a victory for the more conservative wing of the hierarchy.

In the "Brief History" of the evolution of the present-day national episcopal conference authored by its own staff, it is stated that:

this model continued until 1966 when the National Conference of Catholic Bishops (NCCB) and the United States Catholic Conference (USCC) were established. The NCCB attended to the Church's own affairs in this country, fulfilling the Vatican Council's mandate that Bishops "jointly exercise their private office" ("Decree on the Bishops' Pastoral Office in the Church, #38). NCCB operated through committees made up exclusively of Bishops, many of which had full-time staff organized in secretariats. In USCC the Bishops collaborate with other Catholics to address issues that concern the Church as part of the larger society. Its committees included lay people, clergy, and religious in addition to the Bishops. On July 1, 2001, the NCCB and USCC were combined to form the United States Conference of Catholic Bishops (Brief History, USCCB). (May 20, 2004, 2)

It is important to point out that the 1965 publication of *Christus Dominus* ("On the Pastoral Office of Bishops in the Church") constituted a significant victory for progressive Catholicism because it created a national level authority structure dominated by liberals that could serve, practically, if not necessarily theoretically, as a counterbalance to the authority of local bishops in the respective dioceses (Varacalli 1983, chap. 7). Michael Warner notes the nature of the "changing witness" on public policy of the American bishops through the National Conference of Catholic Bishops/United States Catholic Conference bureaucracy initiated in 1966. For Warner:

The Bishops' reorganization of the N.C.W.C. into the N.C.C.B. and U.S.C.C. brought in new personnel, processes, and ideas. . . . In the late 1960s, the reformed and expanded U.S.C.C. secretariat took in new advisors who reoriented the message of the Bishops' conference. Inspired by European notions of a "political theology," the U.S.C.C. staff prompted the Bishops to take critical stands on newly designated "moral issues," particularly poverty and the Vietnam War. The new political theology was not a true reading of Vatican II, however. . . . The old N.C.W.C. had promoted Catholic social doctrine as the fulfillment of reason—as the full and true expression of the natural law that was attainable on in the light of Christ. The N.C.C.B., however, . . . has regarded the Church's God-given wisdom more as a "resource" than as an imperative. . . . Conference statements after the 1960s only rarely tried to show how the truth revealed by Jesus Christ benefits all society; instead they emulated the policy pronouncements of secular lobbies and interest groups by criticizing current policies, advocating new ones and calling generally for cooperation, planning, and peace. (1995, 167–68)

Michael Warner concludes his analysis by comparing what he considers the authentic Catholic stance of Pope John Paul II (1978–2005) with the body of American bishops. He states:

But the social magisterium of John Paul II provides an alternative model: one that transcends the sterile options of cultural accommodation or "pragmatic" compromise with modern ideological error. By focusing the social doctrine of the Church on the moral and cultural foundations of democracy and the free economy, the Pope has diagnosed the pathologies that affect American liberty, and threaten its capacity to promote justice for all. (1995, 170)

Progressive Catholic thinkers, obviously, would dispute Michael Warner's criticism arguing that Catholic social thought has much to learn from secular thought and policies. The most powerful progressive Catholic figure in the newly constituted NCCB/USCC and, for that matter, in Catholic America at the time was Cardinal Joseph Bernardin (1928–1996) who was elected president of the NCCB in 1974 and dominated the American Catholic era in the 1970s and 1980s. Under his tutelage and protection, such decidedly progressive episcopal statements as *The Challenge of Peace: God's Promise and Our Response* (1983) and *Economic Justice for All: Catholic Social Teaching and the United States Economy* (1986) were published. He also personally ushered in the so-called "consistent ethic of life" that puts the Church on the side of both the antiabortion and antinuclear weapon positions, thus crosscutting the political right and left. More controversially, some conservatives felt that Cardinal Bernardin provided cover for other initiatives and organizations that were rejecting radically the Catholic tradition as understood by magisterial authority. The most recent reorganization of the national episcopal conference that combined the National Conference of Catholic Bishops and the United States Catholic Conference could be viewed as a victory for more traditional Catholic leadership as the merger, so it is argued, put the more progressive staff members of the latter under closer control and scrutiny of the former.

The Separation of Church and State

The early American colonists and immigrants—both non-Catholic and Catholic—had come from lands where one official religion was dominant and controlled the governing apparatus of their societies. Despite the carnage wrought by the religious wars of Europe and because of the centrality of their religion in their own personal and social lives, some significant portion of those colonists and immigrants *were*, indeed, interested in re-establishing their religious theocracies in the new world (the Puritans of Massachusetts and the Anglicans of Virginia representing the two most significant cases). It was feared by other religious groups that one religious group in the colonies could dominate the new world outside of their local regions.

There were many other colonists and immigrants who were not sympathetic to the theocratic impulse—for both religious and nonreligious reasons. Regarding the former, the members of certain strains of the Protestant Reformation such as the Anabaptists had biblical reasons for opposing the establishment of one religion over the State and civil life. Early Rhode Island and Pennsylvania were two colonies noted for their relative tolerance of religious pluralism. Yet other early founders of the American experiment were deists believing in a vague, nondenominational God whose only role was to crank start or initiate a physical and social universe based on science, rationality, and naturalistic morality. Finally, among the ranks of the earliest colonists there were not a few outright atheists and nonbelievers, well educated and influential beyond their numbers.

Julia Mitchell Corbett makes the acute observation that "prior disillusionment with established religion and the existence of religious pluralism worked against the continued existence of established religion in the United States" (2001, 21). Nationally, what is now commonly referred to as the "separation of Church and State" finds its alleged defense in the First Amendment to the Constitution which reads: "Congress shall make no law respecting an establishment of religion, or prohibiting the free exercise thereof." This principle was then applied, she continues, to the local states as well: "The Fourteenth Amendment holds that the states as well are not to 'abridge the privileges' of their citizens, including the privilege of religious freedom" (Corbett 2001, 23).

The relationship between the two clauses in the First Amendment

has been the continuing source of much controversy and constant reinterpretation. The "establishment clause" says that the national government cannot make any one religion the official religion of the United
States or give preferential consideration to one religious organization
over another. The "free exercise" clause states that the national government cannot obstruct an individual from the reasonable practice of
his/her religious beliefs. The "establishment" and "free exercise" clauses,
as such, provide only very broad parameters for interpreting the practical significance of the meaning of the "separation of Church and State"
and allow the judiciary branch of government a great deal of room in
interpretation and the ability to emphasize one clause over the other.

Not all present-day Americans accept the idea of separation of
Church and State. There are small religious organizations that still defend the idea of theocracy, and there are small groups of atheists who
want religion either abolished or relegated to the very margins of society. Clearly, however, most contemporary Americans *do* accept the concept of separation, but there remain many strong disagreements over
the constitutionality of specific social policy positions and possibilities
(e.g., school vouchers, nondenominational prayer in school, religious
leaders endorsing specific political candidates, government aid for charitable and social service agencies run by religious organizations, etc.).
In general, proreligious forces desire a low wall and much interaction
and cooperation between religion and government with those antagonistic or suspicious of organized religion desiring a very high wall with
government and religion representing two self-contained and almost
completely independent sectors of society, thus "privatizing" religious
expression and commitment in America.

Of relevance to our present discussion, are two key issues. The first
is the various ways by which the First Amendment has been interpreted
and applied in the United States. The second is the manner by which
Catholics have responded to those interpretations.

Regarding the first issue, it should be pointed out that in the early
days of the Republic the concept of the separation of Church and State
was basically created to institutionalize a compromise and cease-fire between the various dominant Protestant groups while simultaneously
hindering public recognition and assistance to minority religions such
as Catholicism. It was taken for granted, conversely, that America was
a generically Protestant culture, and therefore American public institutions should reflect this form of Christianity. It was assumed in a taken-

for-granted manner, for instance, that the King James version of the Bible was staple fare for American public education.

James T. McGreevy notes the alarm of key American elites as the nation entered the middle period of the twentieth century. As McGreevy notes, "in 1938, the editors of *The New Republic* posed the question, 'Is there a Catholic problem?' . . . the answer was yes" (2003, 165). In fact, as the editors continued, "certain well-defined tendencies and activities in the Catholic Church have recently become so prominent as to force themselves on the attention of thinking Americans and to raise the issue of Catholic policy to the magnitude of a public question" (2003, 165). After World War II, and despite—or perhaps, because of— an increasingly successful, large, and influential Catholic presence in the United States, the wall between Church and State actually became higher. This was the result of the growing influence of an increasingly secular influence in both the American judiciary and among other cultural elite sectors of the society who were firm in their resolve to check "Catholic power" (Hamburger 2002). The political, economic, and cultural opposition to Catholicism was starting to change colors, from a generic Protestantism to secular humanism. Watershed decisions on such issues as the right to abortion and the normalization of homosexuality clearly indicated, at least in the eyes of Catholic orthodox thinkers, the direction of Supreme Court decisions, that is, further away from Christian and natural law thinking closer to the secular humanist ideal of an "autonomous individualism."

Regarding the second issue, in general, it is clear that the primary response of most nominal Catholics to the secularist interpretation of the separation of Church and State has been, variously, one of intimidation, acquiescence, and indifference. Such Catholics have accepted the idea and reality that the faith is operant only within private sphere institutions such as the family and parish and, worse (from the proreligious perspective), only within the realm of private thought. They have done so, in their minds, in order to avoid more overt forms of persecution or in order not to "offer offense" (Cuddihy 1978) and in order to gain societal acceptance and claim a piece of the so-called "American dream."

There are two Catholic exceptions to this acceptance of the privatization of religion, one from the radical Catholic left and one from orthodox Catholicism. The former was most manifest in the Father Daniel Berrigan wing that emerged in the wake of Vatican II which, as James

Hitchcock put it, "insisted on the primacy of religion over politics" (1973–74, 81). Before the Second Vatican Council, this position was most prominently taken by Dorothy Day and her Catholic Worker movement.

The Catholic Worker is a truly radical Catholic movement, espousing pacifism, that rejected politics and saw the solution to society's ills to be primarily spiritual in nature. Still in existence today in an admittedly weakened condition, it was founded in 1933 by two especially charismatic individuals, Dorothy Day, a left-wing journalist and convert to Catholicism and Peter Maurin, a French Catholic agrarian and populist thinker. The movement, which publishes a newspaper, *The Catholic Worker*, centers around the building of various "houses of hospitality" throughout America (once numbering over forty) where the homeless and disenfranchised could find food, sleeping quarters, conviviality, and other forms of material and spiritual support. Historian Jay Dolan summarizes very nicely the heart of the Catholic Worker movement which "put no hope in the modern state, it put faith in the community of the sacred; the spiritual was more central to life than the material; peace was better than war; love in action was superior to love in dreams; the ideal of Christian perfection far surpassed the minimalism of the natural law tradition; personalism outranked pragmatism; and in the end, the primacy of love would redeem history" (1985, 411).

On the other hand and, in their minds, vindicated by Vatican II, orthodox Catholics—including some from the most recent generation—believe that it is their Catholic duty to evangelize within a broad conception of Church-State separation and within the rules of the democratic political process. Scholar Peter J. Donaldson (1988) has also observed, among some slivers of the American Catholic population, a radicalization of orthodox Catholicism as a counterresponse to an American civilization descending deeper into what John Paul II has referred to as a "culture of death."

It should be made clear, however, that the radicalization occurring at both ends of the American Catholic spectrum do not represent, at least at the time of this writing, major social developments within the Catholic Church of the United States. What Mary Hanna argued in her treatise, *Catholics and American Politics* in 1979, and others have since confirmed, is still the operant reality: the chilling effect that even a generalized understanding of Church-State separation has had on the voting activities, public statements, and civic activities of politicians, professionals, and ordinary citizens who have been raised (nominally) in the Catholic faith.

There are some signs at the edges, so to speak, about the possible extension of a radicalized orthodox Catholicism within American society. For one thing, during the most recent 2004 presidential election campaign season, some of the younger restorationist, post–Cardinal Bernardin Bishops admonished pro-choice Catholic politicians and, in some cases, denied them the right to receive Communion for their social policy advocacy of the right to abortion (Varacalli 2004). Only time will tell if this radicalization of the Catholic faith in the United States will continue to grow. The recent election of Benedict XVI to the papacy might be one indication that it will.

The Catholic Attempt to Restore Scholarship in Christ: From the Progressive Era to Vatican II

In an important book, *The Church Confronts Modernity: Catholic Intellectuals and the Progressive Era* (2004), Thomas E. Woods Jr. makes a strong case that Catholic intellectuals during the Progressive Era (i.e., roughly from the years leading into the twentieth century until the outbreak of World War I) were able to mount an impressive intellectual critique of the dominant academic ethos. That dominate academic ethos was a secular and secularizing one shaped by such figures as John Dewey, William James, and leading liberal Protestant social gospel thinkers who undermined traditional religious authority, the classical curriculum, and all recourse to absolutist first principles and natural law analysis. Conversely, the progressivist academic revolution promoted a narrowly scientific outlook, subjectivist philosophies such as Kantianism and pragmatism, the development of a nonreligious, society-wide "civil religion" or "American Way of Life," specialized professional learning, and relativism in the form of a progressive education based supposedly on pure experience and induction which was, also, allegedly "value-free" (Carlin 2003). Put much more simply, the attempt was made to replace a traditional Christian worldview with one more humanistic and scientific.

The Catholic intellectual critique of this secular intellectual and cultural movement, for Woods, was characterized not only by theological commitment to the Catholic Christian worldview but also by philosophical sophistication. The position was put forth that faith and reason are complimentary. Additionally, it was stressed that the Catholic should embrace a selective and well-thought openness to whatever was useful in secular and progressive educational approaches without surrendering to them. Woods argues that the educational approach developed by the Catholic University of America faculty member Father Thomas Edward Shields, quintessentially represented the Catholic reaction to progressivist innovations. Furthermore, Woods makes the case that the substantial critique of Shields and his colleagues laid the seeds for a period of outstanding Catholic accomplishments from the 1920s until the convening of the Second Vatican Council. Woods thus places himself in opposition to the secularist charge that the very idea of "Catholic scholarship" represents a contradiction in terms and the post–Vatican II Catholic progressive claim that all pre–Vatican II scholarship represented little more than an intellectual wasteland.

The Catholic response to secular developments in the general American intellectual climate and educational system of the time was the construction of a Catholic educational network from the elementary to the graduate school level that mirrored secular developments in bureaucratization and professionalization but provided a distinctive and decisive twist through the effort to ground all study through the unifying force of neo-Thomism and neoscholasticism with its God-centered teleological focus. Simply put, the Catholic intellectual attempt, in the felicitous phrase of Pope Pius X, was "to restore all things in Christ" (Salvaterra 1988).

Associated with the development of an alternate Catholic educational fortress was the creation of distinctive Catholic social science perspectives and the establishment of separate Catholic scholarly organizations founded on two specific premises: (1) that Catholics bring distinctive philosophical/theological presuppositions and metaphysical starting points into their intellectual approaches and (2) that Catholics should appropriate anything of worth in secular intellectual approaches for the benefit of the faith. As Jeffrey M. Burns has noted, American Catholic social science initially developed around the turn of the century through the pioneering efforts of the sociologist William Kerby, the economist John A. Ryan, the psychologist Thomas Verner Moore, and the anthropologist John M. Cooper (1988, 10). David Salvaterra also makes the case that mention should be made of the vital role played by historian Peter Guilday in attempting to counter secular misconceptions and faulty interpretations concerning the history of the Church (1988, 237). Salvaterra reports that the American Catholic Historical Association was founded in 1919, the Catholic Anthropological Conference and the American Catholic Philosophical Association in 1926, the Catholic Biblical Association of America in 1936, the American Catholic Sociological Society in 1938, the Canon Law Society of America in 1939, the Catholic Economic Association in 1941, the Catholic Theological Society in 1946, the American Catholic Psychological Association in 1947, and the Albertus Magnus Guild, an organization of Catholics in science in 1953 (1988, 79–80).

The Catholic attempt "to restore scholarship in Christ" was reversed sharply, however, in the wake of the Second Vatican Council as the forces promoting secularization in scholarship within the Catholic institution proved greater that those attempting to integrate education under a sacred canopy of Catholic principles (Varacalli 1991). Most of the various Catholic professional associations fell victim either to a "secularization from without," that is, dissolved as specifically "Catholic" organizations or a "secularization from within," that is, internally transformed into shells of their once authentically Catholic selves while still formally keeping the Catholic label. These secularizing developments, according to the winning Catholic progressivist interpretation of the Second Vatican Council, were legitimated by the requirements of ecumenism, academic freedom, critical thinking, and individual conscience. These latter requirements, the progressive Catholic establishment argued, were used to make the case that distinctive Catholic academic perspectives and separate (but, not again, isolated) Catholic scholarly associations were provincial at best or contradictory at worst. Catholic conservatives and traditionalists, on the other hand, unsuccessfully opposed this secularization arguing that, in reality, Vatican II actually affirmed the need for Catholics to engage in public dialogue about what their religious worldview had to offer both to the world and to the various intellectual disciplines. This debate over the issue of whether or not there is a distinctive Catholic contribution to scholarship was only one of many acrimonious debates brought about by divergent interpretations of the significance of the council. Politically, the liberals won the battles during the period of the 1960s through to the 1980s. There are signs, however, that the conservatives and traditionalists—inspired by the pontificate of John Paul II (1978–2005) and now with another restorationist pope, Benedict XVI—are once again trying "restore all things in Christ," the academic life most definitely included. In 1976, for instance, an important new group appeared on the Catholic horizon in America, the Fellowship of Catholic Scholars and, in 1992, a spin-off association, the Society of Catholic Social Scientists.

The Presidential Election of John F. Kennedy

Easily, the figure in modern American Catholic history that symbolizes worldly political success is the one and only American Catholic president, John F. Kennedy, elected in 1960. It is hard to overstate the sense of euphoria that Kennedy's candidacy aroused among many upwardly socially mobile Catholics of the era. Given the historic and rampant anti-Catholicism deeply embedded in American culture and history, it is easy to understand the emotion aroused when Kennedy finally spiked the ball into the presidential end zone.

However, a debate continues over what is most historically and symbolically important about the presidential election. Was it Kennedy's victory in an inhospitable climate? Liberal writers George Gallup Jr. and Jim Castelli concur. As they assert, "the election of John Fitzgerald Kennedy as the first Catholic President in 1960 was a turning point in American history: with that election, American Catholics came of age politically" (1987, 1).

Or, conversely, was Kennedy's achievement at the direct expense of the Catholic faith as other Catholic thinkers assert? For the latter, Kennedy's ultimate significance was to suggest to all-aspiring Catholic politicians (or, for that matter, to any Catholic "on the make") that no office or position, however, was beyond reach, assuming that one's Catholic heritage would be inoperative in any important aspect of public life. Kennedy made this perfectly clear, his critics assert, to non-Catholic America in his speech to the Houston Ministerial Alliance during the 1960 national election. According to Zoller, Kennedy informed the Protestant preachers of Houston and the surrounding area that "he was not the Catholic presidential candidate . . . but the candidate of the Democratic Party" (1999, 174). He also stated in his speech that "I do not accept the right of any ecclesiastical official to tell me what to do in the sphere of my public responsibility as a elected official" (quoted in Dolan 1985, 421). What President Kennedy did *not* address was the issue of whether or not a public official has a duty to follow his conscience, even if it is shaped (to some significant degree) by some combination of Catholic and natural law worldviews. If the former president was not captive to the latter "socialization," just what set of ideas *did* propel him into service for his country? And would secular or non-Catholic ideas necessarily have been more universal, legitimate, and compelling?

Kennedy's political pragmatism, it is argued by his conservative Catholic critics, has quickly led Catholic politicians down the slippery slope to the more systematized defense of the privatization of the Catholic faith espoused in the 1980s and 1990s and exemplified by former New York governor Mario M. Cuomo (Varacalli 2001). Orthodox Catholic critics pose to the contemporary heirs of the Kennedy/Cuomo mind-set the rhetorical question asked in the Bible, "What does it profit a man to gain the whole world but lose his soul?" (Matthew 16:26).

Suggested Readings

Bellah, Robert N., et al. *Habits of the Heart: Individualism and Commitment in American Life*. Berkeley: University of California Press, 1985.

Cross, Robert. *The Emergence of Liberal Catholicism in America*. Chicago: Quadrangle Books, 1958.

Greeley, Father Andrew M. *The Catholic Experience: An Interpretation of the History of American Catholicism*. Garden City, NY: Doubleday, 1967.

Hamburger, Philip. *Separation of Church and State*. Cambridge, MA: Harvard University Press, 2002.

Hanna, Mary. *Catholics and American Politics*. Cambridge, MA: Harvard University Press, 1979.

Hunter, James Davidson. *Culture Wars: The Struggle to Define America*. New York: Basic Books, 1991.

Kelly, Monsignor George A. *Keeping the Church Catholic with John Paul II*. New York: Doubleday, 1990.

"Plenary Councils of Baltimore." *Catholic Encyclopedia* (1912 version), www.newadvent.org/cathen/02235a.htm.

"Provincial Councils of Baltimore." *Catholic Encyclopedia* (1912 version), www.newadvent.org/cathen/02235a.htm.

Varacalli, Joseph A. "The Constitutive Elements of the Idea of an 'American' Catholic Church." *Social Justice Review* 80, nos. 5–6 (May/June 1989).

————. "The Cultural and Political Impotence of Catholics in Contemporary American Life." *The Catholic Social Science Review* 9 (2004).

Warner, Michael. *Changing Witness: Catholic Bishops and Public Policy, 1917–1994*. Washington, DC: Ethics and Public Policy Center, 1995.

Woods, Thomas E., Jr. *The Church Confronts Modernity: Catholic Intellectuals and the Progressive Era*. New York: Columbia University Press, 2004.

Chapter 21

Contemporary Issues after Vatican II

Vatican II: The Battle over Its Significance

Most Catholic commentators would agree that the documents of the Second Vatican Council (1962–65) were about the Church engaging the modern world—a social context characterized by, among other things, the pervasive influence of science, high technology, bureaucracy, systematic and rational approaches to solving human problems, mass forms of communication and education, and centralized political authority—and the values that derive from such forms of social organization (e.g., this-worldliness, empiricism, materialism). The disagreements start and end with the issue of the *nature* and *purpose* of the engagement.

To begin with, some traditional Catholics have made the claim that there was no need to call a worldwide council in the first place; the Church, they claimed, was respected, vital, influential, and fundamentally sound in its worldview and administration. If anything, the secular world—given its self-destructive tendencies and internal contradictions, according to this logic—would come around eventually to the Church's way of thinking and doing if only the Church would "stay the course," and remain strong and committed to her basically changeless traditions.

Others argued that modernity was such a powerful novelty containing certain new truths about the relationship of man to both society and God that it was incumbent upon the Church to reach out in a spirit of "aggiornamento" (or seeking out agreement and compromise) and selectively incorporate certain features of the contemporary age without, however, abandoning the essential worldview and logic of the Catholic religion. Such Catholics would claim legitimacy for their approach in John Henry Cardinal Newman's understanding of the necessity of an organic development of doctrine (1989).

Still others, more fully accepting of the promises and moral imperatives of modern secular life, saw in the calling of the council an opportunity to alter fundamentally and radically the tenets of the faith. Such Catholics, consciously or not, accepted a basic unilinear evolutionary schema that basically translates into the claim that "the past is inferior, the present is better, and within the future lies the possibility of perfection."

As with any document or set of documents, the written word is subject to selective interpretations, either consciously or unconsciously performed, based on a personal philosophy embraced or a vested set of interests to be protected. What, however, were the issues addressed in the documents of Vatican II that were subject to such diverse appropriations and critical disagreement?

One key issue was that of *authority in the Church*. Was the Catholic Church going to continue to be a "top-down" organization led by the pope and bishops and legitimated by the concept of "apostolic succession"? Or was the Church going to accept a completely contrary position, a "congregational" style of leadership typical of the more radical wing of the Protestant Reformation (the Anabaptist alternative, which vests authority "bottom up" in the congregation/laity)? Or, much more likely in the immediate post–Vatican II era, was the Catholic Church going to evolve into some hybrid or "connectional" form between these two opposing end-poles, somehow trying to incorporate both a "top-down" and "bottom-up" approach that combines both central roles for episcopal leadership and some form of representational democracy, involving the lower echelon clergy (priests), religious (sisters and brothers), and the laity?

These issues of centralization and decentralization are key here. What should be the authoritative relationship between the pope and a bishop or between Rome and a local regional (e.g., Latin America, Africa) or national (e.g., the United States, the Netherlands) branch of the Church Universal? Between a religious order/organization (e.g., Jesuits, Franciscans, Dominicans, Legionaries of Christ, Opus Dei, etc.) and the pope/Church magisterium? Between a bishop and the local diocesan clergy, religious, and laity? Between the priest and the local parishioner?

Another issue brought to the fore, intentionally or not, by the Second Vatican Council was that of *the uniqueness and privileged position of Catholicism in a pluralistic world*. Was the Catholic Church going to continue its defense of the claim that (1) the figure and message of Jesus Christ was at the center of all creation and human history and (2) the Catholic Church was the one and only Church of Jesus Christ? Or, was the Church moving to accept some revolutionary change in her self-understanding by embracing an out-and-out religious and cultural pluralism? Or, more likely, was the Church going to attempt to maintain its claim to uniqueness and privilege while yet acknowledging that some substantial component of truth, beauty, holiness, and utility exists outside of the Catholic religion?

The *locus of salvation* was a concern of importance that was debated in light of the council. Was the Catholic Church going to continue to accept the claim that the purpose of life was to reach some otherworldly heaven or, as Saint Augustine puts it in his *Confessions* (1998), that the intended destiny of each individual soul was for it to rest with the Lord in next life? Or, was the Catholic Church going to change its stance to those—such as the Protestant social gospelers at the turn into the twentieth century and Catholic socialists and communalists—who believed that the purpose of existence was to create "heaven here on earth," that is, to institutionalize a quite this-worldly reign of social justice as the reason d'être of the Catholic faith?

Yet another key consideration hotly disputed in light of the council documents was the respective role of *objective moral reality versus the exercise of conscience in religious decision making*. Was the Catholic Church going to maintain its historic position that the ultimate standard of what is or is not Catholic is set by some objective set of ideas, that is, by sacred Scripture, sacred tradition, and the natural law tradition, all interpreted by the magisterium? Or, was the religion going to adjust itself to the contemporary world, promoting subjectivist philosophies (Varacalli 1997) of one sort or another by agreeing to the principle that the ultimate decision as to what is religious or moral resides with the individual, this amounting to a defense of the secularized version of the "Protestant principle," that is, the modern idea of an "autonomous individualism" or, in David Carlin's translation, "private judgement." For David R. Carlin: "now this American ideal of private judgement is completely incompatible with a key principle of Catholicism, which holds that the Catholic Church is God's great repository of religious truth on earth, and that the popes and bishops and then authorized agents are the ordinary teachers of that divinely revealed truth" (2003, 18).

The Bicentennial Program (1973–83) and Movement (1973+)

At least among the majority of bishops and other elite sectors of the Catholic community in the United States, the liberal or progressive interpretation of the significance of Vatican II had won the day in the immediate years after the council (Varacalli 1983). It did not take long for the progressives to use the Church's official and nonofficial machinery to move to implement their vision for Church and society. It is a vision that more conservative Catholic thinkers consider to be secularizing and this-worldly, either subtly or overtly.

In 1973, an elaborate three-stage ten-year American Catholic Bicentennial Program focusing on the theme of "Liberty and Justice for All" was initiated by the Church's national level bureaucracy, then titled the National Catholic Conference of Catholic Bishops/United States Catholic Conference. More specifically, the idea for a nationwide consultation on the idea of implementing a social justice agenda came out of the bosom of the conference's advisory council, which had been created only as recently as 1970, another of the "collegial" innovations implemented in light of the spirit of the council.

The Bicentennial Program quite consciously sought legitimacy in at least four important post–Vatican II documents seen as elaborations and developments of Vatican II. One was Pope Paul VI's Apostolic Letter, *A Call to Action*, which concerned itself with the requirement to translate Catholic theological principle into Catholic activity devoted to questions of social justice. Second, the program found great inspiration in the synod of bishops 1971 document, *Justice in the World*, which pronounced that "action on behalf of justice fully appears to us as a constitutive dimension of the preaching of the Gospel, or in other words, of the Church's mission for the redemption of the human race and its liberation from every oppressive situation." It was also spurred on by Paul VI's 1967 encyclical, *Populorum Progressio* ("On the Development of Peoples"), which demanded that justice be institutionalized in the relationship between First and Third World nations. Finally, that Catholics in the United States have a theological imperative to actualize such a vision was made clear by one of the Bicentennial Program's most powerful supporters, the then archbishop of Newark, Peter Gerety in his 1973 pastoral letter, *The Day of Peace Restored*. As Archbishop Gerety stated: "We must . . . admit that we have not listened very carefully to Pope John XXIII's teaching or the teaching after him of the Second Vatican Council, of Pope Paul VI and of the Synod of Bishops on matters of justice and peace. Inescapably, they require American Catholics to consider what it means to be the Church in our society."

The Bicentennial Program consisted basically of three, more or less, distinctive stages. The first, supposedly "grass-roots" stage included over 830,000 individual responses from approximately half the nation's dioceses that solicited which issues on the part of Catholic parishioners were perceived to be vital to the contemporary Church. It also entailed the holding of numerous parish and diocesan meetings and seven regional "justice hearings" in which over 500 Catholic clerical and lay leaders presented testimony. Finally, and using as a base the individual responses, the justice hearing testimony, and various Church documents, eight writing committees prepared working papers and proposals along eight separate themes within the overall theme of "liberty and justice for all:" Church, ethnicity and race, neighborhood, family, personhood, work, nationkind, and humankind.

The second stage of the program consisted of the national Catholic assembly held in Detroit in October 1976, the Call to Action Conference. The conference was composed overwhelmingly of liberal Catholic intellectuals, bureaucrats, and activists of one stripe or another with over two-thirds of the voting delegates employed in official Church organizations and over 90 percent claiming heavy involvement in numerous Church groups. The conference debated, voted, amended, and eventually passed an enormously large list of recommendations—a total of 182—along each of the eight subthemes that were to be considered by the National Conference of Catholic Bishops at the subsequent May meetings from 1977 to 1981.

The third period of the overall "Liberty and Justice for All" program (1977–83) was designated by the Bicentennial Committee as a time of "follow-up," to study, discuss, and implement appropriate (from the viewpoint of the bishops) Call to Action recommendations. At their May 1977 meeting, the bishops responded initially to the Call to Action proposals by (1) issuing a pastoral statement addressing some of the more controversial Detroit recommendations and (2) assigning each recommendation to a bishops' committee within the National Conference of Catholic Bishops/United States Catholic Conference. It was then the task of each respective bishops' committee to evaluate each of its assigned resolutions a directive to either study, act immediately, support existing activities, or "respond in light of the universal law of the Church." The pastoral reply also created a bishop's Ad Hoc Committee on the Call to Action within the episcopal conference under the chairmanship of a liberal prelate, Archbishop John Roach. The task of the committee would be to serve as a strong monitoring committee, complete with funds and staff, and which was authorized to receive regular progress reports on the implementation of acceptable proposals.

The 1978 May meeting of the bishops produced the *Call to Action Plan*, later entitled *To Do the Work of Justice*. The plan proposed a six-prong approach on the theme of "Liberty and Justice for All," through its sections on human rights; economic justice; the Church as people, parish, and community; family life; education for justice; and world hunger. Unsatisfied merely to mandate, the plan called for a review of national accomplishments and pitfalls in 1983. The year 1978 also saw the creation of a permanent secretariat within the national level bureaucracy, that of the Secretariat for the Laity, which would be of special assistance to the Call to Action bishops' committee.

In March 1979, the Ad Hoc Committee on the Call to Action, in conjunction with both the Secretariat for the Laity and the staff of the United States Catholic Conference, held a "mini–Call to Action" follow-up conference in Washington, D.C. At this three-day conference over 300 bicentennial diocesan coordinators reported to each other the progress, or lack thereof, in the implementation at the local parish level of the Call to Action proposals. The information was then gathered by the staff of the United States Catholic Conference and disseminated to the various dioceses throughout the country.

In November 1979, the Ad Hoc Committee on the Call to Action Plan indicated that it formally would survey and report on the follow-up activity in 106 dioceses in the nation to the directives in *To Do the Work of Justice*. Based on these results, the committee, now chaired by another liberal prelate, Bishop Joseph Francis, produced the report, *The Diocesan Implementation of "To Do the Work of Justice: A Plan of Action for the Catholic Community in the United States."*

The key question in all of this was whether the Bicentennial Program was a success or a failure from the perspective of the liberal or progressive wing of the Catholic Church that rose to power in the post–Vatican II years. The author of this text has previously answered a definitive "yes" to the question arguing, in his *Toward the Establishment of Liberal Catholicism in America* (1983), that the Bicentennial Program and process strengthened and created a liberal political and social movement that dominated the Catholic Church in the United States through the 1980s and still represented a powerful faction today. The agenda of this liberal Catholic movement included both sociopolitical and economic issues and the attempt to liberate the Church from what it viewed as an unnecessarily narrow and puritan-like stance on sexual morality. The orthodoxy of the movement has been strongly questioned by various traditional, conservative, and orthodox Catholic scholars (Zoller 1999; Kelly 1990, 1995; Hitchcock 1984).

The New Catholic Knowledge Class and Catholic Higher Education

The mission of the scholarly and educational apostolate of the Catholic Church in the United States from the progressive era through to the opening of the Second Vatican Council was, as previously discussed, "to restore all intellectual activity in Christ" (Salvaterra 1988). Such an attempt both utilized and critiqued secular and non-Catholic thought from within a Catholic vision and framework of fundamental Catholic beliefs and sensibilities. Among others, as Thomas Woods (2004) has argued, this attempt was both impressive and sophisticated, if unappreciated and rejected, by the mainstream liberal Protestant and secular educational establishment that dominated the larger American civilization.

The Catholic desire to develop alternative Catholic intellectual models, academic organizations, and distinctively Catholic colleges and universities started to wane a bit during the post–World War II era and, eventually, in the post–Vatican II era, almost disappeared completely (Varacalli 1991, 1997–98). Catholics were leaving their ethnic urban enclaves and moving into the suburbs integrating themselves with non-Catholic neighbors. They were also simultaneously moving up the American socioeconomic ladder. Concomitant with such developments was, at least for many Catholics, a transfer in one's basic frame of evaluative reference, from a Catholic frame of reference to one extolling the standards of American elite society and the secular academy. In short, many Catholic academics assimilated into a non-Catholic academic ethos. American Catholic colleges started more consciously to ape themselves after the American model of higher education (itself based on the ideal of the highly specialized German research university) characterized by significantly compartmentalized, nonhierarchically ordered, and empirically based sources of knowledge. In 1955, the Catholic historian, Monsignor John Tracy Ellis, would pen a lament titled "American Catholics and the Intellectual Life" in which he judged Catholic intellectual life in the United States to be inferior vis-à-vis the larger non-Catholic scholarly community. Monsignor Ellis' analysis spoke for many upwardly socially mobile Catholic academics at the time who wanted to share in the social status of the reigning elite educational establishment.

Another landmark event in the surrendering of the attempt to develop a distinctly Catholic intellectual worldview was the widely successful revolt led by progressive Jesuit educators and by the University of Notre Dame president, Father Theodore Hesburg in their 1967 Land O'Lakes declaration calling for "institutional autonomy" and "academic freedom" for Catholic colleges and universities (Kelly 1995; Varacalli 1997–98). The call was justified in the minds of its progressive proponents by the claim that the Second Vatican Council had fundamentally repudiated the Church's once critical attitude to the outside non-Catholic world. Ecumenically-oriented and secular scholarship was now to be enthusiastically embraced. It was a revolt that, objectively speaking, not only distanced Catholic higher education from magisterial inspiration and influence but also entangled it much further into governmental laws, foundation requirements, and bureaucratic regulations indifferent at best to hostile at worst to the Catholic religion. This newly self-imposed dependency of Catholic higher education on these non-Catholic external sources of authority was, in turn, an important cause in opening up the secular floodgates in terms of personnel, faculty, and ideas much of which turned out to be indifferent at best to hostile at worst to the faith and that, practically and quickly, "de-Catholicized" many colleges and universities. Given the progressive Catholic position that much of the prior 2,000-year-tradition—scholarly tradition included—of the Church was obsolete, such a movement was viewed by reigning Catholic educational elites as necessary, a form of liberation, and an upgrade in intellectual quality.

Ave Maria University School of Law, backed by the philanthropic efforts of Catholic businessman Thomas Monaghan, is considered a large part of the Catholic restorationist movement in Catholic higher education. The goal of the law school is to produce lawyers who are trained to the highest standards of the legal profession and are also inspired by the Catholic intellectual, moral, and religious tradition.
Copyright Bill Shurtliff, 1999.

Part and parcel of the de-Catholicization of Catholic higher education has been the rise of what can be called the "new Catholic knowledge class" composed of progressivist intellectuals, bureaucrats, and social activists who derive their authority from secular credentials and whose material interests are not aligned with that of the Catholic Church. This class is in fundamental conflict with magisterial authority, a class that includes many Catholic college presidents and administrators intent on accepting no interference from traditional religious authority in the attempt to gain acceptance, and various sorts of rewards, from America's cultural elite. The ascendency of the new Catholic knowledge class represented a startling victory for the Americanist wing of the Catholic Church in America and, again, constituted a radical reversal in the operant frame of reference for Catholic scholarly activity, from one essentially Catholic to one secular.

The rise of the "new Catholic knowledge class" cannot be understood apart from changes in both the leadership of the Catholic Church and in the "collective conscience" (Durkheim 1965) of American society. Regarding the first, there was the rise to ecclesiastical power in the post–Vatican II Church of a strategic ally of the new Catholic knowledge class, that is, of the progressive cardinals' (Dearden–Bernardin) wing, which reached its height of influence in the mid-1980s. Regarding the latter, mention should be made of broad changes in American culture such as the emergence and acceptance of such ideas as "autonomous individualism," moral and religious relativism, and a basic materialism that have been disproportionately embraced by most progressive American Catholic elites. Regarding the transformation of individualism that took place in American society at the time, one can argue that the secularization of the "Protestant principle" has been inextricably intertwined with the contemporary new Catholic knowledge class calls for a complete autonomy from Rome (but, importantly, not from the American State) and for the broadest possible definition of academic freedom that appears to have no limits (except, perhaps, outside of the always currently popular as defined by a progressive establishment).

The history of Rome's reaction to these developments, that is, to keep its universities and colleges Catholic (and, increasingly, to recapture them) started in 1968 (a little after the Land O'Lakes declaration). However, Pope John Paul II made a major attempt in 1990 to restore authentic Catholic education in both the United States and throughout the Catholic world through the publication of an Apostolic Constitution on Catholic Colleges and Universities titled *Ex corde Ecclesiae* ("Out of the Heart of the Church"). The title of the Apostolic Constitution makes clear that the university, and especially the Catholic university, has "come out of the heart of the Church" and is therefore tied, in certain constitutive ways, to the mission of the Catholic Church. Each national or regional conference of Catholic bishops was expected to create a suitable set of norms or "ordinances" to move, once again, in the direction of "restoring scholarship in Christ." In the United States, however, a powerful combination of progressive Catholic bishops, Catholic educational administrators, and other components of the new Catholic knowledge class have, to date, successfully frustrated the attempt to implement the Catholic vision of the recently deceased John Paul II for Catholic higher education among the overwhelming percentage of what are now nominally Catholic institutions of Catholic higher education. Orthodox and traditional Catholic orders, communities, and individuals, in response, are in the process of trying to recapture a few smaller Catholic colleges (e.g., Franciscan University, University Dallas, Benedictine College) or build new (mostly small, liberal arts or "great books"–oriented) ones (e.g., Christendom College, Ave Maria College, Thomas More College, Thomas Aquinas, Magdalene College). An exception to this pattern of working with small institutions is the present attempt of Catholic multimillionaire businessman, Thomas Monaghan, who is funding the construction of a traditional Catholic university, Ave Maria University, in Naples, Forida, due to be completed by the year 2006. Another exception is the slow but discernible movement back toward Catholic orthodoxy on the part of the "Bishops' university," that is, Catholic University of America, in which the leading American prelates are members of the university's Board of Trustees. This movement is parallel with that of the general replacement of the progressive cardinals Dearden–Bernardin bishops' wing with more orthodox and conservative prelates appointed during the latter part of John Paul II's pontificate.

The Theology of Liberation: The American Context

The theology of liberation is a left-wing theological and theoretical perspective that attempts to integrate Marxist and other "conflict" perspectives (along feminist, ethnic, racial, sexual liberationist lines) with Catholic/Christian belief. It was popular in the 1960s and for the next few decades due to the combination of social protest/justice movements of the era and the ascendancy of progressive this-worldly theologies among Protestant and Catholic elites. Indeed, the theology of liberation was a quite an ecumenical endeavor among liberal religionists of the era, uniting them, for instance, in common cause in the American Civil Rights movement (headed by Martin Luther King Jr.) and the anti–Vietnam War movement, and other key issues that were debated in American society at the time.

Historically, the theology of liberation is somewhat similar to the earlier religious expression among progressive American Protestant thinkers, the "Social Gospel" movement at the turn into the twentieth century. The optimistic, this-worldly nature of the Social Gospel movement fit nicely into the belief held at the time by many of America's religious elites that it was, indeed, possible to create something close to "God's kingdom her on earth." The Social Gospel movement became severely attenuated in light of the incredible human and physical destruction ushered forth by World War I—a war utilizing science and technology to destroy, not enhance human life and civilization. The effect of World War I was to create an atmosphere more conducive to traditional Christianity with its greater sense of evil and sin in the affairs of humankind.

Originally developed in Germany, the theology of liberation was intellectually transported to Latin America in the immediate post–Vatican II era by upper-middle progressive thinkers and activists. They argued that the gross disparities in wealth, power, and status that characterized the southern hemisphere not only justified intellectually such a perspective but constituted a moral imperative for action given its emphasis on a this-worldly liberation, along socialist lines, from material poverty and physical oppression of all sorts. While most scholars concur with the contention of the now Father Richard J. Neuhaus that the specific synthesis of Gustavo Gutierrez in his *The Theology of Liberation* (1973), is "simply the classic text of the theology of liberation movement" (1987, 178), there were a number of variations created during the 1970s and 1980s given a plurality of the numerous social change and protest movements that took place then in conjunction with the Church's increased emphasis on the "social question" characteristic of the post–Vatican II period.

As discussed elsewhere in this volume, the incarnational, sacramental, and integrationist nature of the Church has implications for Catholic scholarship in that the Church's predisposition is to try to baptize, by transforming in contrast to capitulating to, non-Catholic perspectives and methods. During this era, official Roman authorities, especially Joseph Cardinal Ratzinger of the Congregation for the Doctrine of the Faith (now Pope Benedict XVI), spent much time spelling out the criteria for a successful cooptation of various non-Catholic worldviews into a Catholic vision. Key Roman documents like the "Instruction on Certain Aspects of the 'Theology of Liberation'" (1984), "Instruction on Christian Freedom and Liberation" (1986) and "Guidelines for the Study and Teaching of the Church's Social Doctrine in the Formation of Priests" (1989) provided the proper methodology for judging whether or not various syntheses were successful or not from the position of an official Catholicism. There is one key question, among others, that must be addressed in judging the adequacy of a synthesis of Catholicism with any non-Catholic cultural formation from the viewpoint of an official Catholicism: What is primarily transformative in the exchange, the Catholic vision or the non-Catholic one? In other words, the key issue is what is co-opting what? The majority of what passed for theologies of liberation during the 1970s through the 1980s were judged, from the framework of the guardians of Catholic orthodoxy, to have allowed incorrectly incompatible philosophies, social explanations of reality, and anthropological assumptions about mankind to have excessively and decidedly shaped their essential character.

During much of the early post–Vatican II period of Church history, theologies of liberation were nonetheless considered something of an intellectual rage and a method by which an allegedly outdated religious tradition and structure could update itself and make itself relevant to the needs of the contemporary modern situation, at least in the eyes of the Catholic intellectual avant-garde. It should not be surprising, as such, that various incarnations of this worldview were accepted by American Catholic progressives, especially by what Father Andrew Greeley (1975) referred to as the "new Catholic social action" that emerged during the bishops' Bicentennial Program and Call to Action Conference (1976) and that dominated the national Catholic American scene at least until the early 1990s. At the time, Father Greeley was a defender of what he calls the "old social action," relatively speaking, a more moderate, pragmatic, results-oriented form of Catholic "Americanism" (Varacalli 1983). For Father Greeley, the new Catholic social activism, with its embrace of the theology of liberation, was needlessly ideological, utopian, extreme, and anti-American, and derived its positions not essentially from Catholic social thought and other Catholic sources but from what he derisively referred to as the currently fashionable "radical chic."

The theology of liberation represented an historically important but time-specific manifestation in the religious, Christian, and Catholic history of the United States. Theological formulations like the Social Gospel movement and the theology of liberation can be expected to appear from time to time in American history depending upon the appearance of a constellation of historical and cultural/religious forces that are capable of granting it widescale societal plausibility. Recent more conservative directions in American society are not propitious regarding the immediate reappearance of the theology of liberation as a significant social phenomenon.

Ecumenism

Ecumenism is the theory and practice emphasizing the search for a commonality of vision, purpose, and action between and among differing religions and nonreligious groupings. Ecumenical thinking and activity has been especially pronounced in the Catholic community of the United States in the immediate post–Vatican period, spurred on by both developments in Catholic theology (e.g., Vatican II and post–Vatican II theology) and American culture (e.g., pluralism, democracy, individualism). The key issue, however, is whether or not ecumenism has been implemented within the Church within an orthodox understanding of the faith or if it has been allowed to evolve into religious heterodoxy through the promoting of an out and out religious and moral relativism, itself a reflection of the larger secular civilization.

There is a structured acceptance of what might be called a "minimalist ecumenism" within the Catholic worldview. This is so given the Catholic acceptance, as part of its doctrinal foundation, of the concept and reality of the natural law representative of the constitutive nature of what it means to be human. The truth that the Catholic religion claims it offers to the world certainly does not solely depend on the promulgation of the natural law given that the Church also relies on sacred Scripture and an ever developing sacred Tradition in its understanding of reality. The natural law, however, represents the single greatest tool for ecumenical relations that the Catholic religion possesses in its own arsenal of intellectual weapons. The Catholic philosopher, Ralph McInerny puts it very well in his *A First Glance at St. Thomas Aquinas* (1990). For McInerny, given that "the main principles that should guide human conduct are naturally knowable by men . . . the theory . . . [of natural law] . . . can be seen as the basis of exchange between believer and non-believer on moral matters. There is a common base they share" (1990, 33).

Prior to the Second Vatican Council, the ecumenical impulse on the part of the Church was both limited and constrained, for the most part, to what the Church thought were elements in other non-Catholic ideational systems that, nomenclature aside, were merely repeating eternal Catholic truths. The position taken by Pope Pius XI in *Quadragesimo Anno* (1931), in speaking to "certain Catholic quarters" who hoped that the Church and a "moderated and attenuated form of Socialism" might find some "middle ground," is here instructive.

> But such hopes are in vain. Those who wish to be apostles among the socialist should preach the Christian truth whole and entire, openly and sincerely, without any connivance with error. If they wish in truth to be heralds of the Gospel, let their endeavor be to convince Socialists that their demands, in so far as they are just, are defended much more cogently by the principles [of] Christian faith, and are promoted much more efficaciously by the power of Christian charity.

And a little later on in the 1931 encyclical, the pope continues:

> If, like all errors, Socialism contains a certain element of truth (and this the Sovereign Pontiffs have never denied), it is nevertheless founded upon a doctrine of human society peculiarly its own, which is opposed to true Christianity. "Religious socialism" and "Christian socialism" are expressions implying a contradiction in terms. No one can be at the same time a sincere Catholic and a true socialist.

The tone and perhaps even the substance of the Catholic theological approach to ecumenism was changed in light of the teachings of the Second Vatican Council. This change is manifest in the post–Vatican II Church's orientation to (1) other religions, (2) other nonreligious philosophies, and (3) atheism. Regarding the first, in the Vatican II statement, *Nostra Aetate* (1965), the following is propounded:

> The Church rejects nothing of what is true and holy in theses religions. She has a high regard for the manner of life and conduct, the precepts and doctrines which, although differing in many ways from her own teaching, nevertheless often reflects a ray of Truth which enlightens all men. . . . The Church, therefore, urges her sons to enter with prudence and charity into discussion and collaboration with members of other religions. Let Christians, while witnessing to their own faith and way of life, acknowledge, preserve, and encourage the spiritual and moral truths found among non-Christians, also their social life and culture.

In another key Vatican II document, *Gaudium et Spes* (1965), the strain and tension between Catholic and secular/non-Catholic worldviews is reduced as follows:

> Those also have a claim on our respect and charity who think and act differently from us in social, political, and religious matters. In fact, the more deeply we come to understand their ways of thinking through good will and love, the more easily will we be able to undertake dialogue with them.

And in the same document, ecumenism is extended also to the mind of the nonbeliever:

> [The Church] . . . tries . . . to seek out the secret motives which lead the atheistic mind to deny God. While knowing how important are the problems raised by atheism, and urged by here love for all men, she considers that these motives deserve an earnest and more thorough scrutiny.

Key questions emerge as to the nature and extent of the movement toward ecumenism in the immediate post–Vatican II period of the Church. Some schismatic traditionalists have concluded that the documents of the Second Vatican Council move close to an out-and-out religious and cultural relativism and therefore condemn them as inauthentic and not inspired by God. Extreme progressivists also acknowledge this claim but heartily endorse the direction of the movement arguing that all significant religious and cultural worldviews are essentially equal in their truth content, although perhaps shedding light on different truths or on the partial truths that make up a more comprehensive Truth. Typically, such liberal thinkers simultaneously endorse a selective and progressive interpretation of another Vatican II document, *Dignitatis Humanae* (1965), to the effect that the deliberations of human consciousness are supreme, even in those cases where they contravene established, that is, magisterially endorsed, Catholic theology and the perennial truths of the natural law. Between these two endpoints are a series of positions that range from those moderate traditionalists and conservatives who argue that the documents of Vatican II have changed merely the tone but *not* the substance of doctrine to those neotraditionalists and moderates acknowledging a pluralizing movement within the Church, but one stopping short of denying the Catholic faith a privileged status in understanding the will of God and his design for humankind. Obviously, these various options vis-à-vis the meaning of ecumenicity play themselves out in the context of the contemporary culture war taking place within both Church and society and will have, as such, consequences for the future of both.

Catholics and Politics in the Contemporary United States

The issue of the present-day political participation of Catholics in the United States is a significant one (Varacalli 2001, 2005). It is important to start our discussion by demonstrating just how political participation fits into the overall vision of an official understanding of the faith and, then, to lay out some basic Catholic principles for political involvement in what some have referred to as "the art of the possible."

For an official Catholicism, the ultimate destiny of each human being is not to acquire worldly "success," but to reach heaven. This is expressed beautifully in St. Augustine's prayer and acknowledgment to God in his *Confessions* (1998) that "our hearts are restless until they rest in Thee." For the Church, reaching eternal salvation requires the person accepting God's gratuitous gift of grace, primarily through active participation in the sacramental life and, relatedly, exercising many virtues including some demonstrated commitment to the social apostolate. The social apostolate includes both *individual* (i.e., good works and charity) and *structural* dimensions (i.e., the attempted institutionalization in society of social justice).

Regarding the latter, more systematic commitment, the 1971 statement *Justice in the World*, declared that "a concern for social justice . . . is a *constitutive* feature of the preaching of the Gospel" (italics added). "Constitutive," however, must not be confused with "definitive." From a Catholic perspective, an all-consuming this-worldly political involvement should not represent the be-all and end-all of human existence. To the contrary, the reconstruction of society along authentic Christian principles and lines at least compatible with Catholic social thought, while a *good in and by itself*, nonetheless is not the raison d'être of the Catholic faith. Rather it is a lesser good; it is both secondary to and derivative of the primary mission of assisting individuals in the quest for eternal, other-worldly salvation. In the final analysis, from a Catholic perspective, individuals are seen stumbling to the cross in a this-worldly "vale of tears." But as we stumble, the Catholic logic continues, we are also commissioned by Christ to do so in solidarity with, and concern for, all of His children and for all of His human creation, the political and civil order included. In short summary: Catholic involvement with governmental and political issues is intended to serve what are, for the Church, the ultimate and penultimate ends of human existence, that is, respectively, the salvation of souls and concern and activity for the realization of the common good.

The basic and generic Catholic principles for political involvement are taken from the Congregation for the Doctrine of the Faith's "Doctrinal Note on Some Questions Regarding the Participation of Catholics in Political Life" (2002). Analyzing the "Doctrinal Note," one can derive the following eight principles:

1. Given that morality cannot be separated from politics, it is a religious duty for Catholics to participate in the political process in the attempt to promote the common good. Such participation must be conducted ethically, can take many forms, is contingent upon sociohistorical contexts and circumstances, and is shaped by the particular responsibilities, specific competencies, and personal situations of individuals actualizing different social roles.
2. In a democracy, all citizens are free to base their political decisions on their own religious and philosophical traditions; such a position does not constitute a violation of the "separation of Church and State."
3. Authentic Catholic political participation is based on the premise that all moral choices made must be compatible with the Catholic faith and the natural law.
4. The Catholic Church endorses no specific political party or program and acknowledges a wide role for the Catholic citizen in applying prudential judgments as long as such judgments do not violate the fundamental dignity of the human person. And even on issues involving direct attacks on innocent human life, Catholics are still free to make prudential judgments as to what policy (e.g., an attempted Right to Life Amendment to the Constitution versus a "state's rights" approach to banning abortion state by state) that is most likely to protect human life at a particular sociohistorical moment and place.

5. It is not, religiously or morally, possible for any Catholic citizen to promote or vote for any law that attacks human life such as abortion, euthanasia, and human embryonic stem cell research. Likewise, the "Doctrinal Note" includes the fundamental and inalienable ethical demands to restrict marriage to monogamy, to defend the freedom of parents regarding the right to educate their children, to protect children from such modern forms of slavery such as drug abuse and prostitution, to defend the right of religious freedom, and to promote forms of economic life that are at the service of the human person and the common good.

6. The Catholic must support the whole array of issues addressed by the social doctrine of the Church although some issues, by their very nature, are more contingent and allow more room for the prudential application in terms of means (e.g., privatization vs. government as a means of securing retirement benefits, home-schooling vs. the elementary school as a means for securing primary level education of children) while others, like those involving direct attacks on human life, are relatively more straightforward in application.

7. Catholic participation in political life should be based on realism. This means rejecting both (a) the attitudes of a self-imposed "Catholic inferiority complex" in a non-Catholic social context like the United States, especially in light of the fact that numerous non-Catholic political programs have proved to be so ruinous for American civilization and (b) the utopian perspective, typical of influential left-wing political thought in the United States, that fails to see the inevitability of men and women living in imperfect social situations.

8. That active, intelligent, and faithful Catholic political participation in society is consistent with the call for coherence between faith and life and the Gospel and culture.

The Catholic commentator, Richard Hinshaw usefully summarizes the various obligations that, respectively, both Catholics in public life and the average Catholic citizen should take from the "Doctrinal Note" (Hinshaw 2003). For the former, the obligations are (1) to be guided by Gospel values and the Catholic social teaching in public policy deliberations, (2) to promote the absolute moral prohibition against laws permitting the destruction of innocent human life, and (3) to reject the attempt to separate one's religious faith from public conduct. Regarding the latter, the obligations are (1) to be activity involved in civic affairs, (2) to bring Gospel values and Catholic social teaching to bear on the issues of everyday political and civic life, and (3) to utilize one's vote, one's voice, and one's voluntary organization participation to promote the common good and to reject narrow self-interest.

Based on both studies of American Catholic attitudes and behaviors, it is clear that both many Catholic politicians and the average Catholic citizen have failed to implement Catholic principles in public and civic life. The question is "why is this the case"? How much of it is willful and a conscious rejection of a well-understood religious and moral obligation? And how much of the latter is out of calculating self-interest? Conversely put, how much of the failure to apply faith to political life is out of ignorance of the Catholic principles themselves? And if ignorance is at least a major cause of the failed implementation of Catholic political principles, why is this the case? Who and what is responsible for such a gross failure? The bishops? Those in charge of Catholic formation and catechesis? The present system of Catholic higher education? The Catholic laity themselves? An American central value system progressively becoming more secular? All five? Are there other considerations involved?

Sociologically, whether Catholics in the United Sates "think" in a Catholic way and, derivatively, politically act in a Catholic way depends, *in part*, on the nature of the broader cultural message. In a society such as the United States, the mainstream or dominant culture has never been Catholic and the present broader cultural movement is progressively in the direction of accepting such values as materialism, utilitarianism, moral relativity, and autonomous individualism. The key issue for Catholics that remains is whether or not the Catholic Church, qua institution and community, has the resources, skill, and commitment to construct an internally coherent and consistent Catholic subculture or set of social institutions (e.g., parishes, schools, seminaries, newspaper and other mass media outlets, hospitals and other health care facilities, professional and academic associations, and other Catholic voluntary associations) capable of socializing its adherents into a willing acceptance of the basic tenets of the faith and general Catholic worldview. The purpose of such a Catholic subculture is not merely to shield the religious community from the outer culture, as is typical of a counterculture like the Amish, but to create a mechanism of mediation where Catholics can both selectively accept elements of the broader culture that are life affirming while simultaneously critiquing it and, eventually, shaping it from the logic of its own heritage.

The political failure of Catholic America to shape the broader civilization is rooted in the severe weakening, during the post–Vatican II period in the United States, of a once distinctive Catholic subculture or "plausibility structure." With this weakening, many Catholics have naturally come to be socialized into an acceptance of such secular American commitments as socialism/Marxism, feminism, bourgeois materialism, new age, sexual liberation including homosexuality, the therapeutic mentality, and radical individualism. And as a correlate of this weakening, during the immediate post–Vatican II period, the Catholic Church, qua institution, lost whatever modest political influence and status it had gained during the previous decades—witness a string of defeats from *Roe v. Wade* in 1973 to human embryonic stem cell research in 2001. Secular forces have now advanced their agenda in American society to the issues of the cultural normalization and legal equality of all aspects of the homosexual experience. The next major secularist advance, many Catholic analysts suspect, will most probably be in the area of the promotion of essentially unrestricted biological and genetic engineering. It is important to point out the result, as orthodox Catholics see it, of what is seen as the dialectic taking place between the increasingly secularist monopoly in the American public square and the advanced erosion within Catholic institutional life. The result is the uncritical assimilation of Catholics into a mainstream culture itself moving further away from one Judaic-Christian in nature and accepting of the natural law to one basically secular in orientation.

The dramatic increase in the cultural impotence of the Catholic faith naturally has its corollary in the realm of politics. Despite the facts that the Catholic representation in both houses of Congress and among viable presidential candidates has increased significantly since World War II concomitant with the rising educational, occupational, and income of the general population, Catholics have been anything *but* successful politically, if one defines success in terms of the ability to bring Catholic social thought into the public sphere from which national social policy is forged. The social scientific evidence is that the Catholic politicians have not voted either consistently from a Catholic perspective or as a discernible bloc.

Mary Hanna's 1979 analysis, *Catholics and American Politics*, is probably still the best available in explaining the inability and unwillingness of Catholic politicians to make an impact *qua Catholic*. She notes three reasons. First and foremost, the Catholic faith was not a significant factor in the value orientation of many "Catholic" congressmen. Second, even when congressmen claim a strong allegiance to their faith, internal Catholic pluralism militated against a single vision and concerted activity; for Hanna, "there is indeed no one way to be Catholic; it seems clear that the Catholic Church with its rich and complex history, traditions, and teachings provides a variety of reference points for its adherents. . . . There is then no single thrust that Catholic religious influence takes in the lives and thinking of the Catholic sector of Congress" (86–87). Third, Hanna cites the American normative conceptions of the "separation of Church and State" and of the need to stress the public interest and not the interests of any particular subgrouping as a reason for the lack of a united Catholic political presence.

Hanna's first explanation provides evidence of the fact the Catholic Church simply has lost the hearts and minds of many through an outright secularization. Hanna's second explanation is more subtle and fascinating. It is indicative of an *internal* secularization that reveals that what is really operant—that what is really of paramount importance—in the thought and activity of many "Catholic" politicians is some form of non-Catholic allegiance (e.g., socialism, capitalism, feminism, pragmatism, etc.) that selectively chooses what elements of Catholic social doctrine are to be utilized *ideologically*. The Catholic politician, as such, "can have his cake and eat it too," satisfying some non-Catholic ideological interest which is of primary importance while simultaneously legitimating his/her action to the Catholic citizenry by clothing it superficially in the trappings of the faith. Three reactions are in order in responding to Hanna's third explanation. The first is to note the *false* understanding of Church-State separation, i.e., one that attempts to separate religiously informed thought and action from the political process, that is conveniently assumed by many Catholic politicians. The second is the ignoring, by Catholic politicians, of the natural law tradition accepted by the Church whose principles are both universal in thrust and applicable for the good of all humankind. The third is the blatant "interest group" politics that characterizes much of American political life that is viewed widely today, for better or worse, as acceptable.

The situation regarding the lack of authentic Catholic formation for the Catholic citizen in American life is not superior to that of the Catholic politician and, actually, serves the function of making it possible for Catholic politicians avoid a political penalty for their rejection and ignorance of the Catholic faith. The religious values held by the average Catholic citizen varies across the "orthodox-heterodox" spectrum with no more than perhaps 20 percent of the Catholic population being "orthodox-across-the-board," combining a respect for all aspects of the Catholic faith including, simultaneously, a liturgical and social Catholicism. The rest of Catholic America sociologically should be categorized as different variations of a selective, cafeteria-style Catholicism termed by Father Andrew Greeley (1976, 1977) as "communal Catholicism."

If this sociological analysis of the present state of American civilization and of the Catholic Church in the United States is even close to being correct, there is no "quick fix" that can immediately reverse the situation. The basic, sound, and enduring solution to the Catholic Church in this country righting herself and, derivatively, satisfactorily addressing the issue of Catholic participation in political life is long term and requires painful sacrifice and patience: It is the rebuilding of the "plausibility structure" of the Catholic Church. Only when this strategy produces results, that is, when the future generations of Catholics in America start to think as serious Catholics, will they then act as serious Catholics in the American public square.

The Emergence of a "Communal Catholicism" and the Role of Conscience

Part and parcel of the increased roles of pluralism (religious, social, and moral) and of a hyperindividualism in contemporary American society is the emergence of a selective Catholicism that has been both termed and celebrated by Father Andrew M. Greeley (1976, 1977). The emergence and institutionalization within the Catholic population of this "communal Catholicism," furthermore, has implications for the exercise of individual conscience in both Church and civil affairs and raises the crucial question, for legitimate Catholic authorities, of what is the "proper formation" of conscience (Varacalli 1989).

Both classical arguments in the sociology of religion and by Catholic social theory help explain theoretically the phenomenon of a communal and highly individuated religiosity in the modern world,

American society included. And such arguments also can explain why such developments are quite challenging to the maintenance of the Catholic faith, at least as put forth by traditional Catholics and the Church's magisterium. Regarding the sociology of religion, in addition to Father Greeley's discussion of the developments, the intellectual work of Thomas Luckmann (1961), Meredith McGuire (2002), and Ernest Troeltsch (1931) are important.

In his *The Invisible Religion*, Thomas Luckmann promotes what sociologists call a "functional" definition of religion by describing sociologically an individual's religious commitment as the product of the total socialization experience, as the result of the influence of various "agents of socialization" in shaping and "completing" human beings who are, following fellow German sociologist, Arnold Gehlen (1980), born "instinctually deprived" at birth. From Luckmann's perspective then, the individual's religious perspective or "ultimate concern" (following Protestant theologian Paul Tillich's [1957] functional definition of religion) is made up by the influence of both one's private sphere (e.g., family, neighborhood, religious, voluntary associational, etc.) and public sphere (e.g., government, corporations, mass media, education, etc.) involvements. It is important to point out that, from Luckmann's analysis, the influence that one's religious (traditionally defined) organizations makes on an individual is only one of many agents of socialization and may not—and empirically speaking, often is not—the key shaper of a person's worldview or ultimate concern. Relatedly, sociologist Meredith McGuire in her popular sociology of religion textbook, *Religion: The Social Context* (2002), strikes a similar note in arguing that "religious" allegiances may take either what she refers to as "official" (recognized by society's cultural gatekeepers as such, Catholicism, Protestantism, Judaism, etc.) and "unofficial" (feminism, witchcraft, astrology, political philosophies, psychology not as a narrow intellectual discipline but as a broader worldview, etc.) forms. Furthermore, and quite consistent with Luckmann, she notes that in most cases in the modern American context, either "unofficial" religion is more important to the individual than are any of the "official" options or that individuals who participate in "official" religion bring with them "unofficial" religions that are, in actually, completely transformative of the official religion in question. Crudely put, for some, feminism, witchcraft, astrology, politics, or psychology is their true "religion" whether or not they attend church, synagogue, mosque, or temple. The bottom line for both Luckmann and

McGuire is not only that the sociology of religion is not synonomous with the sociology of organized religion but that most of ultimate meaning in the modern context comes from nonsupernaturally based sources.

The Luckmann and McGuire logic is intimately connected with Father Greeley's discussion of a communal Catholicism; they are examples in which "official" Catholicism may still holds relevance for the individual but not ultimate significance. For Greeley, many modern-day American Catholics pick and choose pieces of Catholic doctrine as they synthesize these with some cultural or subcultural attachment considered more important. Greeley's term can include any number of cultural/individual reductions of the Catholic faith along ideological, ethnic, socioeconomic, and psychological lines. Thus communal Catholics in the United States consist of those whose Catholicism is translated and reduced, for instance, to Marxism or American nationalism (*ideology*); or to Italianness, Irishness, Germanness, Spanishness, Africanness (*ethnicity or race*); or to being upper, middle, or lower class (*socioeconomic background*).

Cultural or subcultural reduction does not exhaust, however, the meaning of a communal Catholicism. It also includes those whose Catholicism is purely nominal but who are, indeed, very religious but very religious in a distinctly "liberal Protestant" individualized way as both predicted and advocated by the liberal Protestant theologian-historian-sociologist, Ernest Troeltsch. Troeltsch posited an evolutionary understanding of an inevitable religious movement from "Church-related" to "sect-related" to a highly individualized "mysticism." Sociologists Nicholas J. Demerath and Phillip E. Hammond describe this movement as follows:

> Troeltsch contrasted both church and sect to still a third type of religious expression: mysticism. . . . Troeltsch pictured it less in terms of a withdrawn contemplation of the world and more in terms of an active antiassociationalism in which the individual departs organized religion to go it alone within the world rather than outside of it. Thus, Troeltsch predicted that mysticism would become a dominant form of religion among the well-educated middle-classes. He saw it as a liberalizing spirit within Protestantism that would eclipse both the church and sect as religious models. (1969, 70)

As Troeltsch put it himself in his *The Social Teachings of the Christian Churches*:

We must not forget that the whole of the later Middle Ages, with the growth of an independent lay civilization in the cities, itself created a powerful competition with the previous world of thought which had been controlled by the Church and particularly by the priests. Its first effort was naturally to limit the power of the ecclesiastical civilization; that, however, was followed by an increasing disintegration of the objective side of religion in general, as it was expressed in the institutional side of the Church. . . . Through all of these movements, however, a sociological type of Christian thought was being developed, which was not the same as the sect type; it was, in fact, a new type—the radical individualism of mysticism. This type has no desire for an organized fellowship; all it cared for was freedom for interchange of ideas, a pure fellowship of thought. . . . In this type, therefore, . . . the isolated individual, and psychological abstraction and analysis become everything. . . . This type, however, only attained its universal historical significance in the later Protestant Dissenters and in their connection with Humanism. (1931, 376–77)

Monsignor George A. Kelly provides the following critique of liberal Protestantism and mysticism from the viewpoint of a magisterially defined Catholicism:

Protestantism by definition was geared to almost any idea that accentuated individual religious experience. Lacking magisterium, by which all new Catholic interpretations must be measured, Protestantism (except its fundamentalists) was forced by its inner logic to make faith concepts and moral precepts almost a matter of scientific determination. Ernest Troeltsch (1865–1923) . . . was an important contributor to Protestant accommodation. He wanted a vital Christianity, and thought its survival depends on a restructured modern dress. "Absolutes" had to go and "personal satisfaction" had to rise as a norm of religious relevance. Troeltsch does not ask: 'How can I find God?' but 'How can I find my soul?.' He did not even think that Jesus was necessary to Christianity, since Christ was more a symbol of a community than a spokesman of God's revelation. Though a Protestant, Troeltsch thought the reformed churches retained too many features of Catholic Christianity. The modern age to him meant the religious autonomy of man—against both Protestant and Catholic worldviews, if need be. (1979, 40)

Communal Catholicism as a concept, then, contains more than the reality of subcultural commitments reshaping Catholicism; it also includes the religious speculations of those nominal Catholics who have accepted the so-called "Protestant principle" stressing the absoluteness of individual interpretation and the idea that the Catholic Church is, against Saint Bellarmine's formulation, primarily an "invisible reality" capable of infinite reshaping and resymbolization.

Catholic social theory also addresses the cognitive and normative issues involved in the empirical reality of communal Catholicism. Like the sociology of knowledge, Catholic social theory does not support any version of what might be called "angelism." As an incarnational religion, Catholicism acknowledges that the soul is inextricably intertwined in bodies, that grace works through nature, that reason is embedded within a matrix of emotions and other nonrational attachments, and that individuals, as with the sociological claim, are necessarily and intimately affected by cultural and socialization influences that are temporally and spatially bound. The spirit, in essence for Catholic social theory, must continually be in a critically self-conscious relationship with both human nature and society if it is to master, or at least reasonably control, these relationships. And, empirically it is obvious that, in many cases, the spirit is subdued both by nature and society.

Put another way, Catholic social theory accepts the claim of social science that the present-day plethora of heterodoxies in the exercise of the Catholic faith on the part of nominal and dormant Catholics involves the inevitable human reality of mediation. That is, it is the case that the Catholic faith is mediated through some distinctive personality orientation or some cultural or subcultural construction (e.g., nationality, ethnicity, socioeconomic class affiliation, philosophy or ideology) that is capable of producing a radically individualistic or communal Catholicism. In these instances, the Catholic faith is understood as a secondary or tertiary (or nonexistent) allegiance that is absorbed selectively into some other moral commitment considered ultimately more significant. Put into psychologist Gordon Allport's framework (1960), a communal Catholicism is an example of an "extrinsic" or "immature" religious expression, one placing emphasis of what a religion can do practically and pragmatically for a group or for an individual and not what the group or individual can do selflessly and sacrificially for the transcendent God.

The Birth Control Controversy

The consistent teaching of the Catholic Church is that sexual activity between a husband and a wife (the conjugal act) must be open to procreation (the "gift of life"). In the words of scholar Julia Mitchell Corbett, "the Church continues to restate its well-known teaching that the use of artificial birth control is sinful. The Church teaches that the natural result of sexual intercourse is the procreation of children and that any method that interferes with this end is against the law of God and the Church" (2001, 87–88). The Church's position on this matter is elucidated in all its complexity in such encyclicals as *Casti Connubii* (1930), *Humanae Vitae* (1968), and *Familiaris Consortio* (1981). Indeed, the official Catholic position was the same position that the total Christian community took officially for two millennia until various Protestant groups started to break away from this hitherto universal Christian doctrine in light of the Anglican's famous Lambeth Conference in 1930.

It is important to point out that many Christian families, both Protestant and Catholic, may have ignored or rejected routinely the official Christian position on birth control. However, it is just as important to understand that what religious organizations do pronounce officially does make a difference in what many adherents think and do. In the words of Monsignor George A. Kelly, the Lambeth Conference "opened the door slightly to the use of contraception in hardship cases" (1990, 30). Today, in 2004, the Catholic Church stands almost alone in the Christian community in maintaining this historical doctrinal stance. How birth control has become "taken for granted" as part and parcel of modern life and has contributed, at least in the eyes of orthodox Catholics, to an dramatic increase in an unlicenced sexuality represents an example of what the latter religionists mean by the effects of "slippery slope" thinking regarding the "contraceptive mentality."

The Catholic Church's almost immediate response to the Lambeth Conference was the publication, later in the same year, of the encyclical of Pius XI, *Casti Connubii* (1930), which stated bluntly that "any use whatsoever of matrimony exercised in such a way that the act is deliberately frustrated in its natural power to generate life is an offense against the law of God and of nature, and those who indulge in such are branded with the guilt of grave sin" (1930, 56). Father Richard J. Neuhaus expresses the official Catholic understanding of human sexuality in, perhaps, a slightly more positive way when he asserts that:

The way of love is openness to the other, and openness to life. It is the uncompromised gift of the self to the other and, ultimately, to God. Against a widespread dualism that views the body as instrumental to the self, the way of love knows that the body is integral to the self. Against a sexuality in which women become objects for the satisfaction of desire, the way of love joins two persons in mutual respect and mutual duty, in which sacred bond respect turns to reverence and duty to delight. Against a culture in which sex is trivialized and degraded, the way of love invites eros to participate in nothing less than the drama of salvation. (1995, 40)

The orthodox Catholic position, rejected by a clear majority of the Catholic population and almost all of a progressive Catholic persuasion, is that the acceptance of birth control leads to a "contraceptive mentality." This, in turn the logic proceeds, fuels a sexual revolution endorsing, among other horrors, the "necessity" of abortion as the birth control of last resort and the weakening and, in some cases, dissolution of the intact traditional family (Wilcox 2005).

The orthodox Catholic scholar, Monsignor George A. Kelly, makes this case as he states that:

Even at Lambeth, the Anglican theologian and bishop, Charles Gore, no friend of Rome, rose to warn his peers that from a Christian viewpoint the separation of sexuality from its God-given procreative reason for existence would free men and women from the need for marriage. . . . And cautioned Gore, if heterosexuals could relish this freedom of sexual fulfillment, why not homosexuals, since procreation no longer was an essential function of sexuality? . . . Later developments in England and in Anglicanism proved Gore correct about effects, personal and social, of abandoning a first principle of Judeo-Christian morality. . . . If a church in Christ's name could endorse contraception, it could be called upon later to endorse fornication, adultery, and pederasty. Henry VIII would have been vindicated on the dissolubility of Christian marriage and Thomas More made out to be fool for the sacrifice of his life. (1990, 30–31)

Two pregnant quotes from the work of Catholic historian John T. McGreevy make clear just how quickly the American Catholic population turned around its position on the acceptability of birth control. On the one hand, McGreevy notes that:

Public dissent from Church teaching on contraception was nonexistent in the United States in the 1940s and 1950s and birthrates for Catholic women remained higher than those for non-Catholic women, even at the height of the post-war baby boom. Catholic women educated at Catholic colleges in particular, continued to desire families of five children or more, defying the demographic rule that increased education for women led to decreased fertility. (2003, 232)

On the other hand, McGreevy notes a sea change in the attitude of the American Catholic population after the publication of *Humanae Vitae* in 1968:

Opposition to *Humanae Vitae*, more vocal and sustained than any other topic in the history of modern Catholicism, inevitably stimulated study of the very meaning of papal authority, sin, and dissent. . . . Most Catholic couples rejected the teaching or ignored it. . . . [A] survey forwarded to the American bishops found a majority of Catholic parents with more than seven children unsympathetic to *Humanae Vitae*. (2003, 246)

Indeed, historian James T. Fisher links the rejection of the Church's teaching on sexuality in general in light of changing social mores to the general fleeing from religious life of many priests, brothers, and sisters. As he states:

Defections from the ranks of the priesthood and sisterhood increased dramatically between the Vatican's conservative position on moral issues and the dramatic changes in American social attitudes during this period, especially those concerning human sexuality. . . . In 1966, some 200 American priests resigned from the active ministry, a number that had grown to 750 by 1969, while the number of ordinations in the same period dropped by more than 15 percent. And the rate of decline increased over time: whereas in 1964 there were 47,500 seminarians in training for the priesthood, by 1984 there would be approximately 12,000. Two hundred Catholic seminaries closed their doors during these two decades. In 1966, there were roughly 180,000 nuns in the United States. By 1980, the number had dwindled to less than 130,000, despite a significant increase in the Catholic population during the same period. (2000, 146)

While the official, orthodox Catholic position on birth control has remained constant over the ages, the overwhelming percentage of the American Catholic population today are either ignorant of its logic and rationale or simply outright reject it. The rejection can range from a feeling that the Church posits an unrealizable ideal to follow to simply that the Church is an agent of sexual repression and archaic thinking. There are both external and internal reasons for the ignorance/rejection of the Church's position on contraception which, it can be plausibly argued, stand in a dialectical or mutually influencing relationship with each other. For one thing, American culture has lost, to a significant degree, its Christian influence and has become far more secular in nature endorsing a radical individualism in thought and action. More specifically, the civilization has become far more sexually emancipated with a kind of quasi Freudian understanding of the sexual "needs" of the individual having become a contemporary cultural staple for significant segments of the American population. Relatedly and institutionally, the mass media promotes overt sexuality in its movies and television shows; and journals, magazines, and academics, throughout the educational system, promote sexual openness and experimentation both subtly and overtly. Demographically, more and more women are working full time in the nation's economy and many upwardly socially mobile married couples consciously desire less (or no) children as a way to further both economic income and what is perceived to be the higher status and prestige associated with full-time employment as a "professional" in the public sphere of society.

For its part, the liberal Catholic establishment, so well institutionalized within the Catholic Church of the United States from the mid-1960s through to the 1990s, has, in its writings and personal lifestyle choices, also pushed the idea that the Church's traditional teaching on sexuality is obsolete, needlessly restrictive, humanly repressive, and, too boot, sexist in nature. Indeed, many progressive Catholic commentators, such as Father Andrew M. Greeley (1976, 1977) believe that Pope Paul VI's reaffirmation of the Church's historic position on birth control in the 1968 encyclical, *Humanae Vitae*—in light of an increased rejection of the idea by the Catholic rank and file—caused a severe alienation from and, in some cases, flight from, the Church *qua* institution. In contradistinction to Father Greeley's analysis, the far more orthodox Catholic scholar, Monsignor George A. Kelly (1990) believes that the majority of the Catholic population was of one mind with the Church on the issue of contraception but that Pope Paul VI made a strategic mistake in the early mid-1960s by supporting the existence of a "birth control commission" whose task it was to make recommendations to the pope about whether or not the Church's teachings could and should change. For Monsignor Kelly, the existence of the commission, whose deliberations were manipulated by the secular mass media and liberal Catholic elites, falsely generated and aroused the hopes of those who wanted the Church to change her course on this issue. When Pope Paul VI rejected the commission's recommendations to relax the strictures against birth control and published his famous encyclopedia, *Humanae Vitae* (1968) defending historic Church teaching, controversy was ignited and a social movement against the Church's teaching coalesced. For Kelly, the birth control controversy in the 1960s and 1970s could have been avoided; for Father Greeley, both external and internal forces made such a controversy inevitable. In the words of Monsignor Kelly, "only naivete can explain how a pope would initiate a procedure which could be misused to propose that what the Church always considers evil might not be evil after all. The infighting which followed the Commission's creation became the platform for undermining popular belief in a firm Catholic doctrine. . . . If the Catholic Church was so sure of its teaching, why a study commission?" (1990, 29–30, 31).

Regardless of who has the better argument in the Greeley-Kelly debate over the impact of a delayed deliberation on the acceptability of birth control on the part of Church authorities during the decade of the 1960s, it is clear that, today, the overwhelming percentage of Catholic Americans, either liberal or nominal, reject the historic teaching. Orthodox Catholics persist in believing, however, that the deleterious effects of the sexual revolution and the "contraceptive mentality" will force a reconsideration of the issue and lead to a significant recovery and acceptance of the Church's teaching on marriage and sexual morality (Wilcox 2005).

The Ordination of Women: A Battle Over the Meaning of "Tradition" and "Equality"

In the official or magisterial Catholic religious tradition, as Julia Mitchell Corbett explains, "the sacrament of orders, or ordination to the priesthood, sets a man apart for the official sacramental ministry of the Church. Catholics believe that it gives the priest the grace required to carry out the demands of his priesthood. Only men are ordained to the priesthood" (2001, 78).

There are a not insignificant number of feminists in the Catholic Church of the United States who oppose the Church's position denying the theological possibility of ordaining women to the priesthood and diaconate. Sociologically, these women are disproportionately influential in society by virtue of their "social location:" They tend to come from the socioeconomic ranks of the upper–middle class and tend, occupationally, to be professionals. They are, to a significant degree, "progressive" politically.

As is made clear in *The Catechism of the Catholic Church* (1994, #1577), the magisterial opposition to the ordination of women in the Catholic heritage is rooted in the historical reality that, during his earthly existence, Jesus Christ chose only men to be his apostles and, furthermore, that the apostles only chose men to succeed them. The official Catholic position, then, is based on the conviction that Jesus Christ, as part of the Trinitarian God, knew what he was doing in his apostolic appointments and in the laying of the groundwork of sacred tradition.

Feminist advocates of ordination counter basically in two ways. First, some feminists point out that Jesus Christ did rely heavily on women during his earthly ministry, witness the key roles of Mary, Mary Magdalen, and Martha. Second, and perhaps more important, the argument is presented that the Church is confusing a nonessential aspect of the patriarchal culture of the apostolic era with the essential Christian truth that posits a full equality between men and women. According to progressive feminists, tradition can and should change in light of new movements in the Holy Spirit that, in turn, influence the culture and should influence the Church. For such feminists, as Julia Mitchell Corbett notes, "the only way for . . . [the] . . . Church to make good on its pronouncements about the equality and full personhood of all people is to grant women full ordination to the priesthood and accept women as equals for ordination to the higher ranks of bishop, archbishop, and cardinal. According to these women, the necessary changes will have not been made until it is possible for a woman to be elected Pope" (2001, 88). Magisterial defenders, for their part, contend that the feminist definition of equality is tantamount to advocating a utopian and unrealistic androgeny, the argument that men and women should be viewed as interchangeable units, each capable of doing what the other does without qualification. Traditional Catholics believe that men and women are equal in dignity but can still serve different functions, by virtue of the social roles they emphasize and exercise in society and the Church. For instance, a wife's emphasis on the "nurturing" function is no less valuable than a husband's "protective" responsibilities. Additionally, women *do* perform many indispensable Catholic tasks in society through different "apostolates" and in the Church through various "ministries"; the fact that woman cannot be ordained, so this logic goes, is not, in essence, a matter of social inequality but reflects a necessary fidelity to sacred tradition and the will of God. In short summary, the battle over the issue of the ordination of women in the Catholic Church is a battle over the seemingly intractable disagreements over the nature and function of "tradition" and "equality."

A few final observations can be put forth. The first is to suggest that a sizable portion of the American Catholic population, including the large group of "nominal" Catholics, have no strong vested interest or ideological concern regarding the issue of the ordination of women. The issue is of strong concern, however, to groups that are sociologically "nuclear" to the institution; just as there are radical feminist groups in the Church pushing for ordination, so there are some traditional groups (e.g., Helen Hull Hitchcock's Women for Faith and Family) defending the magisterial position. Likewise, there is a split among the clergy, in part along generational lines. Some of the progressive bishops and priests who came into power in the mid-1960s and stayed there through the 1980s have sympathy for the ordination cause (even if their support, in many cases, is guarded and behind the scenes). On the other hand, most of the clergy formed, respectively, before the mid-1960s and from the 1990s onwards tend to be supportive of historic Catholic tradition. Indeed, the high water mark in establishment Catholic circles in the United States for some form of demonstrated sympathy and support for the ordination of women came in April 1988. At that time, the National Conference of Catholic Bishops committee statement, forged by the leaders of the progressive cardinals (Dearden–Bernardin) wing, put out the statement, "A Pastoral Response to Women's Concerns for Church and Society" (Kelly 1990, 162). This draft, in lieu of reaffirming the constant tradition of the Church, instead suggested that the issue of the ordination of women remain open as a topic for further study

(Kelly 1990, 164). While such a call is far from radical vis-à-vis the demands of many feminist groups, it was significant given that it came right out of the bosom of the national bureaucracy headed by the Catholic Bishops of America. It is fair to say that, since 1988, magisterial forces, led by John Paul II (and now by Benedict XVI), have reasserted the traditional teaching of the Church regarding the ordination of women, forcing progressive forces to either leave the Church or, much more likely, to put aside—at least temporarily—the issue.

Intermarriage

Sociologists have coined the term "homogamy" to refer to the general tendency of individuals who have similar characteristics to marry one another (Henslin 2004, 332). Some of the most highly predictable examples of homogamous variables or social channels regarding the selection of a marriage partner are those of age, education, social class, race, occupation, cultural lifestyle, philosophical attachment, and religious worldview.

During the 1950s, when Will Herberg was writing and researching his classic analysis of the state of American religion and civilization (1960), he presented the case that religion was a central determinant in marriage selection. His famous "triple melting pot" thesis argued that, to a significant degree, Protestants married Protestants, Catholics married Catholics, and Jews married Jews. Extrapolating from, and consistent with, his argument would be the claim that a little bit earlier in the assimilation process, ethnicity was also a key predictor in marriage patterns for these groups as Italian Catholics married Italian Catholics and Reform German Jews married others in their same designation. Over time, however, the ethnic demarcation within the broad religious categories weakened while the religious identity became more central.

Today, the sociological evidence is overwhelming that, with the exception of the more traditional core of the respective Protestant, Catholic, and Jewish communities, religion is no longer a key factor in socially channeling marriage. Other variables (social class, cultural lifestyle, philosophical attachment, among others) have supplanted religion as the new "ultimate concern" (Tillich 1957) of the now far more secularized contemporary American (and American Catholic) citizen.

Regarding the issue of Catholic intermarriage, the research of Purdue University sociologist, James Davidson, is crucial. In an important article published in *Commonweal* entitled "Outside the Church: Whom Catholics Marry and Where," Davidson states:

> As . . . was reported in *The Search for Common Ground* (Our Sunday Visitor, 1997), today's intermarriage rate for Catholics is at least twice what it was in the pre–Vatican II era. . . . Whereas only 16 percent of Catholics born before 1941 (the pre–Vatican II cohort) are—or, if widowed, separated, or divorced, were—in interfaith marriages, 32 percent of Catholics born between 1941 and 1960 (the Vatican II cohort) are/were in such marriages, and 40 percent of Catholics born between 1961 and 1977 (the post–Vatican II cohort) are/were intermarried. . . . More and more Catholics are involved in interfaith marriages. (1999, 14)

Consistent with this significant trend, for Davidson, are the realities that young Catholics are less attached to the institutional Church, that Church-approved marriages are down, and that more and more interfaith couples are choosing civil ceremonies. The question remains, however, as to *why* the decreased saliency of one's Catholicism in choosing a marriage partner. Some scholars stress the general processes of secularization operating in the society at large while others emphasize an internal weakening or secularization from within the Catholic community.

Regardless of the precise cause of this development, it is clear that, in general, such a dramatic increase in Catholic intermarriage rates is indicative of the weakened state of Catholicism in the contemporary United States. While it is true that, in some cases, the non-Catholic spouse will convert to Catholicism and agree to raise children in the Catholic faith, the other logical possibilities are just as likely to happen. The newly married couple (and their children) can (1) embrace the religion of the non-Catholic spouse, (2) embrace no religion at all, substituting some secular functional equivalent, or (3) convert to a religion other than that of either spouse. In addition to reflecting the eroding of Catholic denominational identity and loyalty, intermarriage obviously also leads to a further "ripple effect," that is, the deterioration in the health of the religious body.

It is important to note a small countermovement occurring among some young contemporary American Catholic youth. In her volume, *The New Faithful: Why Young Adults Are Embracing Christian Or-*

thodoxy (2002), Colleen Carroll observes that emergence of what can variously be referred to as a "dynamic orthodoxy," a "neo-orthodoxy," or an "intentional orthodoxy" on the part of a specialized segment of today's Catholic youth. These Catholic young people have rejected the key American cultural values of hyperindividualism, excessive materialism, an extreme cultural and religious relativity, and a radical utilitarian worldview while at the same time have embraced official Catholic teaching, in some cases, across the board, including the Church teaching on birth control and the acceptance of natural family planning for married couples.

The overall question here is whether the return to religion on the part of some now nominally Catholic American youth will be in the form of a serious appropriation of the Catholic faith, a slightly less radical version of Father Andrew Greeley's communal Catholicism, to some other denominational affiliation, or to some other syncretic religious/philosophical formulation. Religion, for some of these young Americans, is once again a central factor in all of life's key issues, including finding one's marriage partner. This group however is unrepresentative and atypical of the accurate general trend away from the faith as documented by James Davidson and other scholars. Whether some portion of this group represents an intermediate step back to the restoration of a cohesive Catholic subculture in the future remains to be seen.

Abortion: A Case of Competing "Rights"

Over the ages, the Catholic Church has been consistent in its opposition to abortion and, conversely, promotion of a "culture of life" from the moment of conception throughout the individual life cycle. For instance, in one of the key documents of the Second Vatican Council, *Gaudium et Spes* (1965, "On the Church in the Modern World," #27), it is stated that:

> whatever is opposed to life itself, such as any type of murder, genocide, abortion, euthanasia, or willful self-destruction, whatever violates the integrity of the human person, such as mutilation, torments inflicted on body or mind, attempts to coerce the will itself; whatever insults human dignity, such as subhuman living conditions, arbitrary imprisonment, deportation, slavery, prostitution, the selling of women

and children; as well as disgraceful working conditions, where men
are treated as mere tools for profit, rather than as free and responsible persons; all these things and others of their like are infamies indeed. They poison human society, but they do more harm to those
who practice them than those who suffer the injury. Moreover, they
are a supreme dishonor to the Creator. (Abbott 1966, 226–27)

The Catholic population in the United States is, more or less, evenly
split over whether or not the 1973 *Roe v. Wade* decision legalizing abortion was a morally correct one. The majority of parish-affiliated
Catholics support the Church's position with a majority of nominal and
overtly secularized Catholic supporting, with whatever degree of intensity, abortion rights.

However, it is important to point out, however, that a not insignificant percentage of Catholics who are not only parish affiliated
but who are active in the administering of Church-based programs are
supportive of a "woman's right to choose." Indicative of a weakened
Catholic plausibility structure in the post–Vatican II period, such individuals have been subject to a secularization from within. This means
that they have accepted some external philosophy (e.g., hyperindividualism, feminism, utilitarianism, materialism, cultural and religious
relativity, among others), which actually is the operative "ultimate concern" (Tillich 1957) in their lives as members of both the Catholic
Church and society and, as such, has replaced in importance the official Catholic understanding of reality. As Julia Mitchell Corbett stated:

> The Church . . . teaches that the fetus has a soul and is a human being
> from the moment of conception. Therefore, abortion is murder. Fem-
> inists see the Church's position on . . . [this issue] . . . as a violation of
> women's rights to control their own bodies . . . [and represents an] . . .
> unwarranted intrusion of the Church into areas that are best left up
> to individual morality. (2001, 88)

At one level, then, the battle over abortion is a battle over different conceptions of "rights," one religious/classical/natural law in form,
the other radically modern. From the position of an official Catholicism, the fetus is a living human life and the "right to life" trumps all
other "rights," whether lesser or fabricated. On the other hand, the feminist position, in its most extreme formulation, is a "bottom-up," sec-

ular, and "social construction of reality" one (Hunter 1991), arguing that all definitions of life (and death) emanate from human will and other secular sources and therefore individual human beings can both judge and modify these social definitions of what is or is not life. From this position, the right of a woman to decide on whether or not to have an abortion trumps the status of the fetus. Other feminists, arguing again from individualistic premises, propose that the right to choose to have an abortion is supreme, even if it is acknowledged that the fetus in the womb represents life. There are debates, among such feminists, as to whether this life is in any sense "lesser" than after birth.

In her celebrated book, *Abortion and the Politics of Motherhood* (1985), sociologist Kristin Luker adds a useful empirical twist to the debate over abortion. Her research indicates that a key factor in shaping the attitudes of women toward abortion is to be found in the respective "social locations" they occupy in the larger society. Simply put, those more traditional stay-at-home mothers have a propensity, as a reflection of their lifestyles, to be pro–large family and tend to be against abortion while professionally oriented, upwardly social, career women have it in their economic and status interests to favor social policies making it easier for them to control the number of children in their home life, including access to legal abortion.

Of course, it is the case that there are many women who work outside the home who do not view themselves as "career oriented" and who view abortion as undesirable but as a necessary or lesser evil. Such individuals feel they can only provide for a certain number of children given their socioeconomic condition and see the employment of the abortion option within the framework of their ability to provide what they view as adequate provision for their children.

From an orthodox Catholic perspective, the economic argument justifying abortion is morally unacceptable, representing a case of what Catholic moral theologians term utilitarian, or "proportionalist" or "consequentialist" thinking—in which means employed can justify ends—that violates what is viewed as the absolute necessity to guard and protect all innocent human life. Many Americans and many Catholic Americans simply disagree with the position of the Catholic Church on this issue or are unaware of the logic behind its thinking. Regardless of the degree to which religious, moral, lifestyle, and economic background differences affect the debate over abortion, the issue itself nonetheless represents a major battle between incommensurate worldviews and constitutes the fundamental fault line in the present American culture war.

Homosexuality

There are few subjects as controversial in both the society at large and within the Catholic Church as the subject of homosexuality. Historically, within the American nation, it is fair to assert that homosexuality, at least until relatively recently, has been viewed generally by the American population, variously, as either (or both) "sinful" or "unnatural." The sinful designation can be viewed best against a backdrop of a taken-for-granted conservative Christian (primarily Protestant, but including Catholic and Eastern Orthodox Christian) *religious* understanding of reality.

The possible exception, early in American history, to the negative interpretation of homosexuality would most likely be found among those American elites influenced by Enlightenment or Deist ideas. However relatively disproportionately influential such thinkers may have been, their attitudes were not representative of the average Protestant and Catholic "man in the street" (or, more likely, "on the farm").

The "unnatural" designation has two distinct but related sources, one being American *culture* affirming the value of heterosexuality. The other is the acceptance of the *natural law*, in either its high culture (usually Catholic), or low culture, person-in-the-streets versions. At base, both versions—the former in a more articulate and self-conscious fashion—make the case that human reason (and its associated faculties) leads to the conclusion that homosexuality is not only, literally speaking, unnatural but has demonstrable dysfunctional consequences for both the individuals who practice it (hedonism, suicide, mental illness, premature death, AIDS, etc.) and for the general civilization (breakdown of the intact nuclear family, population reduction, dysfunctions for military, etc.) when that practice becomes significantly institutionalized into everyday life.

Since the mid-1960s, attitudes in the general society toward homosexuality have been changing in the direction of greater tolerance, especially in certain sectors. Indeed, an important sliver of America has offered the homosexual lifestyle significant approval and, in a few cases, a higher status than that of heterosexuality. This is what sociologists call a "new knowledge class" of elites consisting of college professors, government bureaucrats, and those in the mass media and arts. These professions are all united as a distinct sector in American life because they are involved in the production and manipulation of ideas and constitute what some sociologists (Berger and Kellner 1974) call a "knowledge industry." Many in the knowledge industry define themselves as a kind of societal avant-guard, with issues of sexual experimentation and liberation most definitely included. Another influential sector of American life, the moderate progressive element of the middle class, does not so much as endorse the homosexual lifestyle but evinces great tolerance of it. This is the "it's not my cup of tea, but if it's OK with you, it doesn't bother me" reaction, a reaction strongest in that sector of American life most accepting of what the philosopher Allan Bloom (1987) and the sociologist John Cuddihy (1978) have referred to, respectively, as the philosophy of moral, cultural, and religious relativism and that of "offering no offense" to lifestyles not one's own.

There are, of course, many Americans who still basically disapprove of homosexuality for the reasons previously stated. This group is strongest among religious conservatives and traditionalists. As the United States turned into the twenty-first century, a fair estimate would be that the country is more or less evenly split on the issue, consistent with the lines of the general culture war and the closeness of the 2000 and 2004 presidential elections between, respectively, Vice-President Al Gore and Texas governor George W. Bush and Senator John Kerry and President George W. Bush. It is important to point out, however, that even those generally opposed to homosexuality overwhelmingly do not desire homosexuals to be subject to various forms of overt abuse; they just do not want homosexuality to become publically normalized. In this regard, it is also interesting to observe that, in 2004, approximately 60 percent of Americans are against the legalization of same-sex marriage. In the 2004 national election, all eleven state referendums rejected the opportunity to legalize same-sex marriage.

On the other hand, two of the more progressive states in the Union, Massachusetts and Connecticut, have moved to legalize same-sex marriages. Many other states and many other Americans, while stopping short of supporting same-sex marriage, do advocate civil unions. The issue of the normalization of homosexuality and the legalization of homosexual marriage and civil unions is presently much in active and contentious debate in the country. The ultimate resolution, if there is to be an ultimate resolution, remains very much an open question.

The general culture war over the issue of homosexuality naturally finds its correlate within the Catholic Church and the Catholic people. Given the official position of the Catholic Church that the homosexual act is "objectively disordered" and "sinful," internal progressive Catholic opposition to the official doctrinal stance oftentimes takes on a latent and "behind the scenes," quality but represents real and effective opposition nonetheless. The debate within the Church and among Catholics involves at least four fronts.

The first is doctrinal, that is, over what the magisterial Church teaches about homosexuality. The second is the theoretical versus practical implication that this contested doctrinal position involves regarding such issues as the ordination of clergy (priests and deacons), the formation of religious life (sisters/nuns and brothers), and in the hiring, employment, and retention policies toward both clergy and lay people who occupy the thousands of positions within the Church's various bureaucracies, ministries, and apostolates. The third battlefront is for the minds and hearts of the American Catholic people. The final area of contention regarding homosexuality is in the Church efforts in forging social policy affecting both American civilization and the American public square.

Doctrinally and officially, the Church's position, as enunciated in a definitive magisterial document such as the Congregation for the Doctrine of the Faith's "Letter to the Bishops of the Catholic Church on the Pastoral Care of Homosexual Persons" (1986), is clear: homosexual activity is both sinful and objectively disordered. In terms of religious status, however, chaste Catholic homosexuals are to be treated indistinguishably from chaste Catholic heterosexuals. Furthermore, while active homosexual acts are considered immoral and unnatural, the active homosexual nonetheless continues to be the object of Christ's love and respect and that of his Church also. As it is often said, the Church "loves the sinner but hates the sin." It is important to point out immediately that almost all progressive and secular thinkers reject the latter distinction, many times claiming it either as unreal or as a mark of hypocrisy.

The official doctrinal position of the Catholic Church finds significant opposition not only in many religious orders, seminaries, dioceses, and colleges and universities but also, perhaps of a more covert, "at the edges" and subtle but real nature within the various committees of the United States Conference of Catholic Bishops staffed by prominent members of what was referred to previously as the "new Catholic knowledge class." Such opposition, most recently, was manifest through a 1997 statement of the bishops' committee on marriage and family titled "Always Our Children: A Pastoral Message to Parents of Homosexual Children and Suggestions for Pastoral Ministers." It should be emphasized that this statement was *not* a creature of any consensus of the Catholic bishops of the United States but by a bureaucratic and quite progressive committee within the bishops' conference. Such a fact is quite consistent with a sociological literature citing the disproportionate influence of internal, elite, and unrepresentative cliques on the larger organization in which they are embedded. According to Bishop Fabian W. Bruskewitz (1998), perhaps America's most up-front orthodox Catholic bishop and a very persistent critic of the bishops' conference, "Always Our Children" pretends "falsely and preposterously that the *Catechism* . . . [*of the Catholic Church*] . . . says homosexuality is a gift from God . . . (and) . . . totally neglected to cite the Catholic doctrine set forth by the Holy See which teaches that the homosexual orientation is 'objectively disordered.' Also, the document's definition of the virtue and practice of chastity is inadequate and distorted. . . . The character of this document is such that it would require a book of many pages to point out all its bad features, which sometimes cross the border from poor advice to evil advice." The point in bringing up the critique of Bishop Bruskewitz is merely to highlight the fact that official Catholic doctrine on homosexuality (like our previous and more general discussion over the battle for the meaning of the Second Vatican Council) is being actively contested by different wings of the Church institution. The end result of this seemingly never-ending contestation of ideas and claims is confusion among the Catholic population at large as to what is the real position of the religious tradition and the diluting of the impact of the Church's official religious worldview on American civilization and the American public sphere of life.

The contested nature of the Church's position on homosexuality has had major implications for the Catholic Church of the United States during the post–Vatican II period. Given that it was the progressive cardinals' (Dearden–Bernardin) wing that emerged victorious—and has held onto its hegemonic status within the institution until recently—the Church's official position on homosexuality has been ignored widely or at least underplayed internally. Michael Rose, in his controversial treatise, *Goodbye, Good Men: How Liberals Brought Corruption into the*

Catholic Church (2002), has argued that active homosexuality has been encouraged or allowed to exist within the life of clergy and priesthood at both the parish and the seminary level. Orthodox Catholic critics such as Monsignor Michael Wrenn (1991) and Monsignor Michael Wrenn and Kenneth Whitehead (1996) have also substantiated the reality that large parts of a liberal "catechetical establishment" have refused to teach the official Church line on homosexuality and on a host of other hot-button doctrinal issues. Monsignor George A. Kelly (1995) and many other orthodox Catholic observers of the scene have similarly catalogued the active dissent from Catholic doctrinal teaching promoted at many Catholic institutions of Catholic higher education. The end result of all this has led to the failure of the Catholic Church to present accurately and effectively its understanding and rationale on the issues surrounding homosexuality to either its own membership or to American civilization at large.

The results of dissent are reflected in the attitudes and behavior of the American Catholic population, which now do little more than basically mirror on homosexuality and other moral and sexual issues the previously discussed divisions of American civilization. Again, some Catholic elites (including some bishops, priests, religious, and Church personnel) have actually embraced the homosexual lifestyle or laud it as a special gift given to an unofficially declared "chosen people." A significant percentage of the Catholic middle class, while rejecting it as a personal option for themselves/their children, accept is as a legitimated societal-wide option. Orthodox Catholics—reflecting their acceptance of authentic Catholic education—and many working-class through lower-middle-class Catholics reject homosexual behavior and view it as, in some sense, pathological/sinful. Overall, it is probably fair to conclude that, as of the present moment in the year 2005, if the current movement to the normalization of homosexuality is to be stopped or reversed, it will be far more the result of a re-energized and conservative Protestant-dominated "Christian Right" than it will be from the efforts of the Catholic Church and the American Catholic population at large.

The final front in the battle over homosexuality involves issues of legality, politics, and social policy. Homosexual activists have it in their interests to define "homophobia" in the broadest possible way and to make, as such, what they define as homophobic acts or sentiments illegal or, at least, socially taboo. Orthodox Catholicism would acknowledge the reality of homophobic acts that are ethically wrong and, in some cases, illegal but would define the reality in a far more limited and constrained manner. Father John Harvey (1987, 1989), for instance, has defined homophobia as any "unreasonable fear" or "insane reaction" to homosexuality. As Father Harvey states, "in all cases, the genuine Christian condemns the intolerant, violent, murderous attitude toward the homosexual person. But . . . [he/she] . . . does not hesitate to condemn homosexual acts, nor does . . . [he/she] . . . shun the duty of protecting persons, especially youth, from being victimized by homosexual activists or a homosexual culture" (1989, 126). From a Catholic frame, homophobic behavior like assault and verbal abuse must be condemned in no uncertain terms while homosexual behavior is to be viewed as disordered and producing many dysfunctional consequences for both the individual and society.

Homosexual activists, given the general secularization of American civilization and the weakened cultural and political status of the Catholic Church, continue to make impressive inroads in gaining the full equality under law and cultural normalization that they desire. This concerted movement is supported by many American citizens, including many American Catholics, who think that it is unconstitutional or simply unfair to deny rights given to heterosexual couples to homosexual couples. President George Bush's call for an amendment to the Constitution defining marriage as the union between one man and one woman was recently supported by a statement from the bishops of the United States (but defeated in its first attempt in a U.S. Senate vote in July 2004 by a vote of 48 for to 50 against). An important point to consider is just what (little) weight the bishops' statement holds with both the American Catholic people and the American population at large.

Religious Education

The purpose of Catholic religious education or "catechesis" is the handing on of an authentic interpretation of the Catholic faith to the Catholic populace, other interested non-Catholic parties, and to the future generations. The problem or "rub," so to speak, is over the issue of what exactly constitutes an authentic interpretation of the faith. As noted earlier, in the immediate postconciliar years, the progressive wing of the Church in the United States at odds with a magisterial understanding of the faith in either quality or degree, won "the battle over the significance of Vatican II." Constitutive of this progressive wing are the claims that "individualism" and "conscience" trump "tradition" and "law," that "experience" is core to religion while "doctrine" is superficial, that religious and moral relativism must be respected while claims to absolute truth are viewed unnecessarily restrictive and narrow; and that "social justice" issues (implemented almost invariably along quasi socialist lines) are far more central to the faith than are "spiritual" and "liturgical" ones (Varacalli 2001). What Monsignor Michael J. Wrenn in his *Catechisms and Controversies: Religious Education in the Postconciliar Years* (1991) has termed the "catechetical establishment" has been a big part in fomenting change along progressive lines in the Catholic Church during the period from the mid-1960s to the early 1990s

Aided and abetted by this catechetical establishment, the progressive dominance during the postconciliar years—and consistent with earlier discussions in this volume—led to a Catholic Church in the United States emphasizing, or at least manifesting sympathy to, left-wing interpretations on such issues as the role of the Catholic university and college, the theology of liberation, ecumenism, the autonomy of the Catholic politician and voter, birth control, the ordination of women, homosexuality, and abortion, among others. Put another way, this period saw the acceptance, on the part of both establishment and nominal Catholics alike, of Father Andrew M. Greeley's discussion and advocacy of the concept of a "selective," "pick and choose," "cafeteria-style" "communal Catholicism" in which the 2,000-year-old Catholic heritage, at very best, serves as a mere "resource" for the Catholic individual or, at very worst, can be simply rejected, *tout court*. From a magisterial-oriented Catholic perspective, this was a period of institutionalized dissent in which the Catholic plausibility structure was both weakened and taken over by those who desired to transform thoroughly the religious institution.

Magisterial forces led by John Paul II, Cardinal Joseph Ratzinger (now Pope Benedict XVI), and others put forth the response that a key presupposition for restoring the Catholic tradition would be the creation and widespread distribution of a universal teaching tool regarding the essentials of the Catholic faith. This turned out to be *The Catechism of the Catholic Church*, published in 1994 and the first of its kind in over 400 years, which was intended to counter the excessive movement of decentralization, pluralism, and individuation unleashed by the progressive implementation of the documents of Vatican II. Unsurprisingly, there was significant opposition to the *Catechism* on the part of progressive scholars and catechetical personnel who saw themselves, in the words of Monsignor Wrenn, as a "new Church magisterium or co-magisterium" (1991, 64). Writing just before the publication of the universal catechism, Monsignor Wrenn predicted that:

> Once the *Catechism for the Universal Church* is finally in place and official, it will never be quite so easy for free-wheeling theologians and scholars to "freewheel" again. . . . And not just theologians and scholars either. Catechists and teachers of religion at every level in the Church will necessarily be held to stricter account in what they are teaching, once there is an overall standard or "point of reference." For it is only too true that catechesis, or the teaching of the faith, has been seriously affected by the unprecedented dissent that has been evident in the Church over the past quarter century, especially since the encyclical *Humanae Vitae*. This era has been characterized by unprecedented confusion in both the manner and the matter of teaching the faith. (1991, 76)

Monsignor Wrenn's prognosis has proven to be right on the mark. The "freewheeling" nature of progressive interpretations of Catholic tradition have been trimmed significantly since the publication of the *Catechism*, although certainly not eliminated. To the degree that "personnel equals policy," there will always been some tendency to articulate liberal interpretations of Catholic doctrine as long as liberals continue to control and populate the key components and locations of the Catholic plausibility structure.

The Controversy Over Mel Gibson's *The Passion of the Christ*: The Culture War in Play in both American Society and within the Catholic Community

The production and release of Mel Gibson's film, *The Passion of the Christ*, during 2004 represented a sociological phenomenon of importance for students of both the American and American Catholic experience. It is one of the most talked about and hotly debated films of recent memory in the United States. Gibson's film depicts the standard traditional account of the Catholic Church of the trial, scourging, and crucifixion of Jesus Christ.

The controversy that surrounded it begs for it to be incorporated into an analysis of the present-day "culture war" taking place within the larger civilization (Hunter 1991) and the Catholic Church in the United States (Kelly 1979) between, more specifically, what I've termed the "progressive modernizers" and the "orthodox ecclesialists" (Varacalli 2005). For one thing, most of the individuals who are, respectively, critical and supportive of the film would take quite similar positions on such other key issues as homosexuality, abortion, and school vouchers. The critics of Mel Gibson's movie come from the ranks of Jews (with the exception of some Orthodox Jews), liberal Protestants, secularists, and liberal Catholics. Conversely, the two groups most strongly supporting *The Passion of the Christ* has been orthodox Catholics and evangelical Protestants, with Eastern Orthodox Christians (e.g., Russian Orthodoxy, Greek Orthodoxy, etc.) also mostly being supportive of the film. (It is important to point out the limited nature of this traditional religious coalition; it extends only to cultural and political issues given the religiously exclusivist claims of the various religions that are orthodox in nature.)

For Gibson's supporters, the opposition to the film represents an opportunity for the "progressive camp" to register a fundamental blow against the plausibility and truthfulness of traditional Catholicism and Christianity. Orthodox Catholics would claim, likewise, that the film's critics—primarily liberal and reform/conservative Jews and liberal Catholics—are the same as those who view Pope Pius XII as either anti-Semitic or indifferent to the plight of the Jews in the face of Adolf Hitler's monstrously murderous activities during World War II. Defenders of the film, moreover, claim a double standard on the part of America's progressive cultural elite as some celebrated, for instance, Martin Scorsese's film *The Last Temptation of Christ* while at the same time condemning the effort of Gibson. Gibson's defenders also question why so little attention has been focused on the artistic quality (or lack of quality) of the film instead of it being used—it is claimed—excessively as a standard to judge anti-Semitism, bigotry, and religious fundamentalism.

Some of Gibson's critics claim that his film lends itself to the collective blaming of Jews for the death of Jesus and, as such, stands as an indictment against the Catholic religion and traditional Christianity. Critics claim that the movie is unfair in its depiction of the Jewish religious authorities of the time, especially the head rabbi, Caiaphas. The claim has also been made that the film is permeated with anti-Semitic images while the character of the Roman leader, Pontius Pilate, is portrayed in a much more sympathetic light. Some on the progressive side of the barricades profess that the Gospel claim of the involvement of Jewish authorities in events leading to the death of Christ are themselves historically inaccurate. Some go further claiming that the Gospel accounts of the Passion of Jesus Christ are themselves anti-Semitic. Defenders of the film provide several counterarguments. One is that all the characters in the film, save Jesus Christ and a few other figures like Mary, are portrayed in a less than fully positive light consistent with the Christian claims regarding all humans being tainted by the effects of original sin. Another is that Jewish religious tradition itself admits to the involvement of Jewish authorities in the trial of Christ in the form of such sources as the Talmud and the respected Jewish philosopher and sage, Maimonides. Another is the argument that the film could not possibly be anti-Semitic simply because all the characters—minus the Romans—are Jewish themselves (e.g., Mary, John, Mary Magdalen, Veronica, the Good Thief, Simon of Cyrene, Joseph of Arimathea) and, furthermore, were portrayed in a positive light. The Gospel accounts of *The Passion of the Christ*, then according to this logic, are not actually reflective of anti-Semitism but of an internecine battle between establishment (Caiaphas) and antiestablishment (Jesus Christ) wings of the Judaism of the era that only eventually led to the formation of a new religion, that is, Christianity. Some defenders of the film also wonder if, *sub rosa*, one major source of Jewish opposition to the film is to be found in the fact that Christianity claims the existence of a "new convenant" between God and man, one, that not destroying the "old covenant" between Jews and God, nonetheless claimed to supercede it. Furthermore, the defenders of the film claim that it is the Roman soldiers who come off as the most inhuman in their treatment of Jesus and the Jewish population.

Critics of the film claim that it will spur violence against Jews in the United States and in Europe and throughout the world much like some passion plays did in the Europe of the Middle Ages. If true, this brings up the issue of whether or not *The Passion of the Christ* (or similar Christian classics such as *The King of Kings, Barabbas,* and *The Greatest Story Ever Told*) should be banned or at least stigmatized and marginalized. Defenders of the film claim that the message of the film *reduces*, not inflames, hatred between religions and groups that differ, in part at least, in their worldviews. A related issue here involves the indisputable fact that, in European society past, a significant number of Catholics (and other Christians) did blame the Jewish people for the death of Christ. The question, however, is whether this anti-Semitism is reflective of official Catholic Church teaching? Critics of the film claim that anti-Semitism came directly from the bosom of the Catholic Church until the Second Vatican Council and the airing of the film represents a return to anti-Semitism. Those opposed to this claim argue that anti-Semitism derives from neither the film nor from official Catholic Church teaching. As many orthodox Catholic theologians and lay people point out, millions of Christians every Sunday at Mass repeat publically the Nicene Creed that states that Jesus Christ "suffered under Pontius Pilate, was crucified, died, and was buried" therefore casting no official Church blame for the death of Jesus on the Jewish people, then or now. Rather, as orthodox Christians claim, the undeniable instances of anti-Semitism that either historically existed or exist presently are a function of individual ignorance and bigotry and of other "socializing" factors (e.g., ethnic and tribal allegiances, socioeconomic factors, cultural attitudes, etc.) that affect the thought and behavior of those who are only "nominally Catholic" in their religious commitments. A key question here is how will the controversy over the film affect Jewish-Christian relations?

Members of the progressive side of the barricades in the culture war also claim that the film is unnecessarily violent and sadomasochistic. Would the film spur on spontaneous acts of violence like those that allegedly occurred to have happened after a viewing of the film *Fort Apache—The Bronx*? Those on the orthodox Christian side respond that the violence was necessary to show the extraordinary lengths that Jesus Christ—for Christians, the son of God and God himself—went to in order to provide the opportunity for mankind to enter the realm of Heaven. Many traditional Christians made the argument that the violent nature of the scouring and crucifixion of Christ is justified as both being historically accurate and necessary to convey the meaning and logic of the Christian message. Yet other traditional Christians went a step further arguing that no amount of violence could satisfactorily address the Christian claim that God died so that his creation could live; for these Christians, the film was simply not violent enough. All traditional Christians claim that seeing the film and witnessing to the demonstration of love and sacrifice that Christ has for all his children will reduce violence and engender sorrow and contrition in recognizing personal sin. Supporters of the film provide an abundance of anecdotal evidence that the almost universal reaction to the film is one of stunned silence, punctuated only by occasional crying and sobbing. Gibson's defenders also point out what they see as a major hypocrisy on the part of those who condemn the violence in *The Passion of the Christ* yet, at the same time, have consistently remained silent over decades of witnessing Hollywood films featuring sexuality, violence, and murder.

Any cultural analysis of the film would also have to address the question as to the significance of the fact that it is one of the best-selling movies in all history. Critics of the film claim that the film has proven to be of sincere interest to only the already converted, that is, to orthodox Catholics, Orthodox Christians, and conservative evangelical Protestants. The large number of movie ticket sales, the progressive critics claim, is only a function of the controversial nature of the film. Some progressives may also actually feel that the film sold so well at the box office because of the claim that American civilization is still characterized by a widespread and diffuse anti-Semitism in American civilization. Defenders of the film claim that its success is attributable to the fact that there is an enormous religious audience in American society that yearns for films that faithfully and professionally portray movies of spiritual and ethical import or, in the case of the movie under analysis, of what many call "the greatest story every told."

Another issue that must be addressed is the significance of the fact that many Hollywood insiders and members of America's cultural elite made great—although ultimately failing—efforts to condemn and marginalize the film and its production and distribution so difficult. Progressives argue that opposition to the film was a sign on the part of Hollywood to protect the American citizenry against anti-Semitism and a violent and harmful film. The orthodox respond, regarding the anti-Semitism claim, by noting that the Academy Awards recently honored Leni Riefenstahl, a propaganda filmmaker for Adolf Hitler. The orthodox response regarding the violence claim is simply to draw attention to the undeniable number of violent films that Hollywood has produced without a hint of opposition. The orthodox claim that Hollywood and the cultural elite are obviously attempting to impose a left-wing morality on the American public and wants not to provide authentically Christian films a chance to survive and perhaps thrive in the marketplace of ideas. (It is important to note that some progressives might point to earlier periods in the history of American film when there was a strong conservative bias prejudicial to a liberal worldview.)

The issue of the explicit and implicit threats of Hollywood elites and insiders to blackball Mel Gibson from ever working again with major production companies is another issue of interest in a cultural analysis. The orthodox wing of the culture war claims that the threat is not ethical and, moreover, that it is hypocritical given Hollywood's previous objections to what it terms a "McCarthyism" of a previous era in American history. Will such a blackball succeed, or has Mel Gibson led a successful revolt again a Hollywood monopoly? Will major movie production companies support future traditionally religious projects by Mel Gibson or by producers and directors with similar philosophies? Or has Mel Gibson provided an end-run around such monopolies, demonstrating how independent films can compete successfully against media goliaths, and perhaps eventually forcing them to change their sponsorship priorities?

Has Mel Gibson's film led to conversions to Christianity or to the strengthening of a dormant/nominal Christianity in others? If it does, how will it then impact on the nature of the cultural war, including national, regional, and local political elections? Was the 2004 presidential victory of George W. Bush, who energized so effectively the "orthodox-ecclesial" sectors of Americans society, a harbinger of things to come?

Dissecting the Sexual Scandal in the Contemporary Catholic Church

As the Catholic Church in the United States turned into the twenty-first century, it was rocked by revelations of sex abuse perpetuated on young children and, very much more so, on teenage youth by a statistically small percentage but, in absolute numbers, a not insignificant number of clergy, religious, and other Church personnel. Compounding this evil greatly was the apparent fact that many times the offending parties were hidden from detection, shuffled from location to location in lieu of being removed, and protected from religious/moral and legal punishment by ecclesiastical leadership. These combined and very ugly realities seemed to cap a general downward trend in the societal respect afforded the Catholic Church in America over the past forty years.

The many issues involved in the contemporary crisis in the Catholic Church with a focus on the sexual scandals can be analyzed from competing perspectives. Questions abound. What *precisely* is the *nature* of the scandal? What are the various *causes* of the scandal and how are they to be respectively *weighted*? How *deep* is the scandal? What *corrective actions* have or should be taken? What are the *realistic prospects* that continual and future corrective actions will be taken? Can the priesthood and ecclesial office *recover*? What have been the various roles or functions that the *mass media* have taken during the scandal? Can the Church *reform* herself given its present leadership in the United States? Will the lines of that reform be some version of a *Protestantization* in terms of either doctrine or organization? Or could the reform be in the direction of a reaffirmation and revitalization of the Catholic tradition, of a *dynamic orthodoxy*, of a Church both eternal and eternally young?

Two sets of quite similar distinctions made by the social scientists James D. Hunter in his *Culture Wars* (1991) and Monsignor George A. Kelly in his *The Battle for the American Church* (1979) provide one useful way to start to grapple intelligently with the set of issues previously enunciated. For his part, Hunter makes the case that American civilization is presently torn between two disparate factions and worldviews, which he terms, respectively, the "progressive" and the "orthodox." The progressive worldview is essentially based on an Enlightenment understanding of an unfettered and nonsupernaturally based reason, "autonomous individualism," and ultimately that social reality is nothing more than a social construction that can and does constantly change. The orthodox worldview is based on some combination of the Judaic-Christian heritage and natural law thinking and is anchored by a belief that there are certain absolute truths that must be accepted and followed. Focusing on internal affairs within the Catholic Church, Kelly likewise notes that the battle is between what he calls the "modernizers" and the "ecclesialists." For Kelly, the modernizers stress religious immanence, experience, relativity, and pragmatism. The ecclesialists stress religious transcendence, revealed doctrine, the essential role of the Church for salvation, and the nonnegotiable requirement of obedience to the plan of God. Hunter and Kelly are basically dealing with the perennial question of the relationship between society and religion or, more specifically, referring to the work of the theologian H. R. Niebuhr (1951), between Christianity and the surrounding culture. For immediate purposes, the Hunter and Kelly distinctions can be combined and termed, respectively, the *progressive modernizers* and the *orthodox ecclesialists*. The usual qualifiers apply whenever utilizing any type of "ideal typical" sociological analysis as discussed by Max Weber (1946, 1947); ideal types are artificial constructs that are useful in pointing out general tendencies in the civilization. In this case, the terms refer to endpoints in the relationship between the Catholic Church and American civilization. Moreover, these visions are accepted in their pristine versions by only significant slivers of the Catholic population. A majority of Catholics occupy, following Hunter's phrase, a "muddled middle" in which ambivalence, contradiction, indifference, and, on occasion, creative synthesis are characteristic. Indeed, a key issue is whether there is a possible "common ground" between these two worldviews or if they are basically incommensurate. The distinctions are offered as a way, again, to initiate an intelligent discussion of the issues involved in an analysis of the state of the Church and of the sexual scandal leaving plenty of room for later rethinking and reformulation.

These two camps/worldviews tend to see the crisis in the Catholic Church and the associated sexual scandal quite differently on many issues. The progressive modernizers tend to emphasize the key evil as the bishops' cover-up or inactivity in response to the scandal which, in turn, is viewed as a reflection of an allegedly outdated and self-serving oligarchy and hierarchical mode of Church governance. This group would have no problem in accepting enthusiastically the claim of the liberal English Catholic historian Lord Acton that "power tends to corrupt and absolute power corrupts absolutely." Conversely put, what is needed to uncover wrongdoing—sexual, financial, doctrinal, or otherwise—is the acceptance of democracy within the internals of the faith along with its natural correlate, a congregational style of leadership in which the laity and lower echelon clergy and religious are central in decision making. Whatever the pitfalls of attempting to bring democracy to the internals of Catholicism, liberals would argue the attempt is worth it. Democracy is viewed from this perspective as superior to all other empirical alternatives in governing. (Students of American Catholic history might recall the arguments made in favor of congregationalism in the early nineteenth-century controversy over the issue of trusteeism.)

The response of the orthodox ecclesialists is neither that one should ignore nor deny the evil involved in bureaucratic cover-ups—religious or otherwise—but to argue that it is not intrinsic to episcopal leadership per se. Rather it is a function not of any particular system of government but of individuals who fail to carry out their assigned duties. Catholic tradition makes the claim that God makes available to the bishops the necessary graces to lead the Church faithfully and with integrity but only if the bishops cooperate with God's plan and are themselves aligned faithfully with the mind of the Church. Further, the orthodox ecclesialists would not be sanguine about the alleged salutary effects of incorporating lay and lower echelon clergy/religious leadership into Church decision making if that same leadership itself is not religiously formed or socialized into an authentic Catholic worldview. Extrapolating from numerous poll data available, one can conclude that perhaps there are no more than 20 percent of the laity who are in fundamental agreement with the mind of the Church, if one defines the mind of the Church as consistent with magisterial thought. For the orthodox ecclesialists, an unfaithful or doctrinally ignorant laity/clergy/religious is no improvement over an unfaithful episcopal leadership. Indeed, sociologically, the orthodox ecclesialists might well claim that such a democratization of the Church really constitutes no movement toward true democracy at all. Rather, empirically, it would represent a variation of what the classical Italian sociologist Vilfredo Pareto (1965) termed a "circulation of elites" with a dissenting intellectual class replacing an ineffective class of bishops, including some dissenting bishops, in what constitutes a simple, naked power play.

Another issue in which the "progressive modernizers" versus "orthodox ecclesialists" distinction is useful in analyzing the crisis in the Catholic Church and its scandal concerns the issue of the *extent* of the internal corruption within the priesthood and other Church personnel. By implication and by emphasis, the progressive modernizers do not see the corruption as widespread or systemic beyond the current group of bishops; indeed to make such a claim would be to cast light on the consequences of a selective liberal Catholic (and, in many cases, heterodox) interpretation of the Second Vatican Council on the priesthood and the state of Catholicism itself. The progressive modernizers here take one of two tracks. The relatively small number of offending clergy/personnel are either (1) *spiritually or psychologically dysfunctional* or (2) the logical result of the flawed and *sexually repressive anthropology* of the Church. The first answer sees the problem in individualistic and psychological (as compared to cultural/social movement) terms. The second answer assumes a quasi Freudian understanding of sexuality in which the offending parties are the vanguard victims of a disastrous discipline/policy of celibacy as the sexual lid boiled over the pot for at least a few. The "solution" to the first is to eliminate or reform democratically the allegedly self-serving, inward authority structure of the Church with the supposed result being that a new democratized leadership would be more vigilant and faithful in removing dysfunctional priests. Two commonly referred to "solutions" to the second are to allow a married priesthood and to ordain women as priests. The hypothetical end result of these combined solutions supposedly would be the creation of a more modern, pluralistic, democratic, and "relevant" Church, and the reduction, if not elimination, of instances of nonconsensual sex with children.

For the orthodox ecclesialists, both the crisis in the Church and its associated sexual scandals are more extensive than depicted in the worldview of the progressive modernizers and are also seen to be, at base, *cultural* and the unintended consequence of a liberal Catholic social movement with a constitutive focus on sexual liberation. The roots of the crisis, so this logic goes, are *not* to be found *primarily* within individual pathologies or psychological disorders but within an institutionalized *culture of dissent*. The latter itself is viewed as the result of a quite calculating liberal Catholic takeover, during the period from the mid-1960s through the 1980s, of the social institutions of the Church in America. This takeover was aided and abetted by the majority coalition of progressive Catholic bishops in power during that time frame. It was further spurred on by the Bishops' Bicentennial Program (1973–83), with its centerpiece Call to Action conference (1976) which was so crucial in spawning a liberal Catholic social movement that had, at least as part of its agenda, sexual liberation. That the remnant of the episcopal leadership that controlled the American Church at the time and was so indispensable in furthering the progressive modernizer movement is included by the same liberal progressives in the current general attack on bishops is viewed by the orthodox ecclesialists as a delicious irony and regarded by those on the left as a typical concession to the demands of "realpolitik."

For the orthodox ecclesialists, furthermore, the roots of the crisis/scandal are not only cultural and social, but also run deep. They are certainly deeper than the claim of some progressives, both secular and religious, that the sexual scandal involves primarily cases of pedophilia; all the available evidence (Jenkins 2003, esp. chap. 7) is that the overwhelming percentage of sexual abuse cases involve homosexual acts with teenage youth. The orthodox ecclesialists, following at least the rough outline of Michael Rose's *Goodbye, Good Men: How Liberals Brought Corruption into the Catholic Church* (2002), would point to the dramatic increase of active homosexuals into the priesthood over the past forty years and, conversely, the systematic discrimination against orthodox Catholic, sexually straight men entering the seminaries as a major cause of the scandal. According to Rose, for instance, in some seminaries under liberal control, orthodox sexually straight candidates for the priesthood are weeded out during the application/interview process or later encouraged to leave if they somehow gained entrance into the priestly formation program. The logic of the orthodox ecclesialist is not, however, to focus ultimately on the issue of an active homosexual invasion of the priesthood. Rather, the ultimate cause of the problem is viewed as the rejection, on the part of a significant percentage of the priests and other personnel who run the Church's social institutions during the immediate post–Vatican II generation, of the basic doctrines of the Catholic Church, especially those that deal with sexual morality. Too many priests and Church personnel have accepted, from this perspective, the modern American idea of an "autonomous individualism," that, in the final analysis, the ultimate locus of authority resides with the individual embedded in a fundamentally secular society that rejects received revelation and the dictates of conformity to the natural law. The problem is deep for the orthodox ecclesialist then, because the sexual abuse scandal, as evil and wrong as it is, represents for him/her only the egregious tip of an iceberg capable of sinking the Church into oblivion. The crisis within the Church fundamentally is viewed as a *widespread crisis of faith*; a rejection of the idea that what the Catholic Church has consistently taught over the ages is true. For every sexual abuse case, then, there are presumably many more cases of "consensual" heterosexual and homosexual affairs between priests or between priests and parishioners. And, regardless of the issue of personal involvement in sexual scandal, even more prevalent would be the doctrinal dissent perpetuated by priests and Church personnel through their official capacities within the Church. Over the past forty years, from this perspective, the Catholic Church has suffered a massive "secularization from within" with the sexual scandals representing only an externally visible sore on an otherwise diseased body.

Two caveats are immediately in order. The orthodox ecclesialists would not deny that, even at the height of the actual offenses committed, there were innumerable faithful, devoted, and competent bishops, priests and Church personnel serving the Church with distinction and honor. The point to be made, however, is that by, the mid-1980s, the dissenters represented enough of a "critical mass" to weaken severely the Church's ability to serve as a needed leaven for an ever increasing materialistic, utilitarian, and morally relativistic society descending into what John Paul II has referred to as a "culture of death." Second, the high-water mark of dissent has, in all probability, passed. For one thing, the social scientific evidence is that the Church's latest cohorts of priests, seminarians, and nuns in the United States—as modest as these numbers are vis-à-vis the 1950s—are, in the main, both orthodox and sophisticated. And there also has been something of an orthodox renaissance, both intellectually and organizationally, over the past two decades bubbling just under the social radar screen that offers promise for rebuilding the Church down the road. But no one, at least according to the orthodox ecclesial perspective, should underestimate the daunting and unenviable task of putting all the pieces back together again after the post–Vatican II decomposition and restoring integrity to the Catholic house, a task that will necessarily entail cooperative efforts between a laity seeking out saintliness both within the Church and the world and courageous leadership from the current crop of American bishops who would have to be willing to crack more than a few eggs in the restoration process. It is fair to say that most orthodox ecclesialists are more immediately optimistic regarding the former possibility, namely, the revitalization efforts of an orthodox laity energized and ready to rise to the evangelistic demands of the present situation. They believe that they must, in the short run at least, lead the reformation of the Church given both that the problems of dissent are too entrenched within a substantial portion of the hierarchy and that the type of bishop promoted to the episcopate during the past forty years is characterized generally by an overly cautious, bureaucratic-insider, and small-thinking mentality.

Yet another issue in which the two models would produce at least different emphases in interpretation would be on the role that the mass media has played during the scandal. It is important to point out in initiating this discussion that *both* the progressive modernizers and the orthodox ecclesialists would agree that the causes of the scandal are to be found *within* the Church herself and are not mere fabrications of a hostile cultural elite. And both sides are thankful that the mass media has helped to uncover and make public the evil involved in a scandal spanning decades. However, insofar as it has concentrated attention on the gross negligence of the bishops and has depicted the sexual abuse cases as that of pedophilia while, at the same time, ignoring the roles that the culture of dissent and active homosexuality have played in the scandals, the mass media has been cooperating, at whatever level of self-conscious awareness, more with the agenda of the progressive modernizers. Solid social scientific evidence has well documented that the mass media hold values that are far more liberal than that of the population at large, and therefore are sympathetic with the progressive modernizer cause. One need not be a sociologist of knowledge to understand that such considerations as motivation, topic selection, tacit philosophy embraced, language chosen, evidence accepted, mode of interpretation, and social policies recommended, color all intellectual activity, the journalistic enterprise included.

There is one final issue in which the progressive modernizer versus orthodox ecclesialist distinction might provide different and varying interpretations regarding the sexual scandal. The issue involves the *motivation* for the bishops covering up the sordid details of the scandal and for not taking immediate corrective and punitive actions against the perpetuators of abuse. A list of possible generic motivations would include: (1) to "protect" the name of the institution; (2) to "protect" Church personnel, in the sense of any organization "taking care of its brotherhood"; (3) to allow time for the sexual offenders to be psychologically rehabilitated; (4) to allow time for the indelible mark of sacramental grace of the office of the priesthood to reassert itself given that "once a priest always a priest"; (5) to protect individuals whose understanding of the nature and direction of the Church the local ordinary has personal sympathy with; (6) more specifically, to protect individuals whose philosophy of sexual liberation the local ordinary has personal sympathy for; (7) to protect the bishop himself from blackmail, either due to some doctrinal violation the bishop himself has perpetuated/allowed or because he himself is an active homosexual or active homosexual involved in child abuse; and (8) to protect the culture of dissent promoted by the contemporary Catholic knowledge class because at least a few bishops are themselves active co-conspirators in the rejection of the historic faith.

Again, let it be restated that both the progressive modernizers and the orthodox ecclesialists, in light of recent disclosures associated with the scandals, have demonstrated empirically hostility to the bishops. For the former, the scandal provides a golden opportunity to destroy/transform the very office of the bishop and to "update," structurally and doctrinally, the nature of the Church. For the latter, the opposition is *not* to the office of the bishop per se, but to what constitutes an unfaithful (at worst), to ineffective, (at best), body of bishops who have failed in their leadership duties. While these conclusions are admittedly speculative and tentative, the logic of each perspective would suggest that, in the main, the motivation to cover up the scandal on the part of those bishops who, on the surface appear to be loyal to magisterial thinking, would be explanations one through four. Those bishops more open to a radical rejection of the historic nature of the faith would be motivated by explanations five through eight. Many Catholics believe that nothing less than the future of the Catholic Church in the United States depends on whether or not it finds the ability to address clearly and forthrightly the host of issues involved in the sexual scandals.

Suggested Readings

Abbott, Walter, ed. *The Documents of Vatican II*. Washington, DC: America Press, 1966.

Carlin, David R. *The Decline and Fall of the Catholic Church in America*. Manchester, NH: Sofia Institute Press, 2003.

Dolan, Jay P. *The American Catholic Experience: A History from Colonial Times to the Present*. Garden City, NY: Doubleday, 1985.

Greeley, Father Andrew M. *The American Catholic*. New York: Basic Books, 1977.

Hanna, Mary. *Catholics and American Politics*. Cambridge, MA: Harvard University Press, 1979.

Hitchcock, James. *The Decline and Fall of Radical Catholicism*. New York: Image, 1972.

Hunter, James D. *Culture Wars: The Struggle to Define America*. New York: Basic Books, 1991.

Kelly, Monsignor George A. *The Battle for the American Church Revisited*. San Francisco: Ignatius, 1995.

PART VI

WHAT LIES AHEAD? CHARTING OUT DIFFERENT POSSIBLE SCENARIOS FOR THE CATHOLIC CHURCH IN THE UNITED STATES

All exercises in "futurology" are, by their very nature, precarious and unsure. The future is open and, theoretically speaking, just about anything can happen, at least in the long run. Nonetheless, it is an appropriate way to end our analysis of the Catholic experience in America by venturing forth about the nature and prospects of various possible future scenarios for the Catholic Church in this country.

Scenario One: Dissolution. For most Catholics, that the Catholic Church in the United States could dissolve literally on the American scene in the immediate future is surely almost impossible to imagine. It is almost equally hard for them to imagine such an end result even in the long run. As many observers of the Catholic institution have noted, to date, the Church has a history of burying her enemies, both literally and figuratively. (In the twentieth century, for instance, David R. Carlin [2003] notes the demise of both communism and Nazism while questioning the ability of the Church to defeat her most contemporary adversary, that is, liberal secularism.) Nonetheless, it is useful to spend some time on the possibility of the dissolution of Catholicism in America for two reasons: (1) it is not literally impossible and (2) there are powerful forces in society that have both predicted the complete demise of the institution and have advocated such an end.

The more strident cheerleaders of Enlightenment thinking have long pronounced the imminent end for any organization led by supernatural and religious premises in a world that, it is argued, is and should be led by scientific or positivisitic thinking. Positivism is a philosophy that argues that the only things in life that are "real" are the things that the scientist can explain, predict, and eventually control. One of the key historical figures of positivism is the putative "founder" of sociology, the Frenchman Auguste Comte (Lenzer 1983) whose intent was to institutionalize a "religion of humanity" to replace the comprehensive role that Catholicism once played in French and European civilization. While Comte rejected the supernaturalist content or message of Catholicism, he was nonetheless impressed with the hierarchical structure and organization of the Catholic Church. For Comte and his contemporary followers, the trick is to replace religious elites (e.g., the pope, bishops, and other clergy) with scientific leaders who, from this positivistic position, would be the new "priests of humanity" and should be both the interpreters and implementers of an ultimate truth that was based on scientific fact and not on religious myth. Crudely put, Comte was no believer in democracy; he advocated what other sociologists would call a "circulation of elites," that is, in this case, from religious to secular scientific elites. The dissolution of Catholicism and all other forms of supernaturally based religion could, then, dissolve from two causes, not mutually exclusive in nature. One cause is that modern populations could imbibe uncritically the Comtian myth that brings to mind the vision of a this-worldly paradise being generated by the widespread application of scientifically based ideas to all aspects of life—in the physical world, in society and in social relations, and even in the personal lives and psyche of individuals. A second cause, which is perhaps more likely, is a secular totalitarian political leadership that could coercively force a positivistic worldview on a societal population in the short run hoping that future generations would willingly accept a world without religion, mystery, the intuitive, and the supernatural. In this latter scenario, the power of the state/government would play a role in pushing religion out of existence as was attempted by various Communist regimes during the twentieth century.

Scenario Two: An "American" Church. This scenario is more likely. It is one in which Catholicism consciously sheds philosophies, concepts, doctrines, rituals, and organizational arrangements that seem, to the modern upper–middle-class American, to be obsolete, old-fashioned, and part and parcel of some traditional, medieval-like past. Conversely, it is a scenario in which the Catholics would consciously mirror the vision of mainstream, upper–middle-class Americans, highlighting such values as individualism, freedom, moral relativism, and materialism. Such a scenario would constitute a victory for what has been termed and discussed in this book as the "Americanist" wing of the Catholic Church, a proassimilationist wing that has been present historically in American Catholicism but was contained in its influence in the Church at least until the mid-1960s. It is one that would replicate the previous movement of mainstream Protestant and liberal Judaism toward a much more secularized and less traditional religion. As David R. Carlin states, this movement can "be observed in an old liberal religion like Unitarianism, but also in churches that first turned in a liberal direction in the twentieth century, such churches as the Congregational, the Episcopal, the Presbyterian, the United Methodist, and the Evangelical Lutheran Church of America—in short, all the 'mainline' Protestant churches" (2003, 7). Some observers would claim that, if this option were to become dominant, it would most likely closely mimic the high Church tradition of the Episcopal Church, that is, a church that maintains certain externals of the Catholic religion but strongly endorses what the Protestant theologian, Paul Tillich (1957), referred to as the "Protestant principle" or the positing of the ultimate supremacy of individual conscience in all matters religious and moral. This option is plausible because it has a strong appeal to the American middle class, which historically is the class that dominates the American landscape, religious institutions included, and certainly presently strongly influences the contemporary middle-class Catholic population. This "Americanist" solution represents a variation of what H. R. Niebuhr would term a "Christ of culture" option in which it is assumed that, to refer to the phrase of the liberal Baptist theologian Harvey Cox, the dominant culture is "out in front" of the churches and implies that it is culture and not the historic religious traditions that should "wag the tail of the dog." A full-blown Americanist option for American Catholics is already widely a practical, if not theoretical, reality and has not, surprisingly perhaps, been too overtly opposed by Roman authorities. (This passivity on the part of Roman authorities may, perhaps, change with the recent election, on April 19, 2005, of Pope Benedict XVI, the former Cardinal Joseph Ratzinger and former head of the Congregation for the Doctrine of the Faith.) Speaking of the contemporary Catholic population in the United States, as a matter of fact, David R. Carlin observes that:

it is almost certainly true that a vast number of American Catholics—
that is, people who identify themselves as Catholic—are not so much
Catholic in their doctrinal and moral beliefs as they are generic Christians. Why is this? Because generic Christianity is the dominant religion in the United States today, and Catholics (except for recent
immigrants from Latin America) are fully Americanized. If one is fully
American, is it surprising that one would embrace the dominant American religion? (2003, 15)

However, there would be some serious defections from the implementation of this Americanist option on the part of some in the
working-class, minority, and ethnic immigrant communities that have
an affinity for the more traditional/conservative religiosity found in
American Protestantism. As we have noted previously, for instance, a
not insubstantial number of Hispanic Catholic immigrants have rejected
the "Anglo-Catholic" option and have defected to conservative and
pentecostal Protestantism. Defecting Catholics would join either conservative Protestant or traditional sectlike religious options consistent
with the theme in Dean Kelley's volume *Why the Conservative Churches
are Growing* (1972). Kelley's argument is, at base, that only conservative or traditional religions grow in numbers in the modern context
given that only they provide some distinctive alternative to contemporary worldviews. Put another way, the question is this: "Why join a liberal religion that is only mirroring the dominant societal ethos?"
Relatedly, another point is that conservative or traditional religions better provide for the "meaning" function of religion in that they offer a
philosophy undergirded by the claim of an objective moral order based
on absolutes and, thus, provide a clearer answer to the ultimate questions of human existence as compared to the more "open-ended" and
more obviously "socially constructed" nature of liberal religiosity.

There would also be smaller but important defections from the
"Americanist" option on the part of some quite sophisticated and formally educated Catholic Americans who have consciously made the decision as to the religious, moral, and intellectual superiority of the
Catholic faith vis-à-vis other available options. The irony would be,
however, that while significant numbers of Catholics would defect from
a victorious Americanist Church, the Americanist Church establishment
could still dominate society given the prestige, power, and economic co-
ordinates of its middle-class base and because the ideas and lifestyle of

that base would confirm and validate those of the reigning secular cultural elites of American society. Put another way, social location would likely trump numbers in terms of influence if this scenario were to take root.

Scenario Three: Retreat to a 1950s Pre–Vatican II Church or to a Rural Sectlike Existence. This is the possible response of those "discontents of modernity" (Berger, Berger and Kellner 1974), who would consciously reject central aspects of modern American life as it is presently constituted in the twenty-first century and who also would disagree with most, if not all, of the documents of the Second Vatican Council. This response, sociologically, would come close to accepting a sectlike withdrawal from modern life and would take two forms. The first would be to live physically in the midst of "the world" but not to be "of" it; such Catholic discontents would practice their form of pre–Vatican II religiosity in parishes that have broken not only with the Americanist Church but with Churches that have remained loyal to Rome and the historic Catholic tradition that would still be real in other parts of the world, most probably in the so-called "Third World." The second and related option would be, as far as possible, to "drop out" of society and find rural nooks and crannies from which to live and practice their faith. Fundamentally inward in orientation, both strategies would reject the imperative to dialogue and partially co-opt elements of other religions and philosophies, thus refusing the challenge to navigate the waters of relativity. Suspicious even of organic change in Cardinal Newman's sense of development (witness the rejection of Vatican II and of most Catholic changes since the pontificate of Pope Pius XII on the part of some extreme Catholic traditionalists), these options would be an attempt to re-create a microcosm of the 1950's style of Catholicism that was dominant just prior to the Second Vatican Council. As such, its appeal would be limited necessarily given the conformist tendencies of the majority in any society. Many of its advocates would be people of high intelligence who have come to the self-conscious conclusion, consistent with the worldview of the Amish, that Christ is simply not to be found in the surrounding society. Conversely put, the claim would be that salvation is to be found within the sacramental, traditional, communal, and physical boundaries of a religious option whose foundation was forged in the Middle Ages, which serves as a kind of utopian ideal, and for whom a 1950's Catholicism represents the closest American approximation to that ideal. The plausibil-

American cardinals join thousands of worshipers for outdoor mass during World Youth Day, Denver, Colorado, 1993. A key question here is, can an older generation of Catholic leadership connect in a positive manner with the younger American Catholic generation?

ity of this option would actually increase for some individuals if either of the previous options gain strength, that is, the general dissolution of the Church or its takeover by progressive Americanist forces.

Scenario Four: Neo-Orthodoxy. This is the vision of those who accept the official understanding of the Catholic Church regarding the relationship between permanence and social change. Simply put, the neo-orthodox believe that the Church was founded and depends on a set of eternal and unchangeable principles, derived from various sources (e.g., the Bible, sacred tradition, natural law, all under the authority of the Church magisterium). These are implemented necessarily and applied prudentially by magisterial directives in different ways in response to a changing world and changing social contexts (Varacalli 2001). Such implementation and application are, from this perspective, necessarily "organic" in nature; they must be logically derived from, connected to, and consistent with an evolving Church tradition rooted in permanent Truths (Krason 1991). The Church, according to this position, is "eternally young" as the absolute truth of the Catholic faith is constantly mediated, thought somewhat differently, in a world of different cultures and structural arrangements.

The widescale plausibility of this scenario assumes several crucial developments. First and foremost, it would require that the Catholic Church in the United States restore integrity to its own house through the application of discipline and through successful efforts in socializing the Catholic faithful in a Catholic tradition that has, through neglect, been lost on the majority of American Catholics whose religion is now largely nominal. Related to this, there would also have to be growing unrest on the part of a significant percentage of Americans—whether Catholic or not—with the vision and promise of a modern, secular America. Simply put, the restoration of the Catholic Church to one of society-wide respect presupposes that a significant percentage of its members are open to rejecting what they would see as the false promises of a materialistic age. Conversely put, it presupposes a widespread yearning for a philosophy that stresses commitment to, community with, and service for something higher than oneself. The former development is quite possible and, indeed, may very well be underway as there is some sociological evidence emerging that the contemporary children of those who were young adults in the 1960s era are, to a some degree, rejecting the antinomian viewpoints of their parents. In their volume, *Millennials Rising: The Next Great Generation* (2000) co-authors Neil Howe and William Strauss argue, among many other findings, that violence, illegal drug use, and teen sexual promiscuity have declined for those born into American society since 1982. The authors also claim that the "rising millennials" are more conservative politically and socially than are their parents and they are more pro-family also. Combined with Colleen Carroll's recent analysis (2002) suggesting that some segments of present-day young adults are once again embracing Christian orthodoxy suggests that there is some possibility for a come-back for a religion such as Catholicism in the United States. As James T. Fisher notes in his *Catholics in America*, "as the 20th century drew to a close many younger Catholics long for a revival of traditionalist religion, favoring a renewed emphasis on the Church's teaching authority, which they hoped, would lead to a Church as unified as that known by their grandparents in the 1930s and 1940s" (2000, 163). The latter possibility, however, is very problematic given the weakened condition of the present Catholic Church, *qua* institution and community, in America. On the other hand, the new American generations might well find an integrated and orthodox Catholicism quite attractive.

It is also important to mention, in passing, that developments in world Catholicism might provide some assistance to the Catholic neo-orthodox cause. The fact that there has been a startling growth of Catholicism in significant parts of what has been referred to as the Third World or "less industrialized societies" (Henslin 2004) might suggest to some Catholic Americans that the Catholic vision is still real for millions of individuals around the globe and hence provide them some emotional support. Furthermore, there is the reality that American bishops will have the option, in the indefinite future, to bring in thousands of priests from around the world to serve in Catholic dioceses in the United States. American religious orders, likewise, will continue to have the option to shuffle their personnel to America and the West if they see fit. The neo-orthodox option in the United States might be energized, ironically, as the United States is progressively becoming viewed as a "mission territory" for the Church Universal.

Scenario four is possible to imagine but still represents a long-term project. It is, however, the vision of the official Church and of its incredibly charismatic leader, Pope John Paul II who recently passed away on April 2, 2005. John Paul's vision, almost assuredly, will be continued to be implemented by his like-minded successor, Benedict XVI. This vision has generated the unwavering support of a small, but highly educated and devoted, segment of the Catholic population and perhaps can draw upon the varied resources of a world Catholicism for its successful implementation.

Scenario Five: Formal Schism. Another possibility that is very real is one that would see multiple formal schisms. In this case, Roman authorities and their American Catholic allies would support with vigor the efforts of Catholic neo-orthodoxy with the result that the Catholic Church in the United States would neither dissolve nor be taken over those who would either secularize the Church or move it in the direction of some version of liberal Protestantism. If the outer American culture doesn't move in the direction of some kind of religious revival conducive to promoting religious orthodoxy, then one could see the forces behind the "Americanization" of the Church leaving formally the Catholic Church and setting up their own "American Catholic Church" similar to the Church of England breaking with Rome in the sixteenth century. This development would possibly coincide with the continued defections of the sectlike pre–Vatican II remnant Catholics. One would then see three religious options claiming to be Catholic and competing with each other: an "American" Catholic Church, Catholic neo-orthodoxy, and a pre–Vatican II traditionalist remnant. In terms of numbers, the first group, initially, would be the largest and most "respected" in terms of legitimacy granted by secular elites, but the second and third would be more vigorous, with the Catholic neo-orthodox having significant growth potential given that they represent a plausible alternative to full-fledged secularist participation in modern life. Indeed, the growing strength of the neo-orthodox option eventually could well be at the expense of the traditionalists as some of the latter may become impressed with the restoration of the Catholic faith and reconvert under the leadership of the Catholic neo-orthodox restorationist movement.

Scenario Six: Pluralism. This is the basically the option of the "status quo" that presently exists today, of a "do your own thing," and of a "live and let live" philosophy as applied to the Catholic Church in the United States. This option has been made the current reality by the unwillingness or inability of episcopal authority in both Rome and the United States to clearly articulate and enforce just what is or is not official Catholic doctrine. It is one in which the claim of Catholic unity is publicly pronounced by Church officials but is sociologically unreal. It is an option in which there would be as many "Catholicisms," disparate in what they stand for, in the United States as there are leaders and organizations willing to organize and create them. In essence, this would represent the ultimate "Protestantization" or individualization of the Catholic Church in the United States. Such a development assumes a totally ineffective, weak-kneed, or perhaps abolished papacy and centralized authority in the Church Universal.

Suggested Readings

Carlin, David R. *The Decline and Fall of the Catholic Church in America*. Manchester, NH: Sophia Institute Press, 2003.

Carroll, Colleen. *The New Faithful: Why Young Adults Are Embracing Christian Orthodoxy*. Chicago: Loyola University Press, 2002.

Howe, Neil, and William Strauss. *Millennials Rising: The Next Great Generation.* New York: Vintage Books, 2000.

Kelley, Dean M. *Why Conservative Churches Are Growing.* New York: Harper, 1972.

Varacalli, Joseph A. *Bright Promise, Failed Community: Catholics and the American Public Order.* Lanham, MD: Lexington Books, 2001.

Postscript: Staying the Course with Benedict XVI in a Post-John Paul II Church

On April 2, 2005, the pontificate of John Paul II ended with his return to the Lord. Starting in 1978, the accomplishments of his reign were numerous and impressive. Perhaps most outstanding, John Paul demonstrated that the incredibly sophisticated Catholic worldview was not, in any real sense, antimodern, but actually constituted an alternative, healthy, and balanced way to be modern. John Paul's many encyclicals both reaffirmed and organically developed the long tradition in Catholic social doctrine. Philosophically, the pope's integration of Thomism and phenomenology successfully incorporated objectivist/realist and subjectivist/personalist worldviews. He triumphed over communism as he had, earlier in his life, overcome Nazism; at the time of his death he was focused on addressing the intellectual and moral weaknesses of secular liberalism.

Throughout the globe, John Paul II steadfastly advocated a "culture of life" by promoting the spiritual and material needs of the human being from the moment of conception until natural death. Conversely, he did everything possible to oppose the ruthlessly utilitarian philosophy behind the encroaching "culture of death," whether manifested through the exploitation of the socially marginal (the poor, the aged, the uneducated, the unemployed, the physically disabled, the mentally ill, the baby in the womb) or through the evil possibilities ushered forth by the latest revolution in the realm of biotechnology. John Paul II, in short, made strong contributions to the Catholic tradition by advocating and demanding socioeconomic justice and fundamental and universal human rights for all.

The Polish pope was always involved as an active agent for peaceful relations between governments and civilizations through diplomacy and conflict resolution. During his reign, the papal and Catholic presence at the United Nations was real, palpable, and effective. John Paul II was notably successful in bringing many young people back to God. Within a Catholic theological and philosophical anthropological framework, he was a strong supporter for the equality and dignity for women. He had a quite modern genius at employing the mass media as an agent of Catholic evangelization.

John Paul II had many accomplishments in the area of ecumenical relations, especially with the Jewish and Muslim faiths. He tried hard, but was less successful, in his attempts to reach out to the Eastern Orthodox Churches.

Internally, John Paul II internationalized the College of Cardinals, a reflection of his appreciation of the universal composition of the Church and the promising future he saw for the Catholic faith in the less developed countries of the Third World. He was also extraordinarily successful in promoting an appreciation for the many gifts that the Eastern Catholic Churches bring to the Church Universal. Inheriting a rather sick institution and community confused and disoriented during the post–Vatican II era, John Paul II brought the Church back to some semblance of health by the time of his earthly departure in 2005.

On the other hand, relatively speaking, John Paul II's reign was unsuccessful in two areas. The first was in failing to stem the tide regarding the de-Christianization of Europe and the second was in not rooting out the institutionalized dissent that has severely weakened the integrity of the Catholic Church in the United States. Interestingly enough, but perhaps unsurprising from a Catholic frame of reference, John Paul II's successor, collaborator, and dear friend, Pope Benedict XVI—the former Joseph Cardinal Ratzinger—seems to be ready to hit the ground running and confront head-on these two problems.

On April 19, 2005, in the second day of deliberations by the College of Cardinals and on only the fourth ballot, Joseph Cardinal Ratzinger of Germany was elected by over a two-thirds majority to succeed John Paul II to the throne of Peter. The fact that the cardinals chose the former pope's closest religious, intellectual, and moral confidant to succeed him is a clear and compelling sign that the leaders of the Church want and expect an organic continuation of the legacy of John Paul II. In other words, they want the Church, basically, to stay the course set for her by John Paul II during his reign.

The fact that Cardinal Ratzinger assumed the name of Benedict XVI links him to the apostolate of Saint Benedict, viewed, in Catholic tradition, as "the patron and protector of Europe." Pope Benedict XVI is expected by many of his supporters and observers to engage in a battle of ideas with secularism in an attempt to re-Catholicize and re-Christianize the European continent.

Also of importance is the fact that the now Pope Benedict XVI headed the Congregation for the Doctrine of the Faith under John Paul II. The ex–Cardinal Ratzinger knows, then, very well the extent of internal dissent that has so eaten away at the soul of the Church, especially in Europe and the United States. Where John Paul II seemed hesitant to discipline wayward bishops, theologians, religious orders, and political personalities, Pope Benedict XVI can be expected, by both dint of his personal disposition and social experience, to be more willing to continue the unpleasant but necessary task of guarding Catholic doctrinal orthodoxy by rooting out dissent, thus reestablishing integrity to what this volume has continually referred to as the Church's "plausibility structure."

The appointment of Pope Benedict XVI was immediately cheered by orthodox Catholics while disappointing and angering progressive Catholics. His reign is expected to increase, at least incrementally, the hopes and chances of the restorationist camp within the Catholic Church organized in the name of John Paul II, both within the United States of America and throughout the world.

Appendix A

Church Documents Discussed

Note: All Church statements do not carry the same weight in the Catholic worldview. Statements emanating from popes, ecumenical councils, and Vatican congregations are considered, in general, to be more binding than those issued by, for instance, regional or national episcopal conferences and individual bishops in their respective dioceses. The documents listed here, of course, represent only a small percentage of the total of Catholic doctrinal and social doctrinal thinking. Of key importance was the publication, in 1994, of *The Catechism of the Catholic Church*, a concise summary of Catholic teaching representing magisterial thinking. Traditional Catholic thinkers saw in its publication a necessary and definitive statement of Catholic teaching. Progressive Catholic thinkers were opposed to any such summary, arguing that it represents an unnecessary restriction on either regional or individual interpretations of the faith. The Sisters of Saint Paul, headquartered in Boston, Massachusetts, have it as part of their apostolate to publish official Catholic Church teaching through inexpensive pamphlets; 1-617-522-8911, www.daughtersofstpaul.com. The web addresses for Church documents are provided, if they are available.

Pope Leo XIII

Rerum Novarum ("On the Condition of the Working Classes"), 1891, www.uscatholic.org/cstline/rerum.htm

Testem benevolentiae ("On the Heresy of Americanism"), 1899, www.ewtn.com/library/PAPALDOC/L13TESTE.HTM

Pope Pius IX

Quanta Cura ("On Current Concerns"), 1864, with attached "Syllabus of Errors" ("on the eighty principal errors of the age"), www.ewtn.com.library.ENCYC/P9QUANTA.HTM

Pope Pius X

Lamentabili Sane ("Syllabus Condemning the Errors of the Modernists"), 1907, www.etwn.com/library/CURIA/CDFAMEN.HTM
Pascendi Dominici Gregis ("On the Doctrine of the Modernists"), 1907, www.ewtn.com/library/ENCYC/P1PASCE.HTM

Pope Pius XI

Casti Connubii ("On Christian Marriage"), 1930, www.ewtn.com/library/ENCYC/PIICASTI.HTM
Divini Illius Magistri ("On the Education of Youth"), 1929; on the rights of parents to educate their own children, see www.cwtn.com/library/encyc/p11divil.htm
Divini Redemptoris ("On the Evil of Atheistic Communism"), 1937, www.ewtn.com/library/encyc/p1divin.htm
Mit Brennender Sorge ("On the Evil of Racism and on German National Socialism"), 1937, www.newadvent.org/library/docs_pi11mb.htm
Non Abbiamo Bisogno ("On Catholic Action in Italy"), 1931, and the evil of Italian fascism, www.ewtn.com/library/ENCYC/P11FAC.HTM
Quadragesimo Anno ("After Forty Years"), 1931, propounds the idea of subsidiarity, www.ewtn.com/library/ENCYC/P11QUADR.HTM

Pope John XXIII

Pacem in Terris ("Peace on Earth"), 1963, www.catholicculture.org/docs/doc_view.cfm?recnum=3369

Pope Paul VI

Humanae Vitae ("On Human Life"), 1968, www.newadvent.org/library/docs_obhv.htm

Octagesimo Adveniens ("A Call to Action"), 1971, Apostolic Letter, www.papalencyclicals.net/Paulo6/

Populorum Progressio ("On the Development of Peoples"), 1967, on the obligation of more advanced industrialized societies to aid those less advanced in not only economic but also in cultural and spiritual terms, www.ewtn.com/library/encyc/p6develo.htm

John Paul II

Centesimus Annus ("On the Hundredth Anniversary of *Rerum Novarum*"), 1991, www.ewtn.com/library/ENCYC/JP2HUNDR.HTM

Christifideles Laici ("On the Vocation and Mission of the Lay Faithful"), 1988, www.ewtn.com/library/PAPALDOC/JP2Laity.htm

Evangelium Vitae ("On the Value and Inviolability of Human Life"), 1994, www.ewtn.com/library/ENCYC/JP2EVANG.HTM

Ex corde Ecclesiae ("Out of the Heart of the Church"), 1990, Apostolic Constitution on Catholic Colleges and Universities, www.ewtn.com/library/ENCYC/JP2VER.HTM

Familiaris Consortio ("On the Christian Family in the Modern World"), 1981, on the family as the basic cell of civilization and as a "little Church," www.ewtn.com/library/PAPALDOC/JPFAMIL.HTM

Fides et Ratio ("Faith and Reason"), 1998, www.catholicculture.org/docs/doc_view.cfm?recnum=592

Laborem Exercens ("On Human Work"), 1981, www.ewtn.com/library/ENCY/JP2LABOR.HTM

Mulieris Dignitatem ("On the Dignity and Vocation of Women"), 1988, on the fundamental dignity and equality of women, www.ewtn.com/library/PAPALDOC/JP2MULIE.HTM

Veritatis Splendor ("The Splendor of Truth"), 1993, www.ewtn.com/library/ENCYC/JP2VER.HTM

Documents of Vatican II

Christus Dominus ("On the Pastoral Office of Bishops in the Church"), 1965,
    www.ewtn.com/library/COUNCILS/V2BISHOP.HTM
Dignitatis Humanae ("On Religious Freedom"), 1965, www.ewtn.com/library/
    COUNCILSV2RELFRE.HTM
Gaudium et Spes ("On the Church in the Modern World"), 1965, www.ewtn.
    com/library/COUNCILSV2MODWOR.HTM
Nostra Aetate ("On Relations with Non-Christians"), 1965, www.ewtn.com/
    library/COUNCILS/V2NON.HTM
Orientalium Ecclesiarum ("On the Eastern Catholic Churches"), 1965, www.
    ewtn.com/library/COUNCILS/V2EAST.HTM

Documents Emanating from the Synod of Bishops

"Justice in the World," 1971, with its central assertion that "a concern for the
    implementation of justice is a constitutive element of the preaching of the
    Gospel," www.osjspm.org/cst/8-jw.htm

Documents from the Congregation for the Doctrine of the Faith

"Doctrinal Note on Some Questions Regarding the Participation of Catholics
    in Political Life," 2002, www.ewtn.org/library/CURIA/CDFPOLIF.HTM
Donum Veritatis ("The Instruction on the Ecclesial Vocation of the Theolo-
    gian"), 1990, on the legitimate role of Catholic theologians, www.ewtn.
    com/library/CURIA/CDFTHEO.HTM
"Instruction on Certain Aspects of the 'Theology of Liberation,'" 1984,
    www.newadvent.org/library/docs_df84lt.htm
"Instruction on Christian Freedom and Liberation," 1986, www.catholic
    culture.org/doc_view.cfm?recnum=1180
"Guidelines for the Study and Teaching of the Church's Social Doctrine in the
    Formation of Priests," 1988, www.stthomas.edu/cathstudies/cst/edu/bish
    ops.html
"Letter to the Bishops of the Catholic Church on the Pastoral Care of Homo-
    sexual Persons," 1986, www.newadvent.org/library/docs_df86ho.htm

Statements from What Is Now Called the United States Conference of Catholic Bishops

"A Pastoral Response to Women's Concerns for Church and Society," 1988

"Always Our Children: A Pastoral Message to the Parents of Homosexual Children and Suggestions for Pastoral Ministers," 1997, www.nccbuscc.org/laity/always.htm

"Call to Action Plan," 1978, later renamed "To Do the Work of Justice"

"Human Life in Our Day" (1968), promoted the idea that there could be a form of "licit dissent" in cases of ordinary noninfallible Church teaching; was later corrected by the 1990 document of the Congregation for the Doctrine of the Faith, *Donum Veritatis* ("The Instruction on the Ecclesial Vocation of the Theologian"), www.etwn.com/library/BISHOPS/USBP SHV.HTM)

Statements from Individual Bishops

"The Day of Peace Restored," 1973, Peter L. Gerety, archbishop of Newark

Appendix B

Glossary of Key Terms Used

"accent on reality": A phrase coined by psychologist William James to indicate that ideas, in order to be effectively received and acted upon, require a perception of plausibility.

"American Dream": A phrase suggesting that the key priority of American society in the second half of the twentieth century involved the acquisition of significant amounts of material wealth and social status.

Americanizers vs. anti-Americanizers: Catholic groups in the United States who took very different positions regarding the desirability and effect of Catholics assimilating into American culture and society; the former seeing this as a positive development, the latter, as a liquidation of the faith.

American Protective Association: A Protestant American group founded to oppose what they saw as an intrusion of Catholic beliefs, practices, and political power in the United States.

anarchist: An individual promoting the philosophy of anarchy, that is, it is desirable to see a society that can operate and survive without some governing authority. This is a position counter to Catholic teaching that argues for the need for government oriented to promoting the "common good."

Anglican: An individual belonging to the Church of England; many of the early colonists in the South were members of the Anglican Church and loyal followers of England and George III.

Apollonian vs. Dionysian forms of religious ritual: Named after Greek gods, the words refer to distinct forms of religious practice, with the former being characterized as being dignified, sedate, and relying on reason and the latter as low brow, loud, and emotional.

apostles: Referring to the original twelve chosen followers of Jesus Christ.

apostolates vs. ministries: Vocations performed in the name of the Catholic Church; the former refers to vocations oriented to the outside world and the latter to work performed to accomplish internal Church imperatives and functions.

apostolic succession: The belief held by the Catholic Church that popes represent divinely inspired successors to the original pope, Peter, and that bishops represent divinely inspired successors to the original twelve apostles.

aristocracy: A privileged class. The Carroll family in the early Maryland colony represented one of the relatively few examples of a Catholic aristocracy in early American history. Some predict that as American Catholics have moved significantly up the American socioeconomic ladder, an American Catholic aristocracy will inevitably develop.

authority: Power viewed as legitimate.

Baltimore plenary councils and provincial sessions: A series of organizational meetings of the Catholic leadership in the United States that commenced in 1829 and ended in 1884 that provided an organizational strategy of the rational development of the Catholic Church in America.

bishop: In Catholic theology, a leader of the Church who stands in apostolic succession to the apostles and whose office is inspired by the Holy Spirit.

bishops' bicentennial celebration: A major, ten-year (1973–83) social justice program initiated by the progressive Catholic wing of the Catholic Church of the United States.

Black Power movement: A social and organizational progressive African American movement starting in the mid-1960s in the United States; within the Catholic Church it led to a temporary movement re-emphasizing segregationism and a radical pluralist posture for Afro-American Catholics.

Buddhism: One of the world religions recently being introduced onto the American and American Catholic scene that emphasizes a stance of inner-worldly mysticism.

Calvinists: Followers of the Protestant Reformation theology of John Calvin. In the United States, a major Calvinist religion is Presbyterianism.

cardinal: A member appointed by the pope to the College of Cardinals, which chooses—according to the Catholic worldview, with the assistance of the Holy Spirit—the popes of the Catholic Church. Cardinals are almost always chosen from the ranks of bishops although priests and lay individuals are eligible to be appointed to the college by the pope.

casaropapism: A case in which some secular political authority has power over religious authority.

"Catholic moment": A phrase coined by Father Richard J. Neuhaus that indicates the belief that a propitious time has arisen for Catholicism to contribute significantly to American public life.

Catholic social thought: A body of Catholic ideas that are suggestive of the ways by which society should be organized properly and by which individuals should lead their own lives.

chain migration: A sociological idea that suggests that immigrants to a country follow the settlement patterns of the earliest immigrants of a particular ethnic or religious group. For instance, in terms of Catholic migration to the United States, many southern Italian Catholics settled in the New York and New Jersey area while German Catholics migrated to the Midwest.

Christian Democracy: A philosophy that believes that governments and societies can best be ordered by the principles of Catholic social thought. Christian Democratic political parties were once somewhat influential in southwestern Europe and in Latin America in the immediate post–World War II period.

"Church as People of God": A phrase extracted from the theology of Vatican II to suggest that the Catholic Church is not co-terminous with the Church hierarchy but must include input from the lower echelon, including lay, sectors of the Church community.

circulation of elites: A sociological idea coined by Italian sociologist Vilfredo Pareto that argues that there is a cyclical relationship between elite groups. In the case of Catholicism in the United States, the argument has been made that the authority of the pope and bishops loyal to the pope is being challenged by a "new Catholic knowledge class" of intellectuals, activists, bureaucrats, and social planners who make claim to their authority on the basis of their command of secular knowledge.

Civil Rights movement: A social movement started in the 1960s to integrate better and bring fuller equality to Afro-Americans and other minorities in American society. The Civil Rights movement has been used by progressive Catholics to make the claim that the Catholic Church should include equal rights to groups such as feminists and homosexuals, some of whose ideas and practices have not all been compatible historically with the worldview of the Catholic Church.

cognitive respect: A sociological idea coined by the contemporary American sociologist, Peter L. Berger, which refers to whether the empirical understandings of reality of a particular group, whether that group be bishops or progressive activists, are to be granted a fair hearing in the prevalent court of opinion.

"collective conscience": A sociological term coined by the classical French sociologist, Emile Durkheim, which refers to the existence of an overarching cultural worldview that shapes the attitudes and behavior of the individuals living in a particular society. Many orthodox Catholics feel that the "collective conscience" of American society, or at least that of its elite sectors, is becoming progressively more secular and especially hostile to a Catholic understanding of reality.

College of Cardinals: The Catholic organizational body, whose members were originally appointed by a reigning pope that decides, the Catholic logic argues, through the assistance of the Holy Spirit, who the next pope will be.

common good: The idea, strongly supported by the Catholic faith, that individuals must be oriented to creating a society based on Truth, Beauty, Justice, and Holiness.

"communal Catholicism": A phrase coined by Catholic sociologist, Father Andrew M. Greeley, who argues that modern-day Catholics both should and do selectively interpret and accept the Catholic heritage according to the dictates of their individuality and conscience.

"conscience as the supreme subjective norm": A phrase abstracted from the documents of Vatican II that argues that the individual conscience must play a role in the way that people appropriate religious and moral imperatives. The nature and degree of latitude that this principle implies is a hotly contested dispute between orthodox and progressive factions within the Catholic Church with the former arguing that freedom must be linked to objective Truth and the latter arguing that the subjective determination of the individual should be the reigning criterion in decision making.

conscientization: A concept created by Paolo Freire to indicate the possibility of raising the consciousness of an individual out of ideology and into truth, as Marxists understand the term. Used by Marxist theorists in an attempt to revolutionize the proletariat and by liberation theologians to oppose the hierarchy of the Catholic Church.

culture: The sum total of all human creation that has become institutionalized in a society. From a sociological perspective, internalized culture directs the thought and practice of individuals socialized in a particular society.

culture war: The idea that a society or an organization (such as the Catholic Church) can be split by groups holding incommensurate theological and cultural conceptions of reality.

deconstructionism: A philosophical/analytical method that claims that one can unmask, uncover, and debunk the personal interests of an individual's thought and behavior. Used by those imbued with a revolutionary mentality to oppose what is seen as a reactionary status quo.

democracy: Literally, "rule by the people." In controversies involving the Catholic Church, the debate questions under what circumstances can democratic procedures apply and under what circumstances can democracy be made compatible with a religious institution that is, at base, hierarchal in nature.

devotional styles: Refers to the manner in which believers practice their religion. Some devotional styles stress the intellect, others emotion, some are highly structured, others allow and encourage innovation. The general application here is the plurality of devotional styles within the Catholic Church.

dioceses and archdioceses: Organizational units within the Catholic Church. Every diocese or archdiocese (a megadiocese) contains many parishes, each headed by a priest/pastor.

"discontents of modernity": A sociological phrase coined by Peter L. Berger to indicate those individuals who reject what they see as the major outlines of modern life. In terms of the Catholic Church, these "discontents" can range from those who are critical of developments in the outer culture and society to those who feel that the Church institution itself has recklessly accommodated itself to practices and ideas that are incompatible with authentic Church tradition.

doctrine (and development of doctrine): Doctrine refers to the basic beliefs of a religious institution. From the official worldview of the Catholic Church, doctrine can only develop or evolve "organically" and not in a way that contradicts the basic beliefs and practices of the religious tradition.

Eastern Catholicism: Those churches, part of the Universal Catholic Church, that have their liturgical practices grounded in the religion and culture of the Christianity of the Eastern Roman Empire. Not to be confused with Eastern Orthodox Christianity.

ecumenical councils: In the Catholic Church, the convening of meetings of all the bishops of the Catholic world, along with theological experts, to decide controversial issues of doctrine and policy.

ecumenism: In the Catholic Church, the belief that, because there can be found "rays of truth" in religions outside of Catholicism and also that all humanity is united by a "natural law written into the heart," it is useful for Churches and secular organizations to discuss controversial issues and try to reach agreement without violating the logic of their basic fundamental principles. Catholic orthodox thinkers charge that progressive Catholic thinkers stretch ecumenism into an out-and-out religious and cultural relativism, thereby equating the truth content of the Catholic religion with other religions and cultural manifestations.

Edict of Milan: Proclamation of Emperor Constantine that legalized the Christian religion in the Roman Empire.

Enlightenment: A period in European history that either downplayed or denied the truth potential found in supernatural religion and stressed, conversely, the idea that society should be lead by a reasoned and scientific outlook that is viewed as in a "zero-sum" relationship with religion.

ethnic revival movement: A movement pushed by some white ethnic lay Catholic leaders as a reaction to the previous Black Power movement of the early 1960s in the United States. This movement should be viewed sociologically as a predictable outcome of the development of an "interest group" society in which the prevalent idea is that in order to have your worldview protected in the public forum, one must organize one's cultural group in order to accrue necessary political power or clout.

evangelization through inculturation: The idea that one can best spread a faith by building on whatever is true, beautiful, holy, and useful in a civilization. Pope John Paul II (1978–2005) was a great believer is this method and has applied it especially to the case of Catholic conversion on the continent of Africa.

existentialism: Philosophical approach, associated with Jean-Paul Sartre among others, that starts from the assumption that no human meaning is given in life but that all humans must create their own personal, subjective understanding of the purpose of life.

feminism: A philosophy promoting the cause of women in social life. It can take many different forms: from one asserting the superiority of women over men; to one implicitly arguing that women should become more manlike in their social roles; to one arguing the movement toward the blending of male and female into something unisex; to one simply arguing that all human beings should have the same opportunities in life. Feminism in the Catholic Church becomes controversial when the claim is supported regarding the Catholic belief that only men can be ordained to the priesthood (based on the historical reality that all of the apostles of Jesus Christ were men). Some Catholic feminists claim this is a gross example of sexism in the Church; orthodox Catholics reply this is only a faithful requirement of living out correctly Church tradition.

Freudianism: A philosophy/psychological approach based on the work of Sigmund Freud. Assumes the existence of a fundamental internal struggle between a more animalistic part of the human psyche, the id, driven by the pleasure principle and the more rational part of the human psyche, the ego, and the socialized part of the mind, the superego. Of particular importance to contemporary Catholic studies because, many times, Freudianism leads to an excessively sex-oriented understanding of the human being, in contradistinction to the Catholic vision that places a higher premium on the idea of a human being as a spiritual creature intended to eventually be with God (the beatific vision) in Heaven.

fundamental dignity of the human person: A basic starting point in Catholic social thought that all human beings, being made in the image of God, are to be treated with respect and are due certain religious, material, and political rights by virtue of their very humanity.

Hinduism: A great Far Eastern religion characterized by a pervasive other-worldly mystical worldview.

Holy Spirit: In Christian theology, the third member of the Holy Trinity, along with God the Father and Jesus Christ, all three together constituting God.

homophobia: A philosophy that represents an irrational hatred of those with a homosexual orientation or those who practice homosexual behavior. Of relevance for the area of Catholic studies is the claim of secular and some Catholic progressives that the official position of the Catholic Church, which states that homosexual behavior is "naturally disordered," represents a case of "homophobia." Orthodox Catholics reply that the Church teaches a fundamental respect for all of God's humanity, preaches neither hatred nor discrimination against active homosexuals, and that mere designation of homosexual behavior as in some sense pathological is not homophobic but an honest representation of reality.

generation gap: A sociological concept that implies that because of the exaggerated forces of social change that exist in modern life, it is not unusual for parents and their children—who were, respectively, subject to very different socialization experiences—to interpret the social world around them in significantly different ways.

gnosticism: A subject in Christian studies referring to an early philosophical camp; widely used to make the argument that certain religious individuals consider themselves a privileged elite who have access to religious knowledge or insight not capable of being apprehended correctly or fully by the average religious believer.

grace: A Christian theological concept meaning power and inspiration given by God as a gift to mankind.

immigrants/new immigrants: Immigrants are people leaving their lands of origin and resettling in another country usually for either economic or political reasons. The early Catholic immigrants—from England, Ireland, France, and Africa—found themselves in a mostly Protestant America. Many Irish and German Catholics came to American in the early part of the nineteenth century while Catholic immigrants from southeastern Europe came between the 1880s and the 1920s. The phrase "new immigrants" refers to those Catholic immigrant groups from Africa, Latin America, Puerto Rico, Haiti, Vietnam, and the Philippines that came to the United States after President Lyndon B. Johnson loosened immigration restrictions in the mid-1960s.

incarnational: In Christian theology, the idea that the divine can be integrated into things of the world. That the Catholic religion is an "incarnational" religion means that it believes that God's grace can inform, for instance, art, architecture, music, liturgy, scholarship, and reason itself.

individualism (biblical, Republican, expressive, instrumental, autonomous): Various types of individualism manifest throughout American history as discussed by sociological thinkers such as Robert Bellah and David Riesman. The general movement in American society is to forms of individualism that are less oriented to some public or social concern hence becoming especially problematic for a Catholic social thought stressing a concern for the common good, solidarity for one's fellow human beings, and duty to something greater than oneself.

integrationist: A policy of mixing different races and ethnic groups together. In the history of the Catholic Church in the United States, there were times in which the institutional Church favored a policy of separating Catholic racial and ethnic groups from each other, and there were other times in which the policy was integrationist. Likewise, the leaders of the various ethnic and racial groups within the Catholic community historically alternated between wanting their respective groups to be either integrated or separated from other Catholics and the larger society.

Jesus Christ: In a Christian understanding, one person in the Holy Trinity, both God and the son of God and, during his earthly existence, both God and man simultaneously.

judiciary: Referring to the legal branch of government in the United States, as compared to the executive and legislative branches. Of particular concern for orthodox Catholicism is the claim that the judiciary branch of government is increasingly creating laws that are inconsistent with the natural law and the common good and that are opposed to the will of the majority of the American people. The *Roe v. Wade* decision legalizing abortion in 1973 is cited by orthodox Catholics as one particularly egregious example of an judicial usurpation of authority in the United States.

juridical: Referring to the legal authority derived from some accepted authority; in the Catholic Church, the pope and the bishops have a juridical control of much of the Church organization derived from charismatic and traditional sources.

Know-Nothing Party: A Protestant anti-Catholic party prominent in American history.

Ku Klux Klan: Originally a Protestant native group formed to fight the influence of blacks, Jews, Catholics, and other non-Protestant "foreigners" in the United States.

Lambeth Conference: A very important conference held by Anglicans in 1930 that initiated exceptions to the historic prohibition of the use of contraception; between 1930 and the present the overwhelming percentage of Christian denominations, unlike the Catholic Church, have delegated the use of contraception to individual conscience. While the Catholic Church reaffirmed its injunction against contraception in Pope Paul VI's 1968 encyclical *Humanae Vitae*, a large majority of Catholic Americans either have defied the Church's injunction or are ignorant of the Catholic logic behind it.

Land O'Lakes Declaration: A declaration made by progressive Catholic educators in the United States in 1967 to the effect that Catholic educations of higher institution must accept the principles of academic freedom and institutional autonomy. The way these principles have been applied in Catholic higher education since then has led, in the thinking of many Catholics, to a massive secularization of religion within these institutions.

liberalism: The philosophy that makes the claim that society must be based on the exercise of individualism and freedom. There are versions of liberalism that accept that individualism and freedom takes place within a large government or welfare state activity, and there are versions that claim that the exercise of individualism and freedom is sacrosanct and must brook no interference from outside sources.

libertarian: That philosophy of radical individualism and freedom that argues that individuals must be free to make their own choices in life freed from any governing authority, including government.

life chances: A sociological concept suggesting that, given certain ascribed factors (gender, race, socioeconomic background, country of origin, religion, sociohistorical era, etc.), individuals have differential opportunities for material and status achievement in society.

life course: A sociological concept arguing that individuals will go through several distinct social stages, depending on historical and biographical circumstances, throughout their biographical existence. These stages include childhood, adolescence, early adulthood, early and later middle age, and old age.

Lutheran: One of the major branches of Protestantism; named after the first major Protestant reformer, Martin Luther.

magisterium: The official teaching authority in the Catholic Church, consisting of the pope and those bishops in loyal communion with him.

martyrs: In Christian history, those believers who have given their lives or suffered greatly to maintain and defend their religious faith.

Mass: The central religious ritual of the Catholic faith both celebrating and witnessing the actual sacrifice of Jesus Christ through the administration of the sacrament of the Holy Eucharist.

"mature/intrinsic vs. immature/extrinsic religion": Terms in the psychology of religion coined by Harvard psychologist Gordon Allport. A mature/intrinsic religious expression is one that is selfless and characterized by devotion and duty to God; an immature/extrinsic religion is a religious expression used primarily to meet some social/political/emotional need.

ministry: In religious terminology, a job or vocation dealing with one of the internal tasks of the institutional Church.

monarchy: A hereditary form of government led by kings or their equivalents, which predominated during the European period of feudalism.

moral, cultural, and religious relativism: The idea that all morality, social ideals, and religious claims are deserving of equal respect.

multiculturalism: An approach that argues that as many different philosophies and historical customs as possible should be respected and incorporated in all forms of activity (intellectual, educational, religious, governmental, corporate, etc.).

Muslim: A member of the religion of Islam, the latter based on a belief in Allah as the One God, the Holy Qur'an as the word of God, and Mohammad as the last and greatest of God's human prophets.

Mystical Body of Christ: A theological formation of an ideal version of the Catholic Church that utilizes an organic and communal image consisting of mutually interdependent parts of the body with Christ as head.

National Catholic War Council: A national Catholic organization formed in response to a request by President Woodrow Wilson to coordinate U.S. Catholic relief efforts during World War I; after the war, the organization evolved into the national coordinating agency for the bishops of the United States and has gone through numerous name changes.

nativism: A historical movement used to indicate the reactionary attempts of the citizens and organizations of a particular nation to maintain its imaged historical purity by opposing new immigrant groups. In American history, much of the history of nativist movements was organized against Catholics, Jews, blacks, and Mormons.

natural law: The belief that there is structured into human consciousness and human nature a sense of right and wrong that can be used in the moral judgment of social arrangements.

Nazism: An extreme right-wing nationalist philosophy created by Adolf Hitler in Germany during the 1930s and 1940s based on the belief that a super-race was destined to rule civilization and also justified the genocide of supposedly inferior categories of people. Diametrically opposed to the Catholic belief positing the fundamental dignity of human beings.

neo-paganism: A modern form of post-Christian paganism rejecting any subordinate relationship of individuals to a supernatural source of authority and emphasizing the priority of individualism, materialism, political, and status acquisition.

new Catholic knowledge class: Emergent Catholic group of intellectuals, activists, and bureaucrats who claim the right to lead the Church based on their credentials legitimated by the modern secular academy and, as such, are in fundamental opposition to the idea of apostolic succession, that is, the pope and bishops, "appointed from up on high," who should lead the Catholic community.

Nicene-Constantinopolitan Creed: One of the fundamental explanations of the basics of the Catholic faith.

nominal Catholics: Literally, "Catholics by name only": sociologically refers to those Catholics baptized into the faith but who have been socialized fundamentally and shaped by some non-Catholic source of authority (secularism, Protestantism, etc.).

novena: Religious ritual involving nine meetings.

"official" vs. "unofficial" religion: Sociological terms coined by sociologist Meredith McGuire to indicate groups in society that are acknowledged as either "religious" or not. A belief in witchcraft or in astrology would be examples of "unofficial religions" that can perform all the functions of officially recognized religious groups (e.g. Judaism, Islam) for the individuals involved in such groups. Many times "unofficial" religion operates, sotto voce, within an official religion. In Catholicism, there are some Catholics who are more influenced by their unofficial attachments to, say, their feminism, capitalism, nationalism, Marxism, or Freudianism than they are by their Catholic faith.

"options in social engineering": A sociological phrase coined by Peter L. Berger suggesting the options that a supernaturally based religious community faces in a secular, modern world characterized by religious and cultural pluralism.

organizational styles—hierarchal, congregational, connectional: Topics in religious studies to indicate the options in the way religious communities can organize themselves in terms of authority relations. The Catholic Church represents, at base, the hierarchal option, that is, "top-down" authority while the Baptist community represents, at base, the congregational option, that is, "bottom-up" authority. The connectional option, finally, represents a hybrid or compromise formulation of the first two.

Orthodox Christianity: Religious communities, originating in the old Eastern Roman Empire, which broke with the Catholic Church in the year 1054 over a series of religious, political, cultural, and linguistic disagreements. A key issue was over papal authority, which the Orthodox reject.

orthodoxy vs. heterodoxy in religious commitment: Literally "correct" versus "incorrect" religious belief and practice; in the contemporary Catholic Church, the "orthodox" are those that follow Catholic tradition, and the "heterodox" are those trying to "update" tradition or replace tradition with more modern ideas and ways of living.

paganism: A pre-Christian this-worldly philosophy emphasizing the priority of things of this world.

patriarch: The leader and head bishop of any one of the Eastern Orthodox Churches; the patriarchs of Eastern Orthodoxy acknowledge the Catholic pope as one of many patriarchs of Christianity but one who has no authority over any other.

"plausibility structure": A sociological term developed by Peter L. Berger to suggest the necessary social structural prerequisites (institutions, organizations, apostolates) necessary to socialize effectively individuals and groups into the belief structure of some religious or secular group. In the United States, given that the larger civilization was first dominated by a generic Protestantism and presently by an overarching secularism, the Catholic Church can only maintain an effective presence in society if it maintains an intact and functioning "plausibility structure." Orthodox Catholics claim that, since the 1960s, the plausibility structure of the Catholic Church in the United States has been weakened severely by an internal secularization.

pluralism: The existence of competing belief systems and organizations. Religions in the United States must deal with, in some way, the challenges posed to them by a radical religious, cultural, and social pluralism.

pope: In Catholic theology, the vicar of Christ or God's representative on earth and the final religious authority for the Catholic Church.

positivism: The philosophical belief that only the things that can be tested by scientific investigation are real; the founder of positivism was the sociologist Auguste Comte who hoped that all supernatural religion would be replaced in the modern world by scientific knowledge as interpreted by a scientific elite who would, in essence, replace older religious authority.

principle of religious freedom: A principle endorsed by the Second Vatican Council, especially in *Dignitatis Humanae* (1965), to the effect that all individuals in society should have the political right to choose freely and exercise their own form of belief, whether it be religious or nonreligious in nature.

Progressive era: An era at turn into the twentieth century in the United States dominated by thinkers such as John Dewey who promoted a pragmatist philosophy opposed to the Catholic positing that all of social life should be undergirded by certain basic universal truths derived from both the natural and the divine law. According to the historian Thomas Woods Jr. the Catholic Church of the era, as part of its process of putting together its plausibility structure, developed sophisticated intellectual approaches both critiquing and attempting to co-pt the best of pragmatic and modern thinking.

"progressive modernizers vs. orthodox ecclesialists": A phrase indicating the present-day "battle for the Catholic Church" between liberals and conservatives as discussed by, among others, the Catholic sociologist, Monsignor George A. Kelly.

Protestant: A member of one of the numerous religious communities spawned by the Protestant Reformation during the sixteenth century in Europe. Almost all present-day Protestant groups spring from one of the four original reformational groupings: the Lutheran, the

Calvinist, the Anglican, and the Anabaptist. Given the logic of Protestantism, based as it is on an individual appropriation of Christianity, Protestantism has since the Reformation continually multiplied into hundreds of groupings.

Protestant principle: The belief that one's conscience should be the ultimate arbiter of what one decides to believe and how one ought to live. Based originally on Martin Luther's thought.

racism: The belief that some groups with distinctive physical traits are innately superior to others. The Catholic Church in the United States has historically tried but only partially succeeded in countering the racist attitudes and behaviors of some Catholics toward Afro-Americans, Native Americans, and Asians.

religious orders: Within the Catholic Church, religious groups, usually founded by some charismatic or saintly figure, dedicated to pursing and perfecting any one or more of the many apostolates or goals of the Church.

"restorationist movement": A term coined by historian Paul Johnson to indicate the attempt of Pope John Paul II and, now, Pope Benedict XVI and their supporters to reorient the Catholic Church in the United States and throughout the globe back to religious orthodoxy.

rites: Religious rituals; Western and Eastern Catholicism accept the same doctrine and leadership under the pope but have somewhat different religious rituals.

***Roe v. Wade*:** Supreme Court decision in 1973 legalizing abortion in the United States. The Catholic Church originally took the leading role in fighting the decision and now orthodox Catholics are joined by many conservative evangelical Protestants and Orthodox Jews in trying to reverse the decision and encourage U.S. citizens to reject abortion as a practice.

sacraments: In the Catholic, Orthodox Christian, and Protestant Anglican religious traditions, there are seven distinct channels of God's grace that are necessary to assist the individual Christian in both living a good religious and moral life here on earth and in eventually gaining entrance into Heaven. Other Christian groups accept the two sacraments of "baptism" and "communion."

Sacred Scripture (the Old and New Testaments of the Bible): All Christians believe that God has spoken to humankind through the Bible, consisting of the Old Testament (basically the Jewish Torah) and the New Testament (the recordings of the life and witness of Jesus Christ by his followers). Many Protestant Christians advocate a "sola Scriptura" approach that believes that God's truth is only communicated through the Holy Word of Scripture. Catholics, on the other hand, accept the divinely inspired nature of the Bible but believe that God communicates to humankind, additionally, through sacred tradition (that is, the writings of some of the early fathers of Christianity, worldwide ecumenical councils, papal and other episcopal pronouncements), and through the natural law written into the heart of the person.

saint: In official Catholic theology, an individual who has imitated successfully some key attribute of Jesus Christ during his/her lifetime and can serve, after death, as an intercessor for individuals to Christ. Being officially canonized as a saint is a long and careful process involving much research and the proving of at least two miracles. Many non-Catholic religionists in the biblical orbit view the Catholic concept of sainthood as a retrograde pagan practice that divinizes the human. The official Catholic response would be to make clear that Catholic theology does not view saints as divine or as, in any sense, a "semi-god." The Catholic worldview urges all followers of Christ to strive for sainthood and through the process of santification, to be as Christlike as possible.

saint veneration vs. saint worship: The Catholic Church teaches that one should respect, utilize, and venerate the saints as intercessors or go-betweens to Christ. Conversely put, saint worship, that is, the making of a saint into a divine or semi-godlike figure, is heterodox from a Catholic framework. Some Catholics uniformed by official Catholic teaching and many times from rural, premodern contexts have and do practice saint worship.

scientism: The philosophical belief, practiced by convinced positivists, that everything can and should be explained by science and that all social policy and, indeed, individual decision making, should rest on scientific findings.

Second Vatican Council (1962–65): One of the universal, worldwide councils convened by the Catholic Church during its lifetime to address some important theological issue or controversy. The sixteen documents of the Second Vatican Council addressed many issues of vital importance but one was viewed as particularly central, that is, the relationship of the Church to the modern world.

sect: A designation coined by sociologist-theologian Ernest Troeltsch to indicate a religious group in fundamental opposition to whatever passes for mainstream civilization in a society. Many times sects refer to religious groups in a society such as the Amish who believe that Christ cannot be found in the world outside of their circles; in other cases, a sect can refer to groups such as the hippies of the 1960s or the early Black Panther Party, secular groups in opposition, respectively, to what they saw as an American society dominated by capitalism and white oppression. Of note is that Christianity started out as a sect but became mainstream when the Roman Emperor Constantine converted to the faith and promulgated the Edict of Milan.

secularization/secularization from within: Secularization means the loss of religious influence at both the level of human consciousness and on social institutions. European society has experienced a widespread secularization over the past fifty years; in American society secularization is advanced among certain sectors of the civilization but not throughout the total nation. "Secularization from within," a term from the intellectual corpus of sociologists Peter L. Berger and Thomas Luckmann, refers to a situation in which the processes of secularization are masked but still real. Many conservative Catholics feel that the Catholic Church in the United States, while overtly claiming to maintain an authentic Catholic presence, has suffered a severe case of secularization from within.

socialism: A form of government in which ruling political elites make all the fundamental decisions regarding economic life, when, in other words, the government runs a command economy and controls the means of production.

socialization: A sociological concept referring to the ability of a society or organization to pass on its central values and vision to its members. All sociological studies indicate that, presently, the Catholic Church in the United States is failing to socialize successfully its members into the fundamental tenets of the Catholic religion.

subcultures vs. mainstream culture vs. countercultures: Sociological concepts indicating the relationship of a group/individual to society. Subcultures represent variations of mainstream culture (Catholic Americans, Jewish-Americans, Protestant-Americans, Afro-Americans, yuppies, farmers, jocks, southerners, etc.). Mainstream culture represents those values and ideas that set the standard for a civilization. Countercultures represent groups at variance with the mainstream vision of any particular society. Some Catholic sociologists such as David Carlin, believe that, given the widespread secularization of American society, the Catholic Church, if it maintains its orthodox beliefs, will be moving from a subcultural designation to one that is countercultural.

syncretism: The process of integrating various belief systems. In an American context characterized by a fundamental pluralism in religious and cultural beliefs, a certain amount of syncretism is inevitable for all but the most countercultural of groups.

synod of Bishops: Periodic meetings of all the bishops of the world to deal with a specific topic of importance to the Catholic Church (family life, social justice, etc.).

theology of liberation: A synthesis of Marxism and Catholicism, imported to Latin American by German theologians in the 1960s through to the end of the century. Very popular with progressive Catholics as it argued that the constitutive purpose of the Catholic religion was the institutionalization of socialist and, later, feminist social policies.

theology (versus religion): Theology is the systematic and rational study of religion. In Anselm's definition, it is "faith seeking understanding." Conversely, religion refers to the actual beliefs and practices of a particular group. Many "average" religious individuals have only an imperfect understanding of abstract and technical theological issues and debates.

therapeutic mentality: A subjective philosophy oriented not to duty to God or country but to meeting the emotional and personal needs of the individual. The Catholic Church acknowledges a salutary side to therapeutic concerns but is wary of a movement in the direction of selfishness, hedonism, and a radical individual autonomy.

Third World or "least industrialized societies": A sociological phrase coined by sociologists to characterize those nations in the contemporary world characterized by a low degree of science, technology, industrialization, capitalism, and a low standard of living. Sociologist James Henslin likes to employ the phrase "least industrialized societies" because he thinks the more common terminology, "Third World" society, is prejorative. There is a healthy and heated debate in sociology and within Catholic circles regarding the issue of whether or to what degree Third World poverty is the result of the policies of the dominant Western "First World." Catholic encyclicals such as *Populorum Progressio* (1967) make clear that, in the eyes of the Church, wealthy nations have an obligation to assist poorer nations in their development, both economically and in terms of the spiritual and cultural needs of the individual.

totalitarian: A system of government in which political elites control all essential sectors, organizations, and institutions of society. Totalitarian societies can come from the extreme political left (communism) and the extreme political right (Nazism).

Triune God: The Christian belief that God is made up of three persons, the Father, Son, and Holy Spirit.

trusteeism: A movement that periodically appears in an American society infused with a democratic ethos in which parishioners want control of such basic issues as the appointment of pastors, the acceptance of a certain form of liturgical practice, and financial expenditures. Trusteeism is, by definition, part of a "congregational" form of Church organization but provides problems for those religious bodies such as the Roman Catholic Church and the Eastern Orthodox Church that are characterized by a hierarchal and "top-down" form of authority.

"ultimate concern": A theological term coined by the Protestant theologian Paul Tillich, to define what a person's most central religious/philosophical commitment represents.

utilitarianism: A philosophy that views it as acceptable to utilize—or as Catholics would say, abuse—human life as "things," whether in the case of immigrant labor, the exploitation of women by men, or in the execution of abortion and human embryonic stem cell research.

"vale of tears": A Christian phrase indicating that life on earth is but a temporary cross or period of trial and suffering on the way to where the "real action" is, that being the beatific vision or meeting God face to face in Heaven.

vicar of Christ: A belief of the Catholic Church that the pope represents the central nexus between heaven and earth.

worldview: A philosophical description indicating the basic underlying philosophy of an individual, group, or civilization.

Appendix C

Key Voluntary Organizations in the Catholic Church of the United States

Of course, this list is not exhaustive but does introduce the reader to some of the major noneccthe sial, that is, independent of direct Church authority, Catholic organizations in the United States.

Scholarly

Fellowship of Catholic Scholars (founded by Monsignor George A. Kelly, Ph.D., in 1976; first president, Father Ronald Lawler) based at the University of Notre Dame; address: P.O. Box 495, Notre Dame, IN 46556, www.catholicscholars.org. Current president is Dean Bernard Dobankski, Professor of Law at Ave Maria School of Law, 3475 Plymouth Road, Ann Arbor, MI 48105; 1–734–827–8040 voice mail; bdobranski@avemarialaw.edu. Created to provide the Catholic Church an authentically Catholic voice in intellectual and scholarly matters in light of a pervasive secularization of Catholic intellectual and scholarly activity during the post–Vatican II period. Publishes annual proceedings and *Fellowship of Catholic Scholars Quarterly*.

Cardinal Newman Society (founded by Patrick J. Reilly in 1993 who presently serves as president and CEO); address: 10562 Associate Court, Manassas, VA 20109; www.cardinalnewmansociety.org; 1–703–367–0333 (voice mail): 1–703–396–8668 (fax). The Cardinal Newman Society is a national organization dedicated to the renewal of Catholic identity in Catholic higher education in the United States. Publishes monographs and the *Turnaround* newsletter.

Society of Catholic Social Scientists (co-founded by Stephen M. Krason and Joseph A. Varacalli, 1992); address: Stephen M. Krason, Ph.D., Esq., President, SCSS, Department of Political Science, Egan Hall, Franciscan University, Steubenville, OH 43952, www.catholicsocialscientists.org; 1–740–283–6245, extension 2366 (voice mail); 1–740–283–6401 (fax); scss@franciscan.edu. Founded with the dual purposes of promoting the social teachings of the Church in American civilization and public policy and providing a Catholic contribution to social science activity. Publishes *Catholic Social Science Review*, monographs, and a major encyclopedia project *Catholic Social Thought, Social Science, and Social Policy*.

Research and Policy

Catholic Family and Human Rights Institute (founded by Austin Ruse); address: 866 United Nations Plaza, Suite 427, New York, NY 10017; 212–754–5948; 212–754–9291 (fax); c-fam@c-fam.org or www.c-fam.org. The Catholic Family and Human Rights Institute is a nonprofit family and human rights organization operating from a Catholic worldview designed to serve the needs of United Nations delegates, extragovernmental and nongovernmental organizations.

Center of Concern (founded in 1971 by Bill Ryan, S.J., present president is James Hug, S.J., Ph.D.); address: 1225 Otis Street NE, Washington, DC 20017–2516; 1–202–635–2757; 1–202–832–9494 (fax); www.coc.org. A progressive Catholic international research center and policy institute providing theological reflections from a theology of liberationist and feminist perspective. The Center of Concern is devoted to analyzing and exploring global issues and social structures from an ethical perspective based on Catholic social teaching and involves itself in strategies and projects that promotes the good of the entire global community and the integrity of every individual. It involves itself in the struggle to end hunger, poverty, environmental decline, and injustice in the United States and around the world.

Benevolent and Fraternal

The Knights of Columbus (founded in 1881 by Father Michael J. Mc-Givney as a Catholic men's fraternal benefit society that was formed to render financial aid to members and their families; present Supreme Knight is Carl Anderson); address: One Columbus Circle, New Haven, CT 06510; 203–752–4000; www.kofc.org. The Knights of Columbus presently has more than 12,000 councils and 1.6 million members throughout the United States and around the world. The Knights of Columbus is devoted to supporting the pope and clergy and is very active in charitable, social welfare, educational, and religious enterprises. Publishes *Columbia* magazine monthly.

Antidefamation

Catholic League for Religious and Civil Rights (founded by Rev. Virgil Blum of Marquette University in 1973; presently headed by William Donohue, Ph.D.); address: 450 Seventh Avenue, New York, NY 10123; 1–212–371–3191; 1–212–371–3394 (fax); www.catholicleague.org. The Catholic League is the nation's largest Catholic civil rights organization; its purpose is to defend the right of Catholics—lay and clergy alike—to participate in American public life without defamation or discrimination. The league works to safeguard both the religious freedom rights and the free speech rights of Catholics whenever and wherever they are threatened. The league publishes a monthly magazine *Catalyst* and yearly comprehensive reports on various anti-Catholic manifestations in American society.

Women in the Church

Network (founded by forty-seven Catholic sisters in 1971); address: 801 Pennsylvania Avenue SE, Suite 460, Washington, DC 20003–2167; 1–202–547–5556; 1–202–547–5510 (fax); network@networklobby.org. Network is a women-led progressive national Catholic social justice lobby that was founded to educate, lobby, and organize to influence the formation of federal legislation to promote economic and social justice.

It envisions a social, economic, and political order that ensures human dignity and ecological justice, celebrated racial, ethnic, and cultural diversity, and promotes the common good.

Women for Faith and Family (founded by Helen Hull Hitchcock in 1984); address: P.O. Box 300411, St. Louis, MO 63130; 1–314–863–8385; 1–314–863–5858 (fax); www.wf-g.org or info@wf-f.org. Founded to provide Catholic women a means of expressing unity with the teachings of the Catholic Church, deepening their understanding of the Catholic faith, and transmitting it to others. Publishes a quarterly magazine *Voices* and other materials such as leaflets, family sourcebooks, and policy statements. Thousands of orthodox Catholic women in the United States have signed the organization's *Affirmation for Catholic Women* since its publication in 1984.

Pro-Life Organization

Human Life International (founded by Father Paul Marx, O.S.B., in 1981; present president is Father Thomas J. Euteneuer); address: 4 Family Life, Front Royal, VA 22630–6453; 1–540–635–7884; 1–540–622–6247 (fax); www.hli.org or hli@hli.org. An international organization, the mission of Human Life International is to promote and defend the sanctity of life and family around the world according to the teachings of the Roman Catholic Church. In addition to the United States, the organization has many chapters in Africa, Asia, Europe, Latin America, Oceania, and the Carribean. Publishes a wide variety of material including books and social policy statements.

Publishing

Ignatius Press (founded by its publisher, Father Joseph Fessio, S. J.); address: 2515 McAllister Street, San Francisco, CA 94118; 1–800–651–1531; www.ignatius.com. Largest publisher and distributor of Catholic books, magazines, videos and music. Operating from an orthodox

Catholic perspective, Ignatius Press has been in business since 1978. Among many other products, the press has published 875 individual titles and is the publisher of two large circulation magazines, the *Homiletic and Pastoral Review* (edited by Father Kenneth Baker, S.J.) and *Catholic World Report.*

Pauline Books and Media (Daughters of St. Paul); address: 50 Saint Paul's Avenue, Boston, MA 02130; 1–617–522–8911; 1–617–541–9805 (fax); www.daughtersofstpaul.com. Most noted for their faithful publication of all Catholic encyclicals and other official documents of the Church, this very orthodox publishing house has as its stated goal to communicate the Gospel message through all available forms of media such books, cassettes, CDs, music, videos, and software in both English and Spanish.

Sheed and Ward (founded in 1926 by Australian lawyer Francis Joseph Sheed and his British wife, Maisie Ward); address: 4501 Forbes Boulevard, Suite 200, Lanham, MD 20706; 1–800–462–6420; www.romanlittlefield.com. In recent years Sheed and Ward has become a major publishing vehicle for progressive Catholic thinkers. Presently it is an imprint of Rowman and Littlefield Publishers, Inc.

Paulist Press (The present editorial director is Father Lawrence Boadt, C.S.P.); address: Paulist Press, 997 Macarthur Boulevard, Mahwah, NJ 07430; 1–800–218–1903; www.paulistpress.com. The Paulist Press is a major component of the work of the Paulist Fathers, a society of missionary priests founded for and by Americans in 1858. Paulist Press has been in business since 1913. Since the Second Vatican Council, the press has taken a decidedly progressive perspective publishing in the areas of ecumenical theology, Roman Catholic studies, and books on Scripture, liturgy, church history, philosophy, and the connection between faith and culture.

Sophia Institute Press; address: Box 5284, Manchester, NH 03108; 1–800–888–9344; www.sophiainstitute.com. One of the many small but growing Catholic presses part of the recent orthodox Catholic "restoration movement" within the Catholic Church of the United States with the stated goal of producing faithful Catholic books.

National Catholic Newspapers

National Catholic Reporter (established in 1964; present editor in chief is Thomas Roberts); address: 115 East Armour Boulevard, Kansas City, MO 64111; 1–816–531–0538; 1–816–968–2268 (fax); www.natcath.com. This newspaper is very progressive.

National Catholic Register (present editor in chief is Father Owen Kearns, L.C.); address: 432 Washington Avenue, North Haven, CT 06473; 1–203–230–3800; 1–203–230–3838 (fax); editor@circlemedia.com or www.ncregister.com. Policies and perspective consistent with official magisterial teachings.

Our Sunday Visitor (present editor is Gerald Korson); address: 200 Noll Plaza, Huntington, IN 46750; 1–800–348–2440; www.osv.com. Policies and perspective consistent with official magisterial teachings. Also publishes books, magazines, bulletins, pamphlets, and other material.

The Remnant (founded in 1967 by Walter Matt, former editor of *The Wanderer*, given his belief that Vatican II represented a reversal of 2,000 years of authentic Catholic tradition; now edited by Walter Matt's youngest son, Michael J. Matt); address: 336 280th Street, Osceola, WI 54020; 1–651–462–8323; 1–651–462–4764 (fax); www.Remnant newspaper.com. Policies and perspective critical, from a radically traditionalist perspective, of magisterial teachings in the post–Vatican II period.

The Wanderer (founded in 1867; presently edited by Alphonse J. Matt, Jr.); address: 201 Ohio Street, St. Paul, MN 55107; www.thewandere rpress.com. Policies and perspective consistent with official Magisterial teaching.

Periodicals and Magazines

America Magazine (the present editor-in-chief is Drew Christensen, S. J.); address: 106 West 56th Street, New York, NY 10019–3803; 1–212–581–4640; 1–212–399–3596 (fax); www.americamagazine.org. Once a vehicle of orthodox Catholic thinking, has become much more progressive in orientation since Vatican II; dominated intellectually by present-day Jesuit thought.

Commonweal (present editor is Paul Baumann); address: 475 Riverside Drive, Room 405, New York, NY 10115; 1–212–662–4200; 1–212–662–4183 (fax); editors@commonwealmagazine.org or www.commonwealmagazine.org. Progressive review of religion, politics, and culture, based on the belief that Catholicism and America have much to learn from each other.

Crisis Magazine (present editor is Brian Saint-Paul); address: 1814½ North Street NW, Washington, DC 20036; 1–202–861–7790; mail@crisismagazine.com or www.crisismagazine.com. Dedicated to the proposition that the crisis of modernity can be answered by a Christian humanism rooted in the teachings of the Catholic Church, the stated mission of *Crisis* magazine is to interpret and shape the direction of contemporary culture from a standpoint of Catholic tradition.

Lay Witness (edited by Leon J. Suprenant Jr.); address: International Headquarters, 827 North Fourth Street, Steubenville, OH 43952; 1–800–693–2484; www.cuf.org. Orthodox intellectual forum of the Catholic organization, Catholics United for the Faith.

New Oxford Review (present editor is its founder, Dale Vree); address: 1069 Kains Avenue, Berkeley, CA 94706; 1–510–526–5374; 1–510–526–3492 (fax); www.newoxfordreview.org. Orthodox intellectual forum sharply critical of the present state of the Catholic Church in America, including its leadership.

U.S. Catholic (present editor is Father John Molyneux, C.M.F.); address: 205 West Monroe Street, Chicago, IL 60606; 1–312–236–7782; 1–312–236–8207 (fax); editors@uscatholic.org or www.uscatholic.org. Published by the Claretian Missionaries, a progressive magazine oriented to readers the popular level.

Appendix D

Basic Demographic and Statistical Information about the Catholic Church Institution and Community in the United States

Note: The following very useful background information was derived from the Catholic Information Project: *The Catholic Church in America–Meeting Real Needs in Your Neighborhood (CIP)* (December 2003), which was commissioned by the Office of Communications of the United States Conference of Catholic Bishops, 3211 4th Street, Washington, DC 20017–1194, 1–202–541–3000; www.usccb.org/comm/c.p.shtml.

The *CIP* reports that in 2003: there were 63.4 million Catholics (23 percent of the population in the United States); 195 dioceses or eparchies (the latter is the term for dioceses of the Eastern Catholic Church); 19,081 parishes; 43,634 priests; 5,499 brothers; 73,316 sisters; 565 Catholic hospitals treating 83.9 million patients in 2002; 7,142 elementary schools and 1,374 high schools with over 2.6 million students enrolled; and 230 Catholic colleges and universities educating over 720,000 students.

Regarding information about some key ethnic/racial groups in the United States who identify themselves as Catholic, the *CIP* reports that there are 25 million Hispanic Catholics in the United States representing approximately 39 percent of the overall Catholic population. Twenty-five of the nation's 281 active bishops are Hispanic representing 9 percent of the national hierarchy. Hispanic priests represent 6.5 percent of the nation's 44,487 priests. The *CIP* reports that no less than 71 percent of the growth in the American Catholic population since 1960 has been the result of the increase in the number of Hispanics in the U.S. population overall. It also projects that by the second decade of the twenty-first century, Hispanic Catholics will represent over 50 percent of all American Catholics.

Regarding Native Americans, the *CIP* reports that the Bureau of Catholic Indian Missions estimates that, at present, there are 500,000 Native American Catholics. This represents about one-fourth of the Native American population in the United States.

The *CIP* reports that there are currently about 2.3 million African American Catholics with about 1,300 American Catholic parishes being predominately African American. Of the latter, 75 have African American pastors. There are approximately 250 priests, 300 sisters, and 380 deacons who are African American.

Regarding basic information on priests, deacons, and vowed religious, the *CIP* discloses that of the 44,487 priests in the United States, 14,772 (or 33.2 percent) belong to various religious orders, that is, they are not tied to a local diocese under the direction of the reigning bishop or "ordinary." Furthermore, the average age of American priests is 61 years of age. Of the almost 500 new priests ordained in 2003, the average age is 36 with 14 percent of the class being Hispanic. There are almost 14,000 men, almost all of whom are married, who served as permanent deacons. As *CIP* states, "The permanent diaconate, restored by the Second Vatican Council (1962–1965), is a vital ministry in the United States and has grown an average of 10 percent annually. In addition to holding full-time jobs in their places of work, permanent deacons assist in the worship of life of the local faith community by preaching, baptizing, teaching, witnessing marriages, officiating at funerals, and sometimes serving as a parish life coordinator in the absence of a priest" (2003, 5). Regarding American Catholic religious, there are 5,568 religious brothers and 74,698 religious sisters, of which 1,021 brothers and 7,389 sisters teach in Catholic elementary and secondary schools. There are more than 500 religious orders in the United States, each with their own specialized ministries.

Regarding Catholic elementary and secondary education, the *CIP* notes that the Catholic Church in the United States administers the largest network of private schools in the country. Of particular interest, apart from the previous statistics offered regarding overall enrollment numbers, is that in 2003, 13.4 percent or 341,819 students in Catholic elementary and secondary education are non-Catholic. Also, the minority enrollment in Catholics schools numbered 663,682 in

2003 representing 26 percent of overall enrollment. Regarding the latter, 11.2 percent were Hispanic, 7.8 percent were African American, 3.7 percent were Asian American, 2 percent were characterized as "multicultural," .3 percent were American Indian/Native American, and .8 percent were Native Hawaiian/Pacific Islander. For more information, contact the National Catholic Educational Association (www.ncea.org) and the USCCB Department of Education (www.usccb.org/education/index.htm).

Regarding Catholic colleges and universities, the *CIP* includes several facts outside of the overall enrollment figures previously presented that are especially noteworthy. One is that Catholic colleges and universities account for half of all religious-based institutions of higher education in the United States. Another is that, since the conclusion of the Second Vatican Council, almost all are governed by a lay board of trustees. There are other interesting figures. Eleven of the 230 colleges and universities are sponsored by dioceses. Only one institution of higher education, the Catholic University of America in Washington, D.C., is sponsored and partially funded directly by the Catholic Church. All others are sponsored by their founding religious congregations such as the Society of Jesus (the Jesuits) who administer 28 colleges and universities in the United States. Among the more prominent Jesuit institutions of higher education are Georgetown, Boston College, Fordham University, and the University of Scranton. Thirty-five percent of all students attending Catholic higher educational institutions are non-Catholic. Finally, Catholic institutions of higher learning in the United States include 4 medical schools, 26 law schools, 17 schools of engineering, 81 schools of nursing, 177 schools of education, 19 women's colleges, 3 research universities, 13 doctoral universities, and 2 aviation programs. For more information contact the Association of Catholic Colleges and Universities (www.accunet.org), the USCCB Department of Education (www.usccb.org/education/index.htm), the Cardinal Newman Society for the Preservation of Catholic Higher Education and the Fellowship of Catholic Scholars.

The *CIP* also notes the long tradition the Catholic Church has in the United States providing Catholic health care and social services to both Catholics and non-Catholics alike. The Church's 565 hospitals account for 11 percent of community hospitals in the country as well as 16 percent of all U.S. hospital admissions. In addition to hospitals, the Catholic health care network also includes 477 health care centers and

1,534 specialized homes. In the year 2002, the number of Catholic orphanages or residential homes for children totaled 226, serving a total of 714,253 young Americans. For more information, one can contact the Catholic Health Association (www.chausa.org).

The *CIP* also reports that the Catholic Charities network consists of more than 1,400 local agencies and institutions nationwide that provide help for more than 7 million people a year, regardless of religious background. The network consists of 51,000 staff and 175,000 volunteers.

The *CIP* also contains useful information on such topics as humanitarian aid, Catholic involvement in affordable housing, legal and other forms of assistance to migrants, Catholic lay associations with a social apostolate, and Church finances (www.usccb.org/comm/cip.shtml).

Appendix E

Key Locations (Museums, Colleges/Seminaries/High Schools, Basilicas and Cathedrals, Shrines, Monasteries, and Feasts/Festivals)

Note: Information for many of the key locations for Catholic religious, intellectual, and cultural activities in the United States (and throughout the world) can be found on www.catholiclinks.org. A few prominent examples of museums, educational institutions, basilicas/cathedrals, shrines, and festivals/feasts follow.

Museums

John Paul II Cultural Center, 3900 Harewood Road NE, Washington, DC 20017, 1–202–635–5400, www.jp2cc.org. Mission Statement: "The Pope John Paul II Cultural Center exists to bring the wisdom and faith experience of the Catholic Church, as developed through centuries of ecclesial life and thought guided by the Holy Spirit and as articulated by the Church's teaching office, especially by the Popes, to the human search for meaning and purpose in life, righteousness, justice and peace in the world of the twenty-first century with its varied religious, ethnic, and cultural communities."

Mary, Queen of the Universe Shrine Museum, 8300 Vineland Avenue, Orlando, FL 32821, 1–407–239–6600, www.maryqueenoftheuniverse. org/museum.

LaSalle University Art Museum, 1900 West Olney Avenue, Philadelphia, PA 19141, 1–215–951–1221, www.artcom.com/Museums. Statement of purpose: Permanent exhibition of European and American art from late medieval period up to present times.

Colleges/Seminaries/High Schools

Some of the more prominent Catholic colleges and universities are: Georgetown University (in the tradition of the Society of Jesus); St. John's University (run by the Order of St. Vincent); the Catholic University of America (the "Bishops' University"); the University of Notre Dame (run by the Order of the Holy Cross); Seton Hall University (run by the Archdiocese of Newark), Franciscan University (run by the Franciscans); and Christendom College (founded by the layman Dr. Warren Carroll). The newest university, and part and parcel of the Catholic restoration in Catholic higher education is Ave Maria University located in Naples, Florida, and founded by the Catholic layman Mr. Thomas Monaghan.

Some of the more prominent Catholic seminaries are: Saint John Vianney in Denver, Colorado; Holy Apostles in Cromwell, Connecticut (which specializes in late vocations); Mount Saint Mary's Seminary in Emmitsburg, Maryland; Sacred Heart Major Seminary in Detroit, Michigan; Saint Charles Borromeo in Philadelphia, Pennsylvania, and Saint Joseph's Seminary (Dunwoodie), Yonkers, New York.

Three of the most nationally known and respected Catholic high schools can be found in New York: Regis High School in Manhattan, run by the Society of Jesus; and two schools run by the Marianists in Long Island: Chaminade High School and Kellenberg Memorial High School.

Basilicas and Cathedrals

Probably the most famous basilica is the Basilica of the National Shrine of the Immaculate Conception located in the nation's capital, the District of Columbia. Also of special importance is the Basilica of the National Shrine of Saint Elizabeth Ann Bayley Seton, located in Emmitsburg,

Maryland, www.emmitsburg.net/setonshrine/shrine.htm. The University of Notre Dame has its own Basilica of the Sacred Heart. Probably the most famous cathedral, situated on Fifth Avenue in New York City, is Saint Patrick's. Approaching the majesty of Saint Patrick's is the nearby Cathedral Basilica of the Sacred Heart, located in Newark, New Jersey. America's oldest city, Saint Augustine, Florida, is home to the Cathedral-Basilica of Saint Augustine.

Shrines

There are also scores of shrines that dot the American landscape. Just a few would be the National Shrine of Saint Jude, located in Chicago; the National Shrine of the North American Martyrs to be found in Auriesville, New York (www.martyrshrine.org); Philadelphia hosts the National Shrine of Saint John Neumann and, in Doylestown, Pennsylvania, is the National Shrine of Our Lady of Czestochowa and Padre Pio in Balto, Pennsylvania; Mother Cabrini is located in New York City.

Monasteries

Among the numerous monasteries that populate the United States, there is the Monastery of the Discalced Carmelite Order, in Alambra, California; the Immaculate Conception Monastery run by the Passionists of Chicago, Illinois; the Abbey of Gethsemani in Trappist, Kentucky under the direction of the Trappist monks; the Monastery of Our Lady of the Rosary in Buffalo, New York; Belmont Abbey Monastery in Belmont, North Carolina, run by the Benedictine Order; the Queen of Angels Monastery run by the Benedictine Sisters in Mount Angel, Oregon; and the Saint Norbert Abbey under the direction of the Norbertine Order of Depere, Wisconsin.

Feasts/Festivals

As the *Catholic Encyclopedia* explains, Catholic feasts and festivals can be divided roughly into those that are universally celebrated within the

Church and require mandatory attendance at a Church service, that is, they are "holy days of obligation," while others are celebrated more voluntarily by particular religious orders, countries, provinces, dioceses, towns, neighborhoods, ethnic groups, and lay associations (www.new advent.org/cathen). Regarding the former, the more official and obligatory feasts, *The Catechism of the Catholic Church* (1994) makes clear that there are certain "precepts of the Church" that must be followed. As the *Catechism* states: "The precepts of the Church are set in the context of a moral life bound to and nourished by liturgical life. The obligatory character of these positive laws decreed by the pastoral authorities is meant to guarantee to the faithful the indispensable minimum in the spirit of prayer and moral effort, in the growth of love of God and neighbor" (1994, 493). The first precept is that "you shall attend Mass on Sundays and holy days of obligation (#2042). The fourth precept, according to the *Catechism,* "completes the Sunday observance by participation in the principal liturgical feasts which honor the mysteries of the Lord, the Virgin Mary, and the saints" (#2043). The *Catechism* continues, "to be observed are the day of the Nativity of Our Lord Jesus Christ, the Epiphany, the Ascension of Christ, the feast of the Body and Blood of Christ, the feast of Mary the Mother of God, her Immaculate Conception, her Assumption, the feast of Saint Joseph, the feast of the Apostles Saints Peter and Paul, and the feast of all Saints" (#2177). The most obvious examples of the more particular religious celebrations that are not prescribed officially by the Church as obligatory are those promoted by the vast array of America's ethnic communities. The Irish have, of course, their Saint Patrick's Day (which, interestingly enough, has expanded sociologically to include the participation of many Catholic groups outside the Irish clan). The Polish celebrate Our Lady of Czestochowa. Our Lady of Fatima is central for the Portuguese Catholic community. Carpatho-Rusyns pay special homage to Our Lady of Perpetual Help. Eastern Catholics in general venerate three of the great figures of the early Church, the "Cappadocian Fathers" (Saint Basil the Great, Saint Gregory of Nyssa, and Saint Gregory of Nazizus). The Italians have many saints that they venerate and celebrate; one of the more still vibrant Italian American feasts is the "Giglio Feast" ("Feast of the Lillies") celebrated every July to honor both Saint Paulinus of Nola, Italy, and Our Lady of Mount Carmel. This feast has existed for over one hundred years in the Williamsburg section of Brooklyn, New York (www. giglio-usa.org/Brooklyn_Mt_Carmel.htm). Haitians have a central devotion to the feast of Corpus Christi. The central religious celebration of Hispanic Catholics is that of Our Lady of Guadalupe. For an absolutely fascinating and rich discussion of the numerous religious feasts and festivals celebrated by Hispanic immigrants to the United States from Mexico, Central and South America, and the Caribbean, see S. G. Liaugminas, "Catholicism with a Latin Beat," *Crisis* Magazine, September 2001 (www.crisismagazine.com/september2001/cover.htm).

Appendix F

Archival Depositories

Thankfully, there are many archival depositories where those interested in studying the American Catholic experience can find an abundance of valuable and useful material. A few of the most important are listed here under the broad categories of (1) general archival deposits on the Catholic experience in the United States, (2) immigration/ethnic groups, and (3) specific groups within the American Catholic community. The information offered here is certainly not intended to be exhaustive but rather suggestive of the kinds of archival depositories that are available for the inquiring student.

General

The Catholic University of America American Catholic History Research Center and University Archives. Address: 101 Life Cycle Institute, 620 Michigan Avenue NE, Washington, DC 20064; 1–202–319–5065, www.loc.gov.rr/main/religion/cua.html; contact person: Dr. Timothy Meagher, archivist/museum director.

The archives contain the records of such major American Catholic organizations as the National Conference of Catholic Charities, the National Catholic Educational Association, the Catholic Interracial Council of New York, the United States Catholic Conference, the American Catholic Historical Association, the Catholic Anthropological Conference, Catholic Charities USA, the Catholic Commission on Intellectual and Cultural Affairs, the Catholic Theological Society of America, among others. The archives also contain the personal papers of a number of prominent Catholics, including those of Archbishop John Carroll. Among the many smaller archival collections are materials on such important topics as the Americanist controversy, Catholic missions on Native Americans, and anti-Catholic literature. For fuller listings of the collections, http://libraries.cua.edu/index.html.

The Cushwa Center for the Study of American Catholicism. Address: University of Notre Dame, 1135 Flanner Hall, Notre Dame, IN 46556–5611; 1-574-631-5441; 1-574-631-8471 (fax); cushwa.1@nd.edu or www.nd.edu/~cushwa/; contact person: Timothy Matovina, director.

The Cushwa Center for the Study of American Catholicism seeks interdisciplinary and ecumenical cooperation in its many scholar activities which include seminars, conferences, and research and publishing projects. Is especially known for its studies of the Irish experience in America, the growth of Hispanic Catholicism in the United States, and the history of Catholic parish life. Also known for its generation of research on the relationship of American religion and culture, the experiences of women in American religious history, and the impact of the Second Vatican Council on the American Catholic community.

Research Guide for Catholic Resources of the Francis A. Drexel Library. Address: Francis A. Drexel Library, St. Joseph's University, 5600 City Avenue, Philadelphia, PA 19131; 610-660-1900; contact person: Ene Andrilli, Associate Director for Information and Access Services, Saint Joseph's University, eandrill@sju.edu.

Contains a combination of valuable information on world Catholicism, the Catholic Church in the United States, and the Catholic Church in the archdiocese of Philadelphia (e.g., megasites and search engines on the Internet; general resources on the Catholic Church around the world and in the United States; Vatican/papal resources; Church history; Catholic education; journals and newspapers; liturgical resources; Jesuit resources; apologetics; Catholic authors and writings; and Catholic Philadelphia with information on the parishes, organizations, key personages, educational institutions of the archdiocese.

Immigration/Ethnic Groups

Center for Migration Studies Library and Archives. Address: 209 Flagg Place, Staten Island, NY 10304–1199; 1-718-351-8800; 1-718-667-4598 (fax); http://cmsny.library.net.

The Center for Migration Studies maintains a specialized library on international migration, refugees, and ethnic groups. It includes over 27,500 volumes, 150 periodicals, 750 dissertations, 128 newsletters, 60 ethnic newspapers, 1,900 conference papers, and 3,700 journal article reprints. The Center for Migration Studies has excellent resources for the study of ethnic groups, particularly those in the United States. Its collections on Italian Americans ranks among the very best in the world. Also contains collections of the records of both the national and New York offices of the Department of Immigration, United States Catholic Conference (1917–), the USCC's War and Relief Services (1944–71), and the collections of and by the Scalabrini Missionary Fathers in the United States.

Immigration History Research Center. Address: University of Minnesota College of Liberal Arts, 311 Andersen Library, 222-21st Avenue S, Minneapolis, MN 55455–0439; 1–612–625–4800; 1–612–626–0018, ihrc@umn.edu; contact person: Joel Wurl.

In supporting a tripartite mission (teaching, research, and service), the activities of the Immigration History Research Center support the work of its parent institution, the University of Minnesota. The research center develops and maintains a library and archival collection of the American immigrant experience, provides research assistance, produces publications, and sponsors academic and public programs. In partnership with various ethnic communities, historical agencies, research specialists and other educators, it preserves and promotes understanding of the history of the numerous immigrant communities to American shores. In June 1999, the Immigration History Research Center's documentation of the immigrant experience was designated as an Official Project of "Save America's Treasures," a public-private partnership of the White House.

Specific Groups Within the Catholic Community of the United States

Catholic Archives of Texas. Address: 1600 N. Congress Avenue, Austin, TX 78711; 1–512–476–6296; 1–512–476–3715, cat@onr.com.

The mission of this archival center is to collect, preserve, and make available for research those records of individuals and organizations engaged in work reflecting the goals of the Catholic Church in Texas. Records and collections include those of the Texas Catholic Conference and the Texas Knights of Columbus; the Texas Catholic Historical Society; various religious associations, societies, and Catholic clubs of Texas; the papers of prominent individuals including the bishops and clergy of Texas; diocesan and parish information; material on the various religious orders either founded or stationed within the state; newspapers/photographs/sacramental records on microfilm; Texana and Catholic books; and artifacts relating to the history of the Catholic Church in Texas.

Marquette University Department of Special Collections and University Archives. Address: Marquette University, Special Collections/University Archives, Raynor Memorial Libraries, 1355 W. Wisconsin Avenue, P.O. Box 3141, Milwaukee, WI 53201–3141; 1–414–288–5904; 1–414–288–6709 (fax); mark.thiel@marquette.edu; contact person: Mark G. Thiel.

This department within Marquette University library contains an important collection of Catholic records relating to American Indian peoples. Among other material, this collection includes the records of the Bureau of Catholic Indian Missions and the Tekakwitha Conference, as well as other documentation on over 100 native peoples from portions of Canada and the United States. Additionally, the library's general collection holds over 30,000 related titles.

Appendix G

Resource Guides on the Web

www.catholicanalysis.com

There are hundreds of Catholic blogs out in cyberspace that allow individuals to provide their opinions and judgments about the issues and controversies that confront Catholics in America and around the globe. One of the most sophisticated is authored by Oswald Sobrino, a graduate seminary student who routinely posts his in-depth and serious commentaries, essays, and book reviews.

www.catholicculture.org

Another exceedingly useful Catholic website that includes, among other items, a document library of well over 4,500 Church documents and articles, a critical review of over 800 other Catholic websites according to the criteria of comprehensiveness of resources, usability, and fidelity to the Catholic tradition as understood by magisterial authority.

www.catholicdir.com

Since 1817, the Kenedy Directory has served as the basic resource and authoritative guide to much valuable statistical information on the Catholic Church of the United States, including its 208 total archdioceses and dioceses. 1–800–473–7020.

www.catholiceducation.org

The Catholic Educators Resource Center was founded by educator J. Fraser Field. Contains well over 2,000 scholarly and popular articles that deal with Catholic analysis of the social world. The articles are divided into two broad categories.

The first, "Core Issues," includes apologetics, arts and literature, Catholic education, Catholic stories, culture and civilization, facts and misconceptions, history, politics and government, religion and ethics, and science. The second,

"Current Issues," includes abortion, environment, euthanasia, feminism, homosexuality, marriage and the family, media, medical ethics, multiculturalism, parenting, persecution of Christians, population control, sexuality, and social justice.

www.catholicexchange.com

Organized exclusively for religious, charitable, and educational purposes, this web page provides a multitude of resources necessary for understanding the Catholic Church and its varied apostolates.

www.ewtn.com

Site of the Catholic television network founded by Mother Angelica, featuring document library, audio library, Catholic news, and programming information.

www.newadvent.org

Hosts the *Catholic Encyclopedia*, 1913 edition, the *Summa Theologica*, and many other important Church documents.

www.ratzingerfanclub.com

This website deals centrally with one great religious, intellectual, and moral issue confronting the Catholic Church in the United States, that is, its relationship with the dominant political philosophy of liberalism.

www.usccb.org

Official website of the United States Catholic Conference of Bishops.

www.vatican.va

Official website of the Holy See and the Vatican.

www.zenit.org

Daily reports from Rome on happenings in the Vatican and in the global Church.

Appendix H

Timeline on the Catholic Experience in the United States

1565	Celebration of first Catholic Mass in Saint Augustine, Florida
1622	Pope Gregory XV institutes the Congregation for the Propagation of the Faith, under whose jurisdiction the American Catholic Church remained until 1908
1634	Catholic colony settles in Maryland by Cecil Calvert
1763	Spain cedes Florida to England and England gains all land east of the Mississippi River from France
1789	The United States sees its first Catholic bishop, John Carroll, a member of the Society of Jesus, elected and its first and oldest Catholic institution of higher education, Georgetown College and later, University, founded
1829–84	Series of Baltimore plenary sessions and councils convened to organize, standardize, and strengthen the Catholic Church in America
1830s–50	The first major Catholic immigration from Europe, especially Ireland, ensues, thus initiating the processes leading to the making of the Catholic community as the largest religious body in the country and to the "de-Protestantization" of the nation
1842	University of Notre Dame founded by the Congregation of the Holy Cross (C.S.C.)
1848	Diplomatic relations established between the United States and Rome
1856	Bishop James Bayley of Newark established Seton Hall College, later University, the first Catholic institution of higher education under the control of a diocese

1858   Construction begins on Saint Patrick's Cathedral in New York City, a symbol of the new, more impressive posture that Catholics were starting to assume in America

1882   Catholic America's most important fraternal association, the Knights of Columbus, is founded

1889   The bishops of the United States founded the national Catholic university, Catholic University of America in Washington, D.C.

1891   The first of the major "social encyclicals," *Rerum Novarum* ("On the Condition of the Working Classes") is issued thus setting Catholicism off from any simple endorsement of the American capitalist system; Mother Katherine Drexel founds the Sisters of the Blessed Sacrament for missionary work geared to black Americans and Native Americans

1899   *Testem benevolentiae* ("On the Heresy of Americanism") is issued by Pope Leo XIII; debate within Catholic elite circles ensues over whether or not "the heresy of Americanism" is real or not

1907   *Pascendi Dominici Gregis* ("On the Doctrine of the Modernists") is issued by Pope Pius X calling modernism "the synthesis of all heresies"; the combined impact of this document along with Pope Leo XIII's *Testem benevolentiae* holds progressive Catholic forces at bay until the Second Vatican Council

1908   Rome declares that the Catholic Church in the United States is no longer to be considered a "missionary territory" indicating the increased respect that the Church in America was being given by the worldwide Catholic community

1917   The National Catholic War Council founded at the urging of President Woodrow Wilson to organize Catholic assistance to the nation during World War I; organization goes through a series of evolutions in its nature and purpose as the official national bureaucracy of the Catholic Bishops of America and is now called the United States Conference of Catholic Bishops

1921–24   Restrictive immigration legislation passed in the United States, some arguing that it was purposely created by nativist sentiment to stop the influx of millions of poor and formally uneducated Catholics into the country

1928 Alfred E. Smith, governor of New York, is first Catholic presidential candidate of a major political party and is defeated by Herbert C. Hoover

1931 The encyclical, *Quadragesimo Anno* ("Forty Years After"), that is, after *Rerum Novarum*, is published sparking the creation of a host of Catholic scholarly and social service organizations dedicated to institutionalizing and promoting Catholic social thought throughout both Catholic and non-Catholic America; its central concept of "subsidiarity" sets the Catholic Church off from ever accepting, without qualification, socialist ideas

1931–42 Father Charles Coughlin brings his understanding of Catholic issues and concerns to the American nation in widely heard radio broadcasts

1933 Dorothy Day founded the Catholic Worker Movement

1946 Mother Frances Xavier Cabrini becomes the first citizen of the United States to attain official status as a saint

1948 Protestants and Other Americans for the Separation of Church and State formed to oppose federal aid to private religious schools

1952 Bishop Fulton J. Sheen gains fame and many converts to the Catholic faith through his popular program broadcast on mainstream television

1959 Pope John XXIII is elected in Rome to lead the Catholic Church

1960 John F. Kennedy is elected as the first Catholic president of the United States; debate over the years ensued over whether or not his speech to the Houston Ministerial Association and the manner in which he presented his Catholic faith to the American people conceded too much to the practical demands of American politics

1962–65 The Second Vatican Council is held in Rome producing sixteen documents dealing with the relationship of the Church to the non-Catholic world; in-fighting between progressive and conservative forces over the correct interpretation of the council starts with the progressives, at least initially, winning the battle

1965   President Lyndon B. Johnson once again "opens up" America to immigration, bringing in millions of Catholics from the less developed nations of Latin America, Asia, and Africa

1967   The Land O'Lakes document is signed by progressive Catholic leaders in the field of Catholic higher education declaring the absolute need for their organizations to have "academic freedom" and "institutional autonomy" from Catholic religious authorities

1968   *Humanae Vitae* ("On Human Life") is issued by Pope Paul VI; significant dissent against the "birth control encyclical" is initiated by progressive Catholic leaders and quickly gains the sympathetic support of most rank and file Catholics

1968   Catholics United for the Faith, a lay organization of those Catholic supportive of a magisterial defined Catholicism, created and served as noteworthy opposition to dominant progressive Catholic forces of the era

1973   The Supreme Court in its *Roe v. Wade* decision legalizes abortion in the United States; the Catholic community takes the lead in the fight to reduce/eliminate abortion in the country, later to be joined by large sectors of the conservative Protestant community

1975   Mother Elizabeth Ann Bayley Seton becomes the first native-born American to attain official status as a saint

1976   The Fellowship of Catholic Scholars is organized to fight against the secularization of the Catholic Church and, especially, within Catholic higher education

1979   Pope John Paul II starts his papal visits to the United States; coming to, respectively, Boston, New York, Philadelphia, Chicago, Washington in 1979; to Miami, South Carolina, New Orleans, New Mexico, Arizona, Los Angeles, San Antonio, San Francisco, Detroit in 1987; to Denver for World Youth Day in 1993; and, to New Jersey, New York, Baltimore in 1995

1984   President Ronald Reagan opens official diplomatic relations between the United States and the Vatican

1990   Roman authorities issue *Ex corde Ecclesiae* ("Out of the Heart of the Church") in an attempt, in essence, to reverse the secularization of Catholic higher education ushered in by the widespread acceptance of the 1967 Land O'Lakes document; debate between progressive and magisterial forces commence over how to implement the document in the American context

1992   *The Catechism of the Catholic Church*, the first universal catechism in 400 years, is published; viewed as a victory for magisterial forces desiring less latitude regarding the question of what is or is not acceptable Catholic belief and practice

1992   The Society of Catholic Social Scientists is established, another part of the recent "Catholic restoration," geared to integrating Catholic social teaching into the social sciences and social policy

2004   Presidential election between George W. Bush and Senator John Kerry exposes sharp differences in the political beliefs of Church-going verses non–Church going Catholics and the question of the obligation of Catholic politicians to their Catholic faith with a focus on the abortion issue

2005   Upon the death of John Paul II on April 2, Pope Benedict XVI is elected pope on April 19; Benedict XVI is expected to follow the "restorationist" policies of his predecessor

Bibliography

Abbott, Walter, ed. *The Documents of Vatican II*. Washington, DC: America Press, 1966.

Adam, Karl. *The Spirit of Catholicism*. Garden City, NY: Image Books, 1954.

Allport, Gordon. *The Individual and His Religion*. New York: Macmillian, 1960.

American Catholics in the Public Square: A Report to the Catholic Community. Foreword by Margaret O'Brien Steinfels. New York: The Commonweal Foundation, 2004; also an insert in *Commonweal*, July 16, 2004.

Augustine, Saint. *Confessions*. Reprint ed. Translated by Henry Chadwick. Oxford: Oxford University Press, 1998.

Bellah, Robert N. "Civil Religion in America." In *Beyond Belief: Essays on Religion in a Post-Traditional World*. Reprint ed. Berkeley: University of California Press, 1991.

Bellah, Robert N., Richard Madsen, William M. Sullivan, Ann Swidler, and Steven M. Tipton. *Habits of the Heart: Individualism and Commitment in American Life*. Berkeley: University of California Press, 1985.

Berger, Peter L. *The Sacred Canopy: Elements of a Sociological Theory of Religion*. Garden City, NY: Doubleday, 1967.

———. *A Rumor of Angels: Modern Society and the Rediscovery of the Supernatural*. New York: Doubleday, 1969.

———. *The Heretical Imperative*. New York: Doubleday, 1979.

Berger, Peter L., Brigitte Berger, and Hansfried Kellner. *The Homeless Mind: Modernization and Consciousness*. New York: Vintage Books, 1974.

Berger, Peter L., and Richard J. Neuhaus. *To Empower People: The Role of Mediating Structures in Public Policy*. Washington, DC: 1977.

Berger, Peter L., and Thomas Luckmann. *The Social Construction of Reality: A Treatise in the Sociology of Knowledge*. Garden City, NY: Doubleday, 1966.

Blanshard, Paul. *American Freedom and Catholic Power.* Boston: Beacon Press, 1949.

Bloom, Allan. *The Closing of the American Mind.* New York: Simon and Schuster, 1987.

"Brief History." United States Conference of Catholic Bishops, www.nccbuscc. org/whoweare.htm. May 20, 2004.

Brownson, Orestes. "Native Americanism." *Brownson Quarterly Review* (July 1854).

Bruskewitz, Bishop Fabian W. "Editorial on *Always Our Children: A Pastoral Message to Parents of Homosexual Children.*" *Social Justice Review* 89, nos. 3–4 (March/April 1998); also published in *Voices: The Newsletter for Women for Faith and Family* 13, nos. 1–2 (winter 1997/spring 1998).

Burns, Jeffrey M. *American Catholics and the Family Crisis, 1930–1962: An Ideological and Organizational Response.* New York and London: Garland Publishing, 1988.

Caponnetto, Antonio. *The Black Legends and Catholic Hispanic Culture.* Saint Louis, MO: Catholic Central Union, 1991.

Carlin, David R. *The Decline and Fall of the Catholic Church in America.* Manchester, NH: Sophia Institute Press, 2003.

Carlson, Allan. *From Cottage to Work Station.* San Francisco: Ignatius Press, 1993.

———. *The "American Way": Family and Community in the Shaping of American Identity.* Newark, DE: Inter-Collegiate Studies, 2003.

Carroll, Colleen. *The New Faithful: Why Young Adults Are Embracing Christian Orthodoxy.* Chicago: Loyola University Press, 2002.

Catechism of the Catholic Church. New York: Catholic Book Publishing, 1994.

Catholic Encyclopedia. www.newadvent.org/cathen. 1912.

Christensen, Bryce. *Utopia Against the Family: The Problems and Politics of the American Family.* San Francisco: Ignatius Press, 1990.

Cooley, Charles Horten. *Social Organization.* New York: Scribner's, 1909.

Corbett, Julia Mitchell. *Religion in America.* 4th ed. Englewood Cliffs, NJ: Prentice Hall, 2001.

Coulson, William. "Repentent Psychologist: How I Wrecked the I.H.M. Nuns." *The Latin Mass.* Special Issue, 1996.

Cox, Harvey. *The Secular City: Secularization and Urbanization in Theological Perspective.* 25th Anniversary ed. New York: Simon and Schuster, 1990.

Crocker, Harry, Jr. *Triumph: The Power and the Glory of the Catholic Church—A 2000-Year History.* Roseville, CA: Forum, 2001.

Cross, Robert. *The Emergence of Liberal Catholicism in America*. Chicago: Quadrangle Books, 1958.

Cuddihy, John. *No Offense: Civil Religion and Protestant Taste*. New York: Seabury, 1978.

Davidson, James. "Outside the Church: Whom Catholics Marry and Where." *Commonweal* 126, no. 15 (September 10, 1999): 14–16.

Davidson, James D., Andrea S. Williams, Richard A. LaManna, Jan Stenftenagel, Kathleen Maas Weigert, William F. Whalen, and Patricia Wittburg. *The Search for Common Ground: What Unites and Divides Catholic Americans*. Huntington, IN: Our Sunday Visitor, 1997.

Davis, Cyprian. *The History of Black Catholics in the United States*. New York: Crossroad, Herder, 1990.

D'Elia, Donald J. *The Spirits of '76: A Catholic Inquiry*. Front Royal, VA: Christendom College Press, 1983.

D'Elia, Donald J., and Stephen M. Krason. *We Hold These Truths and More: Further Catholic Reflections on the American Proposition*. Steubenville, OH: Franciscan University Press, 1993.

Demerath, Nicholas J., and Phillip E. Hammond. *Religion in Social Context: Tradition and Transition*. New York: Random House, 1969.

Dolan, Jay P. *The American Catholic Experience: A History from Colonial Times to the Present*. Garden City, NY: Doubleday, 1985.

Donaldson, Peter J. "American Catholicism and the International Family Planning Movement." *Population Studies* 42, no. 3 (November 1988).

Durkheim, Emile. *The Elementary Forms of the Religious Life*. New York: Collier Books, 1965.

Eliade, Mircea. *The Sacred and the Profane*. New York: Harcourt, Brace, and World, Inc., 1959.

Ellis, Monsignor John Tracy. "American Catholics and the Intellectual Life." *Thought* 30 (fall 1955).

———. *American Catholicism*. 2nd rev. ed. Chicago: University of Chicago Press, 1969.

Ellis, Monsignor John Tracy, ed. *Documents of American Catholic History*. Milwaukee, WI: Bruce Publishing, 1956.

Fisher, James T. *Catholics in America*. Oxford: Oxford University Press, 2000.

Fox, Father Robert J. "The Catholic Church in the United States of America." In *A Catechism of the Catholic Church: 2,000 Years of Faith and Tradition*. Alexandria, VA: Park Press Quality Printing, 2000.

Friedan, Betty. *The Feminine Mystique*. New York: W. W. Norton and Company, 1963.

Gallup, George, Jr., and Jim Castelli. *The American Catholic People: Their Beliefs, Practices, and Values.* Garden City, NY: Doubleday, 1987.

Gans, Herbert. *The Urban Villagers.* 2nd ed. New York: The Free Press, 1982.

Gehlen, Arnold. *Man in the Age of Technology.* New York: Columbia University Press, 1980.

Gillis, Chester. *Roman Catholicism in America.* New York: Columbia University Press, 1999.

Glazer, Nathan, and Daniel Patrick Moynihan. *Beyond the Melting Pot: The Negroes, Puerto Ricans, Jews, Italians, and Irish of New York City.* Cambridge, MA: M.I.T. Press, 1970.

Gleason, Philip. *Contending with Modernity: Catholic Higher Education in the Twentieth Century.* Oxford: Oxford University Press, 1995.

Greeley, Father Andrew M. *The Catholic Experience: An Interpretation of the History of American Catholicism.* Garden City, NY: Doubleday, 1967.

———. *The Denominational Society.* Glencoe, IL: Scott, Foresman, and Company, 1972.

———. "Catholic Social Activism: Real or Rad/Chic?" *National Catholic Reporter* (February 7, 1975).

———. *The Communal Catholic.* New York: Seabury, 1976.

———. *The American Catholic.* New York: Basic Books, 1977.

———. *The Catholic Myth: The Behaviors and Beliefs of American Catholics.* New York: Charles Scribner's Sons, 1990.

Gusfield, Joseph. *Symbolic Crusade.* Chicago: University of Illinois Press, 1976.

Gutierrez, Gustavo. *The Theology of Liberation: History, Politics, and Salvation.* Maryknoll, NY: Orbis Books, 1973.

Hamburger, Philip. *Separation of Church and State.* Cambridge, MA: Harvard University Press, 2002.

Handlin, Oscar. *The Uprooted: The Epic Story of the Great Migration that Made the American People.* Boston: Little, Brown, 1951.

Hanna, Mary. *Catholics and American Politics.* Cambridge, MA: Harvard University Press, 1979.

Harvey, Father John. *The Homosexual Person.* San Francisco: Ignatius Press, 1987.

———. "AIDS, Morality, and Public Policy." In *Homosexuality, the Questions: Scripture, Church, and Psychiatric Answers,* edited by Joseph A. Dilenno and Herbert F. Smith. Boston: Daughters of St. Paul, 1989.

———. *The Truth About Homosexuality.* San Francisco: Ignatius Press, 1996.

Harvey, Father John, and Gerard V. Bradley, eds. *Same Sex Attraction.* South Bend, IN: St. Augustine's Press, 2003.

Hellwig, Monica. "American Culture: Reciprocity with Catholic Vision, Values, and Community." In *The Catholic Church and American Culture: Reciprocity and Challenge*, edited by Cassian Yuhaus. Mahwah, NJ: Paulist Press, 1990.

Hennesey, Father James. *American Catholics: A History of the Roman Catholic Community in the United States.* Oxford: Oxford University Press, 1981.

Henslin, James M. *Essentials of Sociology: A Down-to-Earth Approach.* 5th ed. Boston: Allyn and Bacon, 2004.

Herberg, Will. *Protestant, Catholic, Jew: An Essay in Religious Sociology.* Garden City, NY: Anchor Books, 1960.

Hinshaw, Rick. "The Political Responsibilities of American Catholics." Radio Interview on the Catholic Alternative Radio Program, WHPC, 90.3 F.M. of Nassau Community College, Garden City, NY (January 23, 2003).

Hitchcock, James. *The Decline and Fall of Radical Catholicism.* New York: Image Books, 1972.

———. "The Evolution of the Catholic Left." *The American Scholar* 43, no. 1 (winter 1973–74).

———. *The Pope and the Jesuits: John Paul II and the New Order in the Society of Jesus.* New York: The National Committee of Catholic Laymen, Inc., 1984.

Howe, Neil, and William Strauss. *Millennials Rising: The Next Great Generation.* New York: Vintage Books, 2000.

Hudson, Winthrop. *Religion in America.* 4th ed. New York: Macmillan Publishing Company, 1987.

Hunter, James. *Culture Wars: The Struggle to Define America.* New York: Basic Books, 1991.

———. *Before the Shooting Begins: Searching for Democracy in America's Culture War.* New York: The Free Press, 1994.

James, William. *The Varieties of Religious Experience.* 1902. Reprint, New York: Modern Library, 1994.

Jenkins, Philip. *The Next Christendom: The Coming of Global Christianity.* Oxford: Oxford University Press, 2002.

———. *The New Anti-Catholicism.* Oxford, England: Oxford University Press, 2003.

Johnson, Paul. *Pope John Paul II and the Catholic Restoration.* New York: St. Martin's Press, 1981.

Kelley, Dean M. *Why Conservative Churches Are Growing.* New York: Harper and Row, 1972.

Kelly, Monsignor George A. *The Battle for the American Church*. Garden City, NY: Doubleday, 1979.

———. *The Crisis of Authority: John Paul II and the American Bishops*. Chicago: Regnery Gateway, 1982.

———. *Inside My Father's House*. Garden City, NY: Doubleday, 1989.

———. *Keeping the Church Catholic with John Paul II*. Garden City, NY: Doubleday, 1990.

———. *The Battle for the American Church Revisited*. San Francisco: Ignatius Press, 1995.

———. *The Second Spring of the Church in America*. South Bend, IN: St. Augustine's Press, 2001.

Krason, Stephen M. *Liberalism, Conservatism, and Catholicism: An Evaluation of Contemporary Political Ideologies in Light of Catholic Social Teachings*. New Hope, KY: Catholics United for the Faith, 1991.

———. *Preserving a Good Political Order and a Democratic Republic: Reflections from Philosophy, Great Thinkers, Popes, and America's Founding Era*. Lewiston, NY: Edwin Mellen Press, 1998.

———. *The Public Order and the Sacred Order*. Portage, MI: PageFree Publishing, 2003.

LaFarge, John. *The Manner Is Ordinary*. Garden City, NY: Image Books, 1957.

LeBon, Gustave. *The Crowd*. Mineola, NY: Dover Publications, 2002.

Lenski, Gerhard. *The Religious Factor*. New York: Doubleday, 1961.

Lenzer, Gertrud, ed. *Auguste Comte and Positivism: The Essential Writings*. Chicago: University of Chicago Press, 1983.

Levine, Donald J., ed. *Georg Simmel on Individuality and Social Forms*. Chicago: University of Chicago Press, 1971.

Liaugminas, S. G. "Catholicism with a Latin Beat." *Crisis Magazine* (September 2001).

Link, Richard. *American Catholicism and European Immigrants*. Staten Island, NY: Center for Migration Studies, 1975.

Lockwood, Robert, ed. *Anti-Catholicism in American Culture*. Huntington, IN: Our Sunday Visitor, 2000.

Luckmann, Thomas. *The Invisible Religion*. New York: Doubleday, 1961.

Luker, Kristin. *Abortion and the Politics of Motherhood*. Berkeley: University of California Press, 1985.

MacIntyre, Alasdair. *After Virtue: A Study in Moral Theory*. Notre Dame, IN: University of Notre Dame Press, 1984.

McGreevy, John T. *Parish Boundaries: The Catholic Encounter with Race in the Twentieth-Century Urban North.* Chicago: University of Chicago Press, 1996.

———. *Catholicism and American Freedom: A History.* New York: W. W. Norton and Company, 2003.

McGuire, Meredith. *Religion: The Social Context.* 5th ed. Belmont, CA: Wadsworth, 2002.

McInerny, Ralph. *A First Glance at St. Thomas Aquinas.* Notre Dame, IN: Notre Dame University Press, 1990.

Morris, Charles R. *American Catholics: The Saints and Sinners Who Built America's Most Powerful Church.* New York: Times Books, 1997.

Morrissey, Gerard. *The Crisis of Dissent.* Front Royal, VA: Christendom College, 1985.

Murray, Rev. John Courtney. *We Hold These Truths: Catholic Reflections on the American Proposition.* New York: Image Books, 1964.

Neuhaus, Rev. Richard J. *The Catholic Moment: The Paradox of the Church in the Post-Modern World.* San Francisco: Harper and Row, 1987.

———. "The Catholic Moment in America." In *Catholics in the Public Square,* edited by Thomas Patrick Melady. Huntington, IN: Our Sunday Visitor, 1995.

Neuhaus, Richard. *The Naked Public Square.* Grand Rapids, MI: Eerdmans Publishing, 1997.

Newman, John Henry Cardinal. *An Essay on the Development of Christian Doctrine.* Reissue ed. Notre Dame, IN: University of Notre Dame Press, 1989.

Niebuhr, H. R. *Christ and Culture.* New York: Harper and Row, 1951.

———. *The Social Sources of Denominationalism.* Cleveland and New York: Meridian Books, 1957.

Pareto, Vilfredo. *The Mind and the Society.* Mineola, NY: Dover, 1965.

Primeggia, Salvatore, and Joseph A. Varacalli. "The Sacred and Profane Among Italian American Catholics: The Giglio Feast." *International Journal of Politics, Culture, and Society* 9, no. 3 (1996).

"Provincial Councils of Baltimore." *Catholic Encyclopedia,* www.newadvent. org/cathen/02235a.htm (1912).

Ratzinger, Joseph Cardinal, with Vittorio Messori. *The Ratzinger Report: An Exclusive Interview on the State of the Church.* San Francisco: Ignatius Press, 1985.

Riesman, David, Nathan Glazer, and Reuel Denny. *The Lonely Crowd: A Study of Changing American Character.* New Haven, CT: Yale University Press, 1961.

Rinehart, Sue Tolleson, and Jerry Perkins. "The Intersection of Gender Politics and Religious Beliefs." *Political Behavior* 11, no. 1 (March 1989).

Rose, Michael. *Goodbye, Good Men: How Liberals Brought Corruption into the Catholic Church.* Washington, DC: Regnery Publishing, 2002.

Rowland, Tracey. *Culture and the Thomistic Tradition.* New York: Routledge, 2003.

Ryan, Mary Perkins. *Are Parochial Schools the Answer? Catholic Education in the Light of the Council.* New York: Holt, Rinehart and Winston, 1964.

"Saint Katherine Drexel." *Catholic Culture,* March 3, 2005, www.catholic culture.org.

Salvaterra, David L. *American Catholicism and the Intellectual Life, 1880–1950.* New York and London: Garland Press, 1988.

Saunders, Father William. "The Eastern Rite Church." *Arlington Catholic Herald,* three part series, March 9, 16, and 23, 2000, www.catholicheral.com.

Scheler, Max. *Problems in the Sociology of Knowledge.* London: Routledge and Kegan Paul, 1980.

Schwartz, Michael. *The Persistent Prejudice: Anti-Catholicism in America.* Huntington, IN: Our Sunday Visitor, 1984.

Shaw, Russell. *Ministry or Apostolate? What Should the Catholic Laity Be Doing?* Huntington, IN: Our Sunday Visitor, 2002.

Sigmund, Paul E. *Natural Law in Political Thought.* Lanham, MD: University Press of America, 1971.

Steichen, Donna. *Ungodly Rage: The Hidden Face of Catholic Feminism.* San Francisco: Ignatius Press, 1991.

Tillich, Paul. *Dynamics of Faith.* New York: Harper and Row, 1957.

Tomasi, Bishop Silvano. *Piety and Power.* Staten Island, NY: Center for Migration Studies, 1975.

Tönnies, Ferdinand. *Community and Society.* East Lansing: Michigan State University Press, 1957.

Troeltsch, Ernest. *The Social Teachings of the Christian Churches.* London: George Allen and Unwin, Ltd., 1931.

Varacalli, Joseph A. *Toward the Establishment of Liberal Catholicism in America.* Lanham, MD: University Press of America, 1983.

———. "The Constitutive Elements of the Idea of an 'American' Catholic Church." *Social Justice Review* 80, nos. 5–6 (May/June 1989).

———. "Neo-Orthodoxy, the Crisis of Authority, and the Future of the Catholic Church in the United States." *Faith and Reason* 15, nos. 2–3 (summer/fall 1989).

———. "Renewing the Battle to Restore Sociology and the Social Sciences in Christ." *Fellowship of Catholic Scholars Newsletter* 14, no. 3 (June 1991).

———. "Multiculturalism, Catholicism, and American Civilization." *Homiletic and Pastoral Review* 94, no. 6 (March 1994).

———. "'Homophobia' at Seton Hall University: Sociology in Defense of the Faith." *Faith and Reason* 20, no. 3 (fall 1994).

———. *The Catholic and Politics in Post–World War II America: A Sociological Analysis.* St. Louis, MO: Society of Catholic Social Scientists, 1995.

———. "The Failure of the Therapeutic: Implications for Society and Church." *Faith and Reason* 23, no. 1 (spring 1997).

———. "Obstructing *Ex corde Ecclesiae*: A Review Essay." *Faith and Reason* 23, nos. 3–4 (fall/winter 1997–98).

———. "Symposium: Catholics and the Practice of Sociology and the Social Sciences." *The Catholic Social Science Review* 3 (1998).

———. "The Saints in the Lives of Italian-Americans: Toward a Realistic Multiculturalism." In *The Saints in the Lives of Italian-Americans: An Interdisciplinary Investigation,* edited by Joseph A. Varacalli, Salvatore Primeggia, Salvatore J. LaGumina, and Donald J. D'Elia. Stony Brook, NY: Forum Italicum of the Center for Italian Studies, 1999.

———. *Bright Promise, Failed Community: Catholics and the American Public Order.* Lanham, MD: Lexington Books, 2001.

———. "Dissecting the Anatomy of the Sexual Scandal." *Homiletic and Pastoral Review* (January 2004).

———. "On Being a Catholic American." *Homiletic and Pastoral Review* (August/September 2004).

———. "Catholicism, Italian Style: A Reflection on the Relationship Between the Catholic and Italian Worldviews." In *Models and Images of Catholicism in Italian Americana: Academy and Society,* edited by Joseph A. Varacalli, Salvatore Primeggia, Salvatore J. LaGumina, and Donald J. D'Elia. Stony Brook, NY: Forum Italicum of the Center for Italian Studies, 2004.

———. "The Cultural and Political Impotence of Catholics in Contemporary American Life." *The Catholic Social Science Review* 9 (2004).

———. "Gibson's *Passion* and the American Culture War." *The Catholic Social Science Review* 10 (2005).

Vecoli, Rudolph. "Prelates and Peasants: Italian Immigrants and the Catholic Church." *Journal of Social History* 2, no. 3 (spring 1969).

Vitz, Paul. *Psychology as Religion: The Cult of Self-Worship.* Grand Rapids, MI: William B. Eerdmans, 1980.

Voeglin, Eric. *From Enlightenment to Revolution*. Durham, NC: Duke University Press, 1975.

Warner, Michael. *Changing Witness: Catholic Bishops and Public Policy, 1917–1994*. Washington, DC: Ethics and Public Policy Center, 1995.

Weber, Max. *From Max Weber*, edited by H. H. Gerth and C. W. Mills. New York: Oxford University Press, 1946.

———. *The Theory of Economic and Social Organization*. New York: The Free Press, 1947.

Wilcox, W. Bradford. "The Facts of Life and Marriage: Social Science and the Vindication of Christian Moral Teaching." *Touchstone* (January/February 2005).

Woods, Thomas E., Jr. *The Church Confronts Modernity: Catholic Intellectuals and the Progressive Era*. New York: Columbia University Press, 2004.

Wrenn, Rev. Michael J. *Catechisms and Controversies: Religious Education in the Postconciliar Years*. San Francisco: Ignatius Press, 1991.

Wrenn, Rev. Michael J., and Kenneth Whitehead. *Flawed Expectations: The Reception of the Catechism of the Catholic Church*. San Francisco: Ignatius Press, 1996.

Zellner, William. *Extraordinary Groups*. 7th ed. New York: Worth, 2001.

Zoller, Michael. *Washington and Rome: Catholicism and American Culture*. Notre Dame, IN: University of Notre Dame Press, 1999.

Index

feminism/feminist, 19, 42, 69, 103, 140–142
Feminist Mystique, The, 110
fetus, 220
Fides et Ratio, 60
"fiery brook" of sociological relativity, 69
Filippino(s), 71, 113
First Amendment to the Constitution, 39, 173
 "free exercise" clause and "establishment" clause, 173
First Glance at Saint Thomas Aquinas, A, 196
Fisher, James, 26–29, 76–77, 80, 113–14, 152, 212, 249
Florida, 26
Fort Apache: The Bronx, 232
Fox, Father Robert J., 115
"frame of evaluative reference," 189–90
France, 25, 75
Francis, Bishop Joseph, 189–90
Franciscan(s), 113, 132–33, 158, 184
Franciscan University, 51, 193
freedom, 19, 68. *See also Veritatis Splendor*
Freemasons, 157
free will (and choice), 7, 67
Freudian/Freudianism, 19, 42, 69, 141–42
French, 71
 Canadian Catholics, 26
 Catholic(s), 113
 French Catholic leadership, 28
 fur traders, 26, 113
 Louisiana, 76
 missionaries, 26
 Revolution, 26, 76
Friedan, Betty, 110
"fundamental dignity of the human person," 20, 62
"futurology," 243

Gallup, George, Jr., 180
Gans, Herbert, 90
"gates of hell shall not prevail," 53
Gaudium et Spes, 198
Gehlen, Arnold, 206

"gemeinschaft," 90
gender, 72, 107, 109
 gap, 107–8
generation(s), 95
 "gap," 95–96
 generational differences as in "pre-Vatican II," "Vatican II," and "post-Vatican II," 65–66, 96
"generic Christianity, "246
genocide, 21
Gerety, Archbishop Peter, 187
"geometric sociology," 89
Georgetown College/University, 132
German(s), 77
 Catholic Americans, 35–36, 76
 Germany, 34
ghetto, Catholic, 33, 41, 46, 169
Gibbons, Archbishop James, 160, 167
G.I. Bill, 90
Gibson, Mel, 52, 145, 229–30, 234
 "giglio feast" of Williamsburg, Brooklyn, 35–36
Gillis, Chester, 89, 91
Glazer, Nathan, 87
globalization, 19, 60
"goal displacement," 170
God, 104
 "God's work must truly be our own," 85
 transcendent, 209
 Trinitarian, 215
 Triune, 3
Good Society, 61, 142
"goods of the earth," 60
Gore, Charles, 211
Gore, Vice-President Albert, Jr., 223
Gospel
 and culture, 201
 values, 107, 201
government power, 55
grace, 14
 of God, working through nature, 209
 "gratuitous gift of grace," 199
Greatest Story Ever Told, The, 232
Greek
 Greco-Roman, 20
 Greek-based, 20
Greeley, Rev. Andrew M., 36, 42, 87,

About the Author

JOSEPH A. VARACALLI, Ph.D, is presently Professor of Sociology and Director of the Center for Catholic Studies at Nassau Community College of the S.U.N.Y. system of higher education. In 1992, he co-founded the Society of Catholic Social Scientists and served as editor-in-chief of its journal, *The Catholic Social Science Review* from 1996 through 1999. An expert in both American Catholic and Italian American studies, he is the author of *Bright Promise, Failed Community: Catholics and the American Public Order* (2000, 2001) and *Toward the Establishment of Liberal Catholicism in America* (1983). In Italian American studies, he is the co-editor of three volumes: *The Italian Experience: An Encyclopedia* (2000), *The Saints in the Lives of Italian Americans: An Interdisciplinary Investigation* (1999, 2003), and *Models and Images of Catholicism in Italian Americana: Academy and Society* (2004). Currently he is co-editing a volume expected to be published in 2006: *Catholic Social Thought, Social Science, and Social Policy: An Encyclopedia*. In 2004, at the Twelfth Annual Meeting of the Society of Catholic Social Scientists, Dr. Varacalli was the recipient of the organization's top honor, the "Pope Pius XII Award for the furthering of a true Catholic social science" as called for in the 1931 Papal encyclical, *Quadragesimo Anno*.

Dr. Varacalli is married to Lillian and has three children: Thomas Francis Xavier (16 years of age), John Paul Varacalli (14 years of age), and Theresa Elizabeth (12 years of age). The Varacalli family resides in Westbury, New York.